THE LIFE AND TIMES OF MR. JOSEPH SOAP

D1385995

Withdrawn from Stock
Dublin City Public Libraries

THOMAS MARTIN

The Life and Times of Mr. Joseph Soap

GREEN THREAD PRESS

The Life and Times of Mr. Joseph Soap
Copyright © Thomas Martin 2018

All rights reserved.
Thomas Martin asserts the moral right to be identified as the author of this book.

This book or any portion thereof may not be reproduced or used in any manner whatsoever without the express permission of the author except for the use of brief quotations in a book review.

This is a work of fiction. Names, characters, businesses, places, events and incidents are either the products of the author's imagination or used in a fictitious manner. Any resemblance to actual persons, living or dead, or actual events is purely coincidental.

Published by Green Thread Press.

First edition, 2018

www.thomasmartin.ie

ISBN 978-1-9999620-1-2 (print)
ISBN 978-1-9999620-0-5 (ebook)

For Siún

CONTENTS

INTRODUCTION

My dearest Conor,

Back when I was a lad, autobiographies were the sole preserve of great achievers. Beginning with a foreword by a peer of similar renown, they would enthral the reader from start to finish by depicting eminent life stories and valuable lessons learned.

Today, however, corners of the literary world have been duped to such an extent that modern so-called 'celebrity autobiographies' have become the great tool with which to air one's dirty washing and these paint-by-numbers anti-classics tend to begin with a foreword by a celebrity of even greater notoriety. Flash-in-the-pan politicians or those with ideas well above their station may even attempt to smokescreen an air of pomp over their titles by referring to them as 'memoirs', but the outcome remains the same.

These days autobiographies, often ghostwritten, are churned out ten-a-penny and I can barely switch on the television set

Leabharlanna Poiblí Chathair Baile Átha Cliath
Dublin City Public Libraries

without getting bombarded with books by actors I can't stand, comedians I don't find funny or musicians I have never heard of. Indeed, is there any other format in the world that would place the contrasting experiences of Martin Luther King and Wayne Rooney's wife next to each other, gathering dust side by side, once used and discarded for all eternity?

The demand from the public appears to be so insatiable that people won't even wait for the life to reach near-completion, with some lives now committed to paper before they have reached the halfway mark. Surely this is nonsensical, as people's decisions and common sense are no doubt influenced by the prospect of causing a scandal, making a scene or merely coming up with another crazy story to fill pages of the inevitable book, for which they will be paid a king's ransom to cobble together.

These books are now even available on tape, or so I have heard from your father, and this revelation only adds further weight to my claim that the world really has changed since my day. It seems the demand for these tales has now begun to bypass even the printed word and people, for who knows what reason, now feel the need for Susan Boyle or her like to actually tell them what she got up to in her youth, as they drive to work or exercise in the park.

I say these things not out of jealousy but out of regret. Regret that some of the people, some of the dare I say 'ordinary every-day people' I've encountered in my lifetime, were never afforded the same opportunity to immortalise themselves in print. As a consequence, we will never get to hear their stories of love, hope, joy and despair, which is a shame like no other as these stories could have been told not with the view of making a profit, but in the hope of maintaining a link in the chain to one's history.

Another much more admirable modern craze seems to be people's desire to trace their family tree, and this prompted me to think as much about the past as I do about the present or indeed the future. What if a lineage could be established and pieced together not just by names of ancestors, but by a written account of their time on earth? The world would surely be a better place, even in the smallest of ways, as these stories would find a wanting audience of relatives curious to learn of their ancestry. Both the author and reader would have a mutual interest in family and love, and each word written and read would have the sole intention of keeping the family's tales and characters alive. What a thing it would be to share joyous moments, great love stories and tales of heartbreak, before they fall victim to memories susceptible to the passage of time.

My reason for writing this autobiography is also a partly selfish one, as I have now had seventy-four years of life and I have not once changed the world or even come close to doing so. Now, through this book, I see an opportunity to cement my place in history, my family's history, and it is one which I refuse to let pass me by.

Your birth, my darling grandson Conor Soap, has for the first time made me aware that my remaining time on earth will surely come and go like a passing summer. I may live long enough for you to see me through sympathetic eyes, but that frail old helpless person you may witness will not be the man I once was, and for the time being at least, still am.

I know your father will tell you all about how I met my wife Audrey, your grandmother, but I'm afraid that he cannot possibly hope to do my finest moment justice. His version of my tale will be told through a second-hand account, tinged with a distant faded nostalgia for a story he has heard so often that repetition will have robbed it of its magic. I see your grandmother's face. I see it every day when I close my eyes and it continues to draw the same smile it drew from me all those years ago when I first laid eyes on her. It is over three decades since her passing, yet time has not changed my most stubborn view, that she was the most perfect creature God ever created and it both puzzles and so deeply saddens me that he saw fit to take her from me so early. We had so much more laughing to do.

I hope you enjoy reading my autobiography and getting to know your old grandad. I feel it is now or never for me to write this book, as I have probably lived about 98% of my life at this point, so now is as good a time as any. It feels right.

One young chap I saw on a television advertisement released his autobiography shortly before Christmas, an American entertainer of some sort or another, Dustin somebody. From his picture he could hardly have been more than fifteen years old.

So you see, Conor, my point is a simple one. My trousers are fifteen years old.

And so begins the life and times of Mr. Joseph Soap...

CHAPTER 1

GETTING STARTED

THE LAST OF THE DUST HAS been wiped from Audrey's old typewriter and it looks marvellous. As I stare at it I am brought back to a time before glowing screens and endless wires sprouting from the backs of the latest contraptions, which for whatever reason people these days feel the need to clutter up their homes with.

I sit and wonder what Audrey must have been thinking the last time she graced this old machine with her presence and as I do so I place my fingers tenderly on the letter keys that are most worn. Audrey used this typewriter solely as a means of helping out with the business, yet here I am now, faced with the daunting task of committing my life to paper, a life filled with people whose memories I pray my words do not sell short.

Unlike a writer who may start a novel unaware of where his imagination is about to take him, my path is set in stone. I know exactly where I must get to, yet still I question my ability to get there, but as it is my story surely there is no one on earth more qualified to tell it. Not one soul has ever or will ever live my life and the memories of conversations once shared and laughter long since bellowed into the sky will forever remain my treasured possessions.

I am extremely fortunate at this stage in life to be able to so vividly remember my past, as though the passing years have been reduced to mere weeks. I know that at seventy-four years of age my time for this world is not the limitless road that once stretched out before me, but I am still very much alive and my mind remains alert and eager to voice its opinion.

Older people do not lose relevance just because we walk a little slower or struggle to keep pace with the modern world, but we are in some ways responsible for the false perception that society has of us. After all, there is not a person over the age of sixty-five, myself included, who has not uttered the words "It was not like that in my day" and by making such a throwaway remark we are unknowingly condemning ourselves to a bygone age. Well I want everyone to know that this too is my day, I'm still here, I'm still alive and just like everyone else in the world I feel the same rain on my scalp and watch the same sun disappear each evening.

Rather than condemnation, sometimes all people need is a chance, especially at the start of life or towards the end of it. Older people will surprise you if you give them a proper hearing and they should be encouraged, never patronised, when afforded a listening ear. I myself want to be heard by those who have an interest in what I have to say, not just by people humouring me because I have been fortunate enough to live my life into old age.

I have always been wary of those people who think it fruitful to broadcast their views on life expectancy, which they claim is seventy-eight years for women, seventy-five for men. These faceless individuals in white coats almost seem glad to be predicting your demise and they no doubt see it as a way of proving their intelligence while they cement their status in high society. I wonder just how smart some of these people really are and I question whether their time and dubious talent would not be better off spent trying to preserve life as opposed to stamping older people with an expiry date.

I imagine the chance to look back upon a happy life is a gift bestowed onto only the truly blessed and I wonder if I would have been as keen to write this book had I led the life of sorrow and regret that so many unfortunate people are condemned to lead. Poverty and criminality have not ravaged my life like they have done others and it has been love and affection that have gripped my life so tightly that they still refuse to let go to this day.

Looking at the many blank sheets of paper beside me, neatly placed on the corner of the writing desk in my bedroom, I can only wonder if they will get branded with the words needed to describe a life that has afforded me so much pleasure. I guess only time will tell.

It feels slightly strange to start to write one's life story as usually 'normal' people's lives are committed to paper only by daily entries into diaries, which some may argue is a much more dignified affair, when compared to selling one's wares in an autobiography. While I agree that the comfort and privacy a diary offers is most welcome for some people as it provides an almost therapeutic feeling for its writer, I do feel that it portrays the person in a rather enclosed light. After all how is a flower meant to grow if it is kept in the shade and never exposed to the sunshine?

I guess the use of diaries shows that regular people live their lives on a day-to-day basis and often we pay little attention to the future that awaits us but ultimately, when pressed, we accept that the time will come when it all has to end. Perhaps living one's life mirrors the experience of reading a good book in so much as we know that it must end at some point, but we just don't want it to.

I applaud anyone who has attempted to put creative words onto paper and I hope that they achieved the goal that their dreams cried out for. Of course, the realist in me suspects that waste paper baskets filled up a lot quicker than the 'New Releases' shelves in bookshops up and down the country, but still I admire anyone who at least has had a go and as the good Lord himself loves a trier, I feel I am in the best of company in that regard.

Although some wealthy folk may look upon my life as a Dickensian nightmare, noticeable only for its lack of finery, I say it is all the more noticeable because of it. My job was that of a shopkeeper and my fruit and vegetable shop provided a good life for my family and me and all that we needed in life was housed inside its four walls.

I never once felt the desire to step on toes, chase up ladders or reach for the stars, as I have always believed that a happy man is a happy man whether he wears a crown or a cap. In fact, I dare say that the man in the cap is the happier of the two should it happen to rain. Over the years I could have spent my hard-earned few bob on all the latest styles but I resisted, as I was always well aware that trends come and go and that one man's designer suit is another man's toga. Fancy cars also failed to entice me, while sprawling mansions would have condemned me to a commute to work, which my home above the shop never asked of me.

In preparation for this book, I delighted in viewing my old photo albums once again. Unlike the typewriter, the albums' leather covers did not require generations of dust to be blown from them as such is their constant movement from my bedroom shelf to my lap, that rarely has a speck of dust been given the chance to settle upon them.

In them, Audrey's smile without fail rises from the paper and illuminates my life as it once did, while the older black and white photographs continue to struggle to do justice to all the blazing colours of my adolescent years. Likewise, the yellow tinge of the even older pictures offers only one of the many colours that my greedy eyes took in during my fledgling years. I hope that the warmth and character of the people, who now live only in my heart, will flow from the pages of this book and that you will then understand why I feel this great desire to further keep their memory alive in yours.

You see, Conor, photography was not as readily available back then as it is today and I wonder if photographs have the same meaning for today's generation as they did for mine. Mobile phones are cameras now and pictures are being taken on a whim, so much so that I recall seeing one young man taking a picture of his dinner while sitting in a restaurant. I noticed that he had ordered the same dish as I had and I was half-tempted to tell him not to bother taking a snap as the beef was nothing to write home about, but in the end I just watched him review the picture on his phone while his dinner went cold.

In my youth if we had access to a camera that alone was enough to make it a joyous day and any old photographs you see shows only fantastic or important scenes, because we could not afford to waste the great gift of being able to capture a moment in time. There was no need for put-on smiles or the forced faking of interest, nor was there a requirement for the person behind the viewfinder to say "cheese" as mile-wide grins were already racing enthusiastically down the lens. It was a time of wonder.

Nowadays the splendid gift of photography has almost been brought to the point of no return and young folks today have chipped away at its relevance through sheer and utter lunacy. Some weeks ago, rock bottom was almost reached when I saw one young lady walking down the street carrying a pole that had a camera perched on the end of it. I watched through disbelieving eyes as she extended it out to the length of a javelin and then proceeded to take a photograph of herself whilst standing outside a newsagent's window. This little madam was obviously so self-obsessed that she had chosen to live her life with an extendable pole as a companion rather than partake in the most basic of human interactions, which was simply to ask a passer-by to take a picture. In my view she couldn't have been any more unsociable if she had run down the street whacking people over the head with the damn thing.

Modern life it seems is retreating back into the shadows and people now even socialise while plugged into a wall. What has the world come to?

All this no doubt stems from people's newly found quest for distraction, and it is this quest which has resulted in us living in an era where celebrity has become the new religion and autobiographies the new Holy Books.

- The Book of Psalms (Samuel L. Jackson, Sam Torrance)
- The Book of Genesis (Phil Collins and his friends) and
- The Book of Job (Steve; the man who makes the computers)

Young Conor, I believe in the spirit of those who you have never met and with this book I will try my utmost to make you feel as though you remember each one fondly. I hope that my words will take you to a place where you have never been and that you are able to share in my emotions, whether happy or sad, as I recount the stories that have made me the man I am today; your auld grandad.

Now let me introduce you to your great-grandparents...

CHAPTER 2

MY PARENTS

I CAME INTO THIS WORLD GIGGLING, or so my mother always told me, when I was born in the back bedroom above the fruit and vegetable shop in Stepaside, County Dublin, which my parents owned and ran. Perhaps I sensed the good fortune that was to come my way in the years ahead or maybe I was just responding in kind to the two smiling faces that beamed with pride and delight at my arrival.

My parents were a handsome young couple named Danny and Angela Soap and in later years they would often say that my birth added to what was already the happiest little family in Dublin. Theirs was a great love and one to be envied but the beginning of their courtship was not so much a whirlwind romance as it was a slight draught from beneath a door.

Father was raised on a small family farm in South County Dublin. My own grandfather, Kenneth, had died relatively young, leaving Father to become a man years before nature had ever intended. As an only child, something of a rarity in those days, he was left with little option but to nurture their small bit of land and he did so in order to look after and provide for my ailing grandmother, Mary-Anne.

To earn a living, he ran a fruit and vegetable stall in the centre of Stepaside from which he sold some of the very produce he had personally freed from the soil. Each morning he would rise at an ungodly hour to begin his day's work and he would pause only to wake the rooster up in order to remind it to later stir all those within earshot.

Father would leave for the dockside first thing where he would go and collect the more exotic fruit that his fair land could only wish to reap, and on his stall, once erected, the rich colours of the fruit sat in total contrast next to the earthy tones of the vegetables, yet each proved as popular as the other.

My mother Angela worked at Clarkthorn shoe factory almost since the day she had left school at fifteen years of age and she was but a tiny drop in a sea of women that flooded in and out through the factory gates each day.

Father had picked a prime location for his stall in the town centre, directly across from a row of factories, which, he figured, would yield hordes of hungry workers from their enormous metal gates. On the morning that would spark the rest of his life Father positioned his little stall directly across from the imposing shoe factory and while separating yellow bananas from green, an unfamiliar voice saved him, temporarily at least, from the most mundane of chores.

The words "one apple please" floated in his direction, striking him dumb, and had poor Father been able to muster a reply with even half of the efficiency he showed in placing an apple in the young woman's hand, he could have saved himself the stress he would endure each working morning for the next three months.

On the wobbly old stall, potatoes were stacked with the skill of a circus performer and more often than not Mother bore witness to Father's early efforts, as bright as a button, she would pay him a visit first thing. With the passing of weeks, Father seemed to sense that Mother's polite chit-chat had elaborated into almost full-blown conversation, yet still the fire failed to catch on. Father knew that he had only the quality of his apples to win the girl's favour as his attempts at flirty charm left a lot to be desired, but he knew that he had fallen for the pretty brunette and felt sure that she was the only girl who could pick him up, dust him down and make him see all the beauty in the world.

Finally, after three months, several abandoned attempts and sixty-three apples, Father eventually plucked up the courage to ask my mother if he could walk her home when she finished work that evening. The book you are holding in your hand should be testament as to how their delicate courtship blossomed into the rest of their lives. Poor Father may not have been a romancer of repute, but through perseverance, luck and quality fruit he got there in the end.

They wed a year later in 1936 in a joyous affair but sadly, less than two months into their marriage and following a long and protracted illness, my grandmother Mary-Anne passed away, leaving Father and Mother to inherit the family home and farm. Father used to say that my grandmother had waited to see him happy before passing over to the next world and he always took great comfort from that belief.

Father and Mother sold up the farm for what it was worth, as they knew that the prospect of raising a family on a farm would all but seal their children's fate and force upon them the never-ending demands of the land. With the proceeds of the sale they bought a small fruit and vegetable shop in Stepaside and they set up home directly above it, while a newly purchased Bedford van saw my father's tired old stall condemned to firewood.

The shop was christened 'Stepaside Fruit and Veg' and almost immediately nosey parkers would pass comment that the name suggested that fruit and vegetables should 'stand to one side' or 'make way' for unhealthier foods such as chocolate or cake, but Father was unperturbed. My parents went on to fill their home with three sons, the first of which was my eldest brother Michael, followed by myself, and then Edward brought up the rear.

With five people living above the shop the place was bursting at the seams and knowing that Father had been raised in wide open spaces, Mother once asked him if he ever felt penned in by the constant barrage coming from his young family.

"I do Angela, but I wouldn't have it any other way," said Father before adding that being surrounded by his family made him happier than she would ever truly know.

My father had always dreamt about owning his own home and business and he was well aware of the hard work he faced because of it, but he was convinced that it was the best thing for his family's future. He continued to travel to the docks each morning to replenish his stock of fruit, and owing to the sale of the farm he now troubled the wholesalers with orders of vegetables which he had previously cultivated for himself.

I vividly remember my early trips to the docks with him. I must have been five years old the first time Father eventually caved in to my constant badgering and agreed to bring me along as he purchased produce of every imaginable shape and size. I was stopped in my tracks by sights I had previously not even dreamt of, as cargo ships, some as big as towns, came in to dock from the four corners of the world. In the distance, ghostly figures hurriedly went about their work at the pace that was demanded of them and men with shades of skin different to my own heaved boxes so large I had thought it impossible. This great drive of human spirit and industry, woven perfectly together by the salty sea air, drew me in immediately and it forever became a place of wonderment for a young boy curious to learn about life.

I wondered how Father could appear to be so at home in such a strange place, especially when the dockers would use language as colourful as the fruit being brought to our shores. The first few times these choice words got an airing in my presence, Father would cup his hands over my ears, to shield me from words I myself would much later detest. As my world went silent I could see men shouting at each other and waving their arms over anything from a spilled box of tomatoes to a misplaced look. I wondered what they were saying but I could only imagine that it was something really important, as the longer the argument went on, the tighter Father would press against my ears.

After a number of visits Father eventually ceased cupping my ears, as often my head would shake with giggles, enough for him to realise that a number of distasteful words had filtered through his fingers to take up permanent residence within my vocabulary. I always made a mental note of the choicest ones after I quickly realised that it was not only Father who could bring things home from the docks and I would later dole them out to my friends in school just like Father did fruit and veg to his customers.

Our home was one built on a foundation of hard work and Father would leave most mornings for the docks long before my brothers and I would wake up. Having left her job at the shoe factory with the view of rearing a family, Mother would start her day's work in tandem with Father's. They would rise to ready the house each morning at half past five and on finishing breakfast, Father would head off in the van to replenish stock, having secured a kiss on the doorstep.

Mother's day within the home was almost set in stone. She would tidy away the dishes and immediately start preparing breakfast for her three boys, boys she was convinced had the appetites of piranha fish.

My brothers and I would later come into the kitchen and like three bears we would charge at the table, towards the three steaming bowls of porridge which lay in wait. We would greedily guzzle down our bowls of porridge and as we did so our eyes would scavenge for more, in the hope that there happened to be some left hiding in the bottom of Mother's pot.

When Mother finally got us off to school, she barely had time to blink. Before opening up the shop, the kitchen had to be tidied for what was already the second time that day and the housework was a never-ending cycle. Without modern-day appliances, chores such as laundry would take their toll and scrubbing and rinsing over a basin were a daily grind. With three boys and a hard-working husband to keep, Mother went about her tasks with steely determination and an admirable air of efficiency and she would not even pause for breath until Father arrived back to the shop.

On his arrival she would down tools and make her way to the yard, whilst seeing if anything needed her attention on the way. Mother would defy her slight build to help unload the boxes and cart them inside, where she would then stack and display the fruit and vegetables in the most inviting manner possible.

With Father back to take the reins of the shop, Mother would then get on to her bicycle and meander through the streets for the mile or so it took to reach Murnaghan's pub, where she would clean for an hour or two before trailing the familiar route back home. Again, she would then help out in the shop, tending to the needs of customers and in the evenings she would compile records of the daily takings.

My mother's life was one of the few exceptions on our road and she knew that. Hers was a labour of love and her efforts were carried out through a personal want. Father worked harder than any man she knew and Mother always sensed that she was the envy of many women on our street, particularly those who faced life's challenges set against a backdrop of alcohol abuse.

Many brave women of that era remained strong and they resolutely tended to their homes while their husbands showed a great weakness and susceptibility to drink. Men, dissatisfied with their lot in life, would often try to drown their sorrows, forever looking for happiness in the bottom of their glass but, predictably, it was a happiness that would forever elude them and many lives were wasted in dimly lit pubs, while wives and children battled the harsh realities of life at the coalface.

My parents went about their day's labour with a sense of pride and they always showed great dignity, even when tasked with the most menial of chores. They were good people and wonderful parents and they forever selflessly put their children's needs high above their own. Neither my mother nor father ever once left Ireland, and they held no desire to, as for them this little island afforded them so much love and happiness that they both knew the grass could not possibly be greener anywhere else in the world.

CHAPTER 3

THE BROTHERS SOAP

I SUPPOSE I AM NOW OF an age where I could be forgiven for
looking back over my life and ruing the fact that the years
have passed so frightfully quickly. Fortunately, I harbour no
such longing as I feel life has been kind to me overall and
mine has been a life I would be both honoured and blessed
to repeat. When you get to my age you feel blessed to still be
alive, having borne witness to so much death that the passing
of friends and family has become an almost frequent and most
unwanted occurrence. I have seen some people taken all too
soon, plucked to the heavens while still in the prime of their
lives. Likewise, I have witnessed others left on earth too long,
allowing illness to grip them in an inescapable hold and leaving
them as shadows of their former selves. My own time on this
planet so far has been charmed and with the exception of a
bit of arthritis and the odd cold here and there, I have been
as fit as a butcher's dog from day one.

My childhood was one of fun and youthful endeavour and I often wonder if having a household full of boys offered my parents the same joys it afforded me. You see there was always a real sense of mayhem whenever the Soap trio were together and noise just seemed to follow us everywhere. At our mother's prompt we would rise in the morning and run at breakneck speed to breakfast, which, once devoured, saw us run off to school. Once there, we would run around the schoolyard and even when inside the classrooms our minds raced with disinterest, before we ran home to torment our besieged mother as she went kindly about her business.

My eldest brother Michael had been born a full three years before I decided to make an appearance and together we lived on a street awash with little faces. It was certainly not commonplace to have such a large gap between siblings as a baby a year (practically every year) seemed to be the norm in other families in those days. Our street was a never-ending conveyor belt of children and once a new bundle of joy drew its first breath, another was in the making. Perhaps my parents needed all their energy and focus as they tried to establish their business, but whatever the reason, it worked to my benefit as Michael and I became inseparable and the best of pals.

When my youngest brother Edward was born, some two years after me, the whole dynamic of our house changed or at the very least that was how it appeared through my juvenile eyes. As the youngest, up to that point, I felt that it was not only my privilege but also my right to be the centre of my parents' focus, yet now, in Edward, I had a younger, cuter rival for their time and affection. Naturally of course both Father and Mother offered little Edward plenty of attention, yet still he appeared to cry constantly and it looked to me like he didn't fully appreciate all the fussing over him, fussing which I had always greedily received with relish.

As Edward grew older I wisely dismissed any sense of rivalry between us and I took on the role of protective older brother as I tried to apply the lessons I had learned from Michael during my own formative years. Just as I had been included in everything Michael did, I set about ensuring that Edward was afforded the exact same opportunities I had been blessed with, yet it is my humble opinion that my younger brother ultimately failed to grasp this opportunity as well as its moral importance.

Very young siblings are often inseparable, as was the case with us, and often innocent minds know no different, yet following several initial years of brotherly togetherness Edward began to spurn both Michael and I, and he always seemed to be indifferent to spending time with us.

Michael to his credit always took his duties as big brother very seriously over the years and I am truly grateful for his bravery in doing so. He ensured that I was never idle, took me fishing on occasion and even to play football with his friends. Some of those boys would mock him for bringing his little brother along but Michael always stood up for both of us and he brushed aside any criticism for the tripe that it was.

I remember one particular day on a patch of land at the bottom of our row, one of the bigger boys in the group took an instant dislike to me and he clattered into me, almost breaking me in two. As I lay on the ground, tearfully checking that both my legs were still attached, Michael by way of retribution proceeded to break the offending boy in four with a fearsome tackle.

You see the easiest thing Michael could have done was to stick with his own pals and try not to show any sign of perceived weakness by showing me compassion, because sentiment is not a luxury that young boys have as there is always pressure to stake one's claim within a group of peers. I would imagine little girls are more accepting whereas little boys can be cruel and even quite brutal in their own way. Michael could have easily dismissed me and left me to forage for myself but courageously he never once shunned me or left me to fight an uphill battle on my own.

I wonder if mixing with those older boys, lads of ten and eleven, brought on my development and shaped me somehow, as even in my eighth year I was always very much an old man of a young boy. I was forever coming up with various schemes, and, if left to my own devices, I could be a right little rascal when I wanted to be. I was, on occasion, bold, but not in a way that brought concern to my parents and thankfully most of my little crimes brought wry smiles to their faces. One such misdemeanour often springs to mind and even after all these years I am both proud and ashamed of my antics in equal measure.

Mrs. Margaret Kirwin, a fearsome lady who lived two doors down from us, would in those days store her milk bottles in an old galvanised bucket outside of her back door. You see back then refrigerators were not all that common so the lovely old milk bottles you don't see any more, were kept outside in a bucket of water to keep them cool. Well, one day I was up for devilment in a big way and with the knowledge of Mrs. Kirwin's method of refrigeration firmly in my mind, I hatched one of my little plans. It was as conniving and sinister as anything a James Bond villain could devise, which was an achievement all the more impressive when you consider that James Bond hadn't even been created at that point.

My plan was to empty the lovely fresh milk out into a separate container and then refill the empty bottles with the smelly stagnant water that was intended to cool them. I would then re-seal the bottle tops with the cloudy water inside, before placing them back into the bucket. Then with the bottles nestled back inside, I would pour the fresh milk from the container out into the base of the bucket, thus creating a vice-versa effect to its original state.

All I needed was an empty container, which I duly commandeered from my father's shed and once in hand I set to work implementing my plan. I sneakily snuck around to Mrs. Kirwin's back garden and I crawled on my belly until I reached her water bucket, which, as I predicted, was by the back door. Jackpot! The bucket contained three full bottles of fresh milk, and with that, the perfect crime commenced.

Firstly, I lifted the milk bottles from the bucket and began to forcefully pull at their foil tops with all the might I could muster. After several failed attempts I eventually managed to free them, before placing each shiny disk on the ground beside me.

I'll need those again later, I thought prudently.

I then proceeded to pour the milk from the bottles out into my container, being careful not to spill a drop. Next up, I filled each bottle to the brim with the putrid water from Mrs. Kirwin's bucket and while doing so, my giggles made me spill some down the sides, but I managed to keep going regardless. I then carefully placed the bottle tops back on, sealing in the slimy water, before gently lowering them back into Mrs. Kirwin's, by now empty, bucket.

I reached over to my container (a washed-out tin of dark wood stain) and I began to pour the milk into the old bucket containing the bottles and as I did so the milk's colour became tainted with orange rust. Once complete, I gathered myself up and headed quickly for the gate, pausing only to have one final look at the three bottles of dirty water, which stood like grey islands in a sea of spoiled white milk. I giggled some more before escaping to the safety of home.

Two hours or so later, just as I sat down for tea with my family, we were collectively startled by the most thunderous noise. Instinctively, I knew it had been sounded with me in mind, so I got up from my chair and ran at breakneck speed towards my bedroom. My mother's calls to return barely registered against the pounding on the front door, while Father walked downstairs to answer the door, which I imagined was shaking on its hinges.

Just as my gut had suspected, it was Mrs. Kirwin who was causing the rumpus and I heard her speak loudly and aggressively to my father. She even used some of the words I thought only the dockers knew.

With a roar to rival Mrs. Kirwin's, Father summoned me down to face the music and the sight that awaited me at the bottom of the stairs is still imprinted on my mind to this very day. Mrs. Kirwin, fine big woman that she was, was standing in our doorway holding a familiar bucket in her right hand and her face was like a storm cloud.

"Look what that little so-and-so has done to my milk bottles!" Mrs. Kirwin bellowed, as she pointed manically between me and the bucket she had by now raised to within two inches of Father's nose.

Father peered into the bucket, where his gaze fell upon a strange pale orange liquid and three milk bottles whose contents appeared so dark they could pass for Guinness.

"Explain yourself, Joseph Soap!" Father said sternly, having turned around to face me.

I stood there in silence and looked at the floor.

"Joseph, are you responsible for this?" Father asked.

"I think so," I offered.

"You think so! I'll give you something to think about!" interrupted Mrs. Kirwin as she moved menacingly in my direction.

Suddenly I felt a protective hand on my shoulder, as Mother appeared at the foot of the stairs and stepped swiftly in front of me, shielding me from the great lump that was Mrs. Kirwin. Although unevenly matched in size, my mother's lack of build would never deter her from taking on all comers when it came to protecting her family, and it was love, not aggression, that made her more than a match for anyone.

Mrs. Kirwin remained livid and she demanded that my parents punish me with force. Worryingly, Father seemed to agree to her demand and after promising to buy her three fresh bottles of milk the very next day, he bid her good evening.

"You leave it to me Mrs. Kirwin, mind how you go," said Father as he closed the door behind the departing old battleaxe.

Father turned and looked at me and I again averted my gaze to the ground, seeking refuge between my feet. Fearing the worst, I tried to come to terms with my impending doom and I found myself closing my eyes in resignation. As my world fell dark I neither saw nor heard sight nor sound, until the faintest of sniggers from above pricked up my ears. Curiosity opened and then raised my eyes skyward and I tentatively cast my gaze towards the heavens in search of answers. Looking up, I found Mother peering down at me and as my nervous eyes met hers, she delightfully and unexpectedly exploded into laughter. Father suddenly followed suit. Not wanting to feel left out I too started to giggle, cautiously at first, but the howls from my parents soon freed me from any nervous restraint. In fact, we all laughed so loudly that I'm sure the departing Mrs. Kirwin must have heard us from outside.

That joyous moment was as nice a time with one's parents as any little boy could ever hope for and it forever proved to me that while crime certainly doesn't pay, mischief can, on occasion.

My parents continued to work hard to provide for all three of their children and due to their considerable efforts we were a real family of note on our street. Mother continued to ensure that we were always turned out in the best of clothes that she could possibly muster for us, and she would persistently keep us all spick and span. I, in particular, had a face as clean as any boy in the county and I often thought that the cleanliness of our faces brought a great sense of pride to my parents, as we were constantly being scrubbed cheek by cheek with a damp cloth. The resulting redness of which, was merely passed off as a healthy glow.

As we all grew older and diverging personalities kicked in, Edward formed a group of his own friends and he went off in a completely different direction to Michael and me. So much so that I once overheard Father jokingly refer to him as the black sheep of the family. At the time I just presumed that he was making reference to the cleanliness of Edward's face, which I often noted ended up in a much grubbier state than my own, but with hindsight I feel that perhaps Father's comment was a lot more telling than it first appeared.

Although the Soap boys were all different, we were in some ways exactly the same, as we were reared to do our best and to know the difference between right and wrong. We were all taught to basically try to be good boys but at times when we failed miserably, the silver lining in the cloud was that at least we knew that what we were doing was the wrong thing to do.

"If you learn from a mistake, than the mistake was well worth making," my parents frequently drilled home to us and I deem them wise words indeed.

Young Conor, I have always taken those words and their sentiment to heart and I honestly believe that if everyone learned a similar lesson then we, as people, would not view lapses in judgement, or those who make them, as failures. Only then would each one of us be seen as equal and the mistakes we all make would remain just as they are – valuable lessons in life.

CHAPTER 4

SCHOOL

ALTHOUGH I AM NOT A MAN for regrets, I often wonder what my life would have turned out like had I applied myself fully during my schooldays. My academic journey was practically over before it had even started, having left school at what is now thought to be the ludicrously young age of sixteen. However, looking back, I do feel that I would have liked to have progressed a bit further, but it was not to be.

Sadly for many children of my generation, education was placed firmly on the back burner, as the harsh demands of everyday life ensured that for most of them, their life's path had already been predetermined and more often than not it led to a life of manual labour or homemaking.

Some say that people from working class backgrounds do not realise that they have gotten the thin side of life's wedge, because everyone they know happens to be in the same boat, but we knew. We knew that we were not well off like some people, but we also knew that in comparison to a lot of other poor unfortunates, we were positively soaking up the sun. We had parents who not only worked hard for us, but also insisted that we try our best to receive a proper education.

My parents always drove home the value of schooling and in some ways I feel that they were overcompensating for their own lack of formal education. As a result, they took what in those days was an unusual interest in their children's tuition when they sent Michael, Edward and I to the local Christian Brothers School, which at the time was deemed to be the finest in the area.

Michael was the first to enrol and I remember feeling jealous every time I saw him in his smart school uniform. Short trousers were all the rage in those days and freshly grazed knees were so common a sight, that they were almost a part of the outfit. I was, however, less jealous of the gigantic satchel that Michael was forced to carry, which housed what I guessed to be a million books or so, and he would come home every day stooped down under the sheer weight of it. I didn't have to wait too long before Michael's uniform found its way onto my back via hand-me-downs and when I was of age, I too was enrolled with the Christian Brothers, a move which was later repeated with Edward.

My parents gave us every opportunity by setting us on a path which they hoped would take us on a lifelong journey of education and academic achievement, but for me and so many like me, the wheels quickly came off the wagon and wishful dreams of a college degree evaporated in the blink of an eye. Despite initial best efforts, I failed to flourish and in terms of exam results, well, the less said about those the better.

My formative years in education are not something which I look back upon with rose-tinted spectacles, and in complete contrast to the vibrant colour of my everyday life, I lived firmly beneath a grey sky during those school hours. The Christian Brothers School was a foreboding place, needlessly ominous, and it always struck me as a very curious place in which to channel a stream of impressionable young boys. Huge dark weather-beaten walls surrounded a dreadful plain old building, a building which in many ways summed up the occupants it employed. It was a structure that did not lend itself to creativity or imagination and its sole purpose, or so it seemed, was to shelter Christian Brothers, so called educators, who merely taught children that verbal, often physical and repeatedly mental abuse was all part of daily life.

A typical school day for me would start almost in denial, as I would eagerly get to the schoolyard early in order to play with my school friends, Donal and Peter (I will tell you about them later). While there, the curse of many, the school bully, was thankfully never an issue for me as I always had Michael on standby during playtimes. I, in turn, would try and keep a watchful eye on Edward but from an early age it was clear that he was to be more of a perpetrator than victim.

Breaks always passed far too quickly and the innocent games of children were cruelly interrupted by the clanging of the bell, which summoned us from yard to desk with noise levels that would rival that of an air-raid siren. Morning prayers were followed by classes teaching (or at least attempting to teach) us Mathematics, English, Irish and of course Religion.

Our main taskmaster was named Brother Leo and he was a type of man that fortunately I have never encountered since. At the time he appeared to me to be about five hundred years old, but looking back he was probably no more than fifty. He was a tall man with a pointed nose and a stare that could free a statue from a block of marble. He ruled his classroom with an iron fist, using the primitive weapon of fear as his only motivational aid.

Violent outbursts were a regular occurrence. The other children and I would frequently cower behind our wooden desks, should another pupil dare to make a spelling error or fail to locate the Mountains of Mourne on the coarsely drawn chalk map of Ireland, which sat on top of a sink unit in the corner of the classroom. Brother Leo would not think twice about hurling his wooden duster at a talkative pupil at the back of the class, or forcefully manhandling (or 'boyhandling' I should say) a poor unfortunate lad who perhaps felt the uncontrollable and unforgivable urge to yawn.

School classrooms, after all, are not the natural habitat for little boys and yet the Christian Brothers never understood this. Young children do not want to be confined to the inside of a building as their natural instincts crave the outdoors, which is why their gaze is usually fixed out the window. Outside, a child's life and imagination are all his or her own, yet for reasons that eluded me at the time, my parents seemed intent on forcing me to sit through hours of unpleasantness day after day, with no end in sight. I often wondered, without answer, why such loving parents would force me to run such an emotional and physical gauntlet, although hindsight would later reveal the method in what I wrongly perceived to be their madness.

Those were dark days for education in Ireland and children today thankfully have no knowledge of the brutality that was commonplace back then. I myself have been on the receiving end of many a cane lashing, and if I were to stand before God himself, I would swear that more often than not, my punishment did not fit the crime.

A memory that stays with me to this day is a caning I received for making an innocent mistake during morning prayers, and the severity of my punishment caused both of my hands to burn as though I had grabbed hold of the gates of hell.

Each morning the loathsome Brother Leo would select a boy to stand before the entire class and recite aloud a prayer of his choosing. Well, one such morning, my heart damn near stopped when I heard a word flung forcibly in my direction.

"Soap!!" bellowed Brother Leo, before pointing to a spot of ground on his left-hand side and ordering me to say 'Angel of God'.

I made my way to the top of the class, eyes fixed on the floor as per usual, and I walked at a snail's pace towards Brother Leo, who up close and with Bible in hand, seemed like a giant. I looked up at him for instruction, but he merely twirled his index finger around for me to turn and face the class.

I manoeuvred myself around at a sluggish pace that would rival that of a turning oil tanker, until I faced the class, which sat silently. Thirty pupils stared my way and I must have looked into all sixty of the eyes before me in the hope of help or inspiration, but I saw only relief on their faces as they were rightly glad that they had not been chosen.

With a gulp, I started to say my prayer aloud:

"Oh angel of God my guardian dear, to whom God's love come't me here…"

Well, the crashing thud of 'the good book' slamming down on to a desk startled me and stopped me dead in my tracks. I quickly looked around for explanation, but all I found was an enraged Brother Leo, who cut me in half with a glare.

"How dare you get the Lord's prayer wrong! How dare you!" raged Brother Leo. "Commence me here… not come't!"

In a flash I felt his huge hands press around my collar, compressing my neck, and I was dragged with considerable force to the far corner of the room. My little feet barely touched the ground, and they struggled to keep pace with my rapidly increasing heart rate, as I was abruptly removed from my position of chief orator and repositioned onto the makeshift gallows beside the sink unit.

I was still to be very much centre of attention though, as Brother Leo now grasped his cane, which he had retrieved from behind the chalk outline of the Macgillycuddy Reeks. I stared at it. I looked nervously back at my fellow classmates, but this time I saw only thirty tops of heads as the other boys knew the fate that lay in store for me. They averted their gazes downward through fear and I must say I would never blame them for that, as who would want to bear witness to another person's nightmare?

A swift series of lashes rained down upon the palms of my little hands with brutal force, and I was almost thankful that the very first strike had hurt so much that the other lashes barely registered, as my pain threshold was already pushing its maximum. As the infamous 'six of the best' pummelled my poor hands, I caught sight of Brother Leo's eyes and he seemed to be almost lost in the moment. His face was red with rage, while his eyes appeared black like a shark's as he inflicted the beating with great gusto and at one stage I would swear blind that his emotions bordered on enthusiasm.

As my own eyes began to well up I tried my best not to cry and I so badly wanted to be a man at that moment. I wanted to be a man so that I would not be small anymore, and I could then stand up to Brother Leo in an even contest.

Would he be so brave against someone his own size?

Would he be such a big man if I had ten more years added on to my then eight?

The thunderous blows eventually stopped and, almost overcome by trembling, I returned towards my seat duly chastised. The shame I felt was at least kept in check by the tremendous burning sensation I felt in my hands and the uncontrollable quiver it sent racing along my arms.

The inaccurately named 'six of the best' must surely have amounted to fifteen, although I will admit to losing count shortly after the tenth blow struck. I remember thinking that smart and all as Brother Leo thought he was, he had just made a glaring mistake of his own, but with unequal justice, his crime went unpunished. Perhaps his counting 'error' was meant on purpose and he used his own twisted judgement to dish out the number of lashes that he himself saw fit.

Crestfallen, I sat back down in my seat and I was left to wonder how a man held in such high regard by both the community and God himself, could show such cruelty to those whom he had a responsibility to nurture. Surely if God is all-forgiving, he could have forgiven me a little slip of the tongue, said while praising him, and saved me from Brother Leo. But he didn't.

When I think now of how Brother Leo seemed lost in that moment, I wonder whether that was his way of dealing with that particular situation, or maybe I am giving him too much credit. Was it a case of him knowing full well the true horrors he was inflicting on a young boy, but that he just felt that it was his godly duty to educate through force, or perhaps he saw himself as a soldier at war, who was merely following orders from above?

Maybe he was able to detach himself emotionally from what he was doing, as he believed that it was all in the best interest of the child, and he may very well have thought that by teaching me such a harsh lesson he was somehow saving me in the eyes of our Lord.

Looking back, I suspect that those thoughts, however deluded they may have been, played only a tiny part in the man's thinking, if at all. Brother Leo and many more like him simply took advantage of their position and in turn used it as a tool to abuse the power that was entrusted to them. The institutions they ran were more like factories than schools and the end product was simply a generation of people too frightened to express themselves or even dare to be different, as individuality was soon corrected under the tutelage of men who knew but one way of thinking.

Young Conor, I don't know what age you will be when you thumb your way through your old grandad's ramblings. You may very well be a grown man with your schooling long since behind you, and if that is the case I only hope that you look back on your years in education with nothing but fondness and a sense of fulfilment.

I hope that you consumed every word from the endless pool of books available and that you feel as though each sentence you have read has in some way enriched your mind's eye and further blessed your imagination.

Of course you might well be a teenage boy with many more years of schooling still ahead of you, and if that is the case, I would urge you to really embrace your education. The era you have been born into has thankfully shed the violent abuse of yesteryear and schools today offer a much more tranquil environment in which to prosper. I am told by your auntie Patricia that the subjects taught are wide-ranging and varied, and that each one offers a depth of knowledge which is designed to both broaden your outlook on life and stoke your curiosity to learn even more.

I myself turned my back on schooling at the first chance I got and I ran all too quickly towards the relative safety of working in my father's shop. Looking back I took the easy way out and although I was never blessed with the emotional strength needed to see out my education, I do sometimes wonder what might have been had I grasped what was there for the taking, and not allowed the system to get the better of me. Maybe I could have achieved a worthwhile education had I just been a little more focused on what really mattered, and I could have done so not because of cruel and callous teachers but in spite of them.

Ultimately I lost my battle with those individuals but I know that you, my darling grandson, will no doubt prove that we Soaps can learn and thrive with the best of them.

CHAPTER 5

FAMILY BUSINESS

THE SUMMER IN WHICH I TURNED thirteen years old proved to be a telling one for me, and when the school bell rang to signal the end of term I sprinted at full pelt to the gate.

I would always escape like a hare from a trap and on arriving home I would fling my satchel against the kitchen wall as though the poor thing had somehow managed to offend me. I would then quickly run downstairs to see if I could help out in the shop. I loved the opportunity it gave me to spend extra time with my family and with each passing year I began to spend more and more time doing so.

Within the four walls of our little shop my imagination and self-belief were allowed to flourish, and as I grew older, I was given more and more responsibility to both learn the ropes and help with the family business. Of course the sweeping-up still had to be done and as the junior shopkeeper I was tasked with it, but I was soon allowed to stack and arrange the fruit that was out on display as I saw fit. There was never much arranging to be done with the vegetables, as their subdued earthy exteriors did not lend themselves to an enticing display, but Father would always encourage me to arrange the rainbow-coloured fruit in as decorative a pattern as I could conjure up. I also carried out other less glamorous chores without complaint, and I was always ready, willing and able to lend a hand to Father, Mother or even my brother Michael for that matter.

Michael you see was now all of sixteen years old and he had left school the previous summer. He had remained with the Christian Brothers longer than most had predicted, solely because he had always enjoyed the sporting aspect that was part and parcel of most boys' schools. The early promise shown for soccer had unfortunately regressed into bog-standard ability and as a result, his decision to leave school was not greeted with any real surprise or resistance by my parents as deep down they knew that his talents lay elsewhere.

Although by no means stupid, it was more than a little apparent that Michael was not exactly going to set the world of academia alight, and as much as my parents loved him, they knew that he would not be making too many creases into the spines of law books, nor would he be worrying the corners of too many medical journals. But Michael was a grafter, make no mistake about that. He would tirelessly lift, scrub, polish, add, subtract and weigh anything that needed his attention, and his stamina and enthusiasm for his work was a constant source of inspiration to me on the shop floor. Michael would also help my father to clear out the store shed or unload the van, which was forever packed with the countless sacks and pallets of every fruit and vegetable imaginable. With Mother now less hands-on in this regard, I would try and assist as best I could, and often the smell of the sea air still lingered amongst the pallets, prompting my senses to transport me back to the dockside.

It really was a great family enterprise and we worked together as one. To his credit, Father always made us feel as though we were a vital cog in the Soap machine, and even if our duties stretched to that of merely tidying up, Michael and I made sure to put our heart and soul into each task.

Michael, being the older brother, was tasked with the more demanding roles and on occasions when my father was busy, he was even entrusted to serve some of the customers on the till. Often my most regular chore was that of 'trying to look busy', as our shop was not large by any stretch of the imagination, and were truth to be told, it's more than fair to say that, between my parents and Michael, they had everything covered, but I just loved being there.

Because of this, the little interest in school that survived inside me was now well and truly on its last legs and the only blackboard which held any relevance for me now, was the one that detailed the price list on our shop's wall, as opposed to one that saw the Lord's Prayer sullied by Brother Leo's hand.

In the back of my mind, whether right or wrong, I always knew that I did not have to worry about achieving good exam results in order to gain employment, as I was already well aware of what career path I wanted to take. I was pretty sure that Father would not seek out too many references in order to give me a job, and even if he did, I was almost certain that Mother would gladly put pen to paper for the good of my cause.

You see the difference between time spent in the shop and that which was confined to the classroom was simply startling to me and, for the first time in my fledgling life, I began to feel a real sense of purpose. In the shop I would get praised by my father for completing even the slightest of tasks, while beneath the school roof, I would get chastised for even daring to show a weakness or a failure to grasp a piece of supposedly simple arithmetic. School made me doubt myself, whereas my family made me believe.

Regardless of my feelings, and my constant protests on the matter, my parents both dismissed the very idea of me leaving school at thirteen years of age, and I was left with little choice but to knuckle down and weather the storm.

As time ticked along I somehow managed to stumble through a further three years of schooling, time enough to pass the milestone of my sixteenth birthday, and were it not for the shop providing a glimmer of hope, I truly believe that I ran the risk of becoming lost in the shadows.

During the latter years of my education I really began to feel as if I were somehow socially and mentally inadequate and this I felt was due in no small part to years of physical and verbal abuse dished out by Brother Leo and his cohorts.

Throughout those subsequent three years, time in which I am sure I forgot more than I learned, I increasingly began to pester my parents about leaving school and I further plagued them with my desire to work full time with them. The tears I cried, as I made my case, eventually struck a chord with my parents and I was relieved and reassured in equal measure when they accepted that my upset was genuine and not put on for theatrical effect.

Mine were real tears, tears of a young lad who was simply turning to his parents for a solution to all his life's woes, but even so, my parents still held deep reservations about the practicalities of it all. I recall, accidently on purpose, overhearing them question whether the shop could sustain us all in full-time employment, particularly in the coming years and they paid further lip service to the fact that Edward would also be approaching maturity in the not-so-distant future. They continued to debate the issue at length, and their collective life experiences, perhaps, acted as both a blessing and a hindrance, as they considered every conceivable pro and con they could think of.

Father and Mother, possibly against their better judgement, eventually decided that I was indeed to be granted my wish and, on hearing the news that my schooldays were forever behind me, my relief on the matter was incalculable. At sixteen years old I unceremoniously condemned my satchel to the family coal shed, where over the years it gathered dust and blackened from within, just as I imagined the souls of Brother Leo and his associates did, to the tune of the school bell.

Once officially a full-time member of staff, I noticed that my role within the shop began to change, and virtually overnight Father began to trust me with a more varied and wide-ranging set of duties. From the onset I threw myself into each task, and while I can't say that my efforts were of any great value, the business at least managed to continue heading in the right direction regardless.

In truth I suspect it would have done so with or without my involvement, but I was still delighted to play a part, no matter how small, in its overall success. We had a loyal and steady stream of customers, who frequented the shop on a near-daily basis, and over time I got to know each by name just as Father did.

The vast majority of our patrons were of course women and, without wanting to sound patronising, they were the true lifeblood of the community. Classed as homemakers, which they were in the best possible way, their tireless efforts ensured that a house was not just a shell to keep the rain off the children, but a place that offered up the best possible environment in which one could raise a family amid challenging times.

I witnessed both sides of society from behind the countertop, and I watched without comment as more affluent women would buy more food than they could possibly need; whereas often I saw poorer women leaving with barely enough. For them every piece of produce was chosen wisely, as they sought out only the largest of each fruit or vegetable available and everything was clinically examined to ensure that it was worthy of the money being handed over to secure it.

The needs of children waiting impatiently at home took precedence over personal pride, and those fine women knew all too well that a child's rumbling belly could not be satisfied by lazily selecting slighter offerings. Noticeably, the smaller pieces of food in stock were always the last to be sold, and I feel that that goes a long way to explaining why early morning was always our busiest time of day.

Mrs. Majella Shields was one such lady. Born and bred in Stepaside, she was a regular visitor to our shop and often the time spent within our walls was the only peace she encountered on any given day. You see Mrs. Shields had to fend for nine children; as well as put up with a husband who was known to be overly fond of a drink. Over the years she had always been extremely choosy when it came to selecting her foods, but I recall one day in particular, when she must have spent all of ten minutes selecting just four potatoes from the barrel of bountiful spuds we had on display. Several other lady customers, who were huddled together in the corner, could be seen and heard passing comment, but Mrs. Shields, undeterred, continued her rummage. Watching in the wings, I felt strangely uncomfortable, as an unfamiliar air of awkwardness infiltrated our little shop.

I clearly remember standing side by side with my father as we watched this puzzled lady agonise over her selection, and each of the many eyes that bore witness to her hesitation clearly saw a vulnerable woman who was afraid to rush even the simplest of decisions. I asked Father why she was taking so long and questioned whether she had perhaps dropped something into the barrel but Father, without taking his eyes off Mrs. Shields, tried his best to explain to me that some people were just not as fortunate as we were.

Just as Father spoke his gaze was met for a faint second by Mrs. Shields herself, and she looked saddened, embarrassed and almost apologetic, until she returned her eyes back to the barrel. Seconds later my father placed his hand tenderly on my shoulder. He then gave me the slightest of squeezes, and by instinct, I immediately raised both of my hands and placed them on top of his. The moment ended when I felt his hand slide from beneath mine and I watched with curiosity as he manoeuvred both of his hands onto the countertop, to greet an approaching customer.

In full view of the nosey women in the corner, Mrs. Shields walked up to my father and placed four large potatoes on the counter, before taking her purse from her shopping bag. I looked on as Father opened the till and as he did so he threw his eyes towards the gossiping women in the corner, before quickly returning his attention back to his serving duties.

"Mrs. Shields, I must apologise to you this morning," said Father.

"Pardon me, Mr. Soap?" asked Mrs. Shields, while opening her purse.

"Yes, you see I'm rather embarrassed about the quality of the potatoes we have to offer here today, in so much as they simply do not match up in size to the ones I usually pride myself in offering," said Father, in a matter-of-fact sort of way.

"Oh, I'm sure that is not the case at all, Mr. Soap," replied Mrs. Shields, too polite to argue otherwise.

Father assured her that it was indeed the case and he then beckoned her to follow him back over to the potatoes out on display. I watched with puzzlement as my father led the nice lady down the middle of the shop, and he paused momentarily, only to politely acknowledge the prying gaggle of women who were observing his every move.

"We have a special offer on today, Mrs. Shields, due to those clearly substandard vegetables, and I hope that you will kindly and with good grace, select a dozen of these puny potatoes for the price of the four that you have already chosen. Also please accept my most sincere apology for any offence or delay caused by your having to trawl through my stock, in search of adequately sized vegetables," Father said, in a tone I was not familiar with.

Father, at this point, had his back turned to me, and as a result, I was not privy to the knowing look, if any, that he may or may not have discreetly given to Mrs. Shields, but reacting to something, or perhaps to the drop of a penny, Mrs. Shields responded in kind.

"Eh, well I really must say that the choice on display here today should indeed be a cause of embarrassment to you and your business, Mr. Soap. I will avail of your offer and I will do so only in the hope that this incident does not happen again, or indeed in future I shall be forced to take my custom elsewhere," Mrs. Shields said, having taken a second or two to reply.

As if unsure what to do next, Father and Mrs. Shields stood awkwardly for a moment, until she paid him the small amount he was due. As she handed him the money I noticed that her hand, which looked to be slightly trembling, remained within Father's for a little longer than was necessary. When the transaction was finally completed, she made a dignified exit, never once taking focus from the door as she went.

"Your custom is always valued here, Mrs. Shields, good day to you!" Father bellowed as the shop door closed.

In that moment I loved my father. I always had done of course, but that small act to another human being only cemented in my mind what I already knew. He was a decent man and he showed me that, by being a shopkeeper, one who cares for his customers, it was possible to serve your community in more ways than one.

It is, of course, important to remember that not every person has the wherewithal to offer grand or elaborate gestures to one's fellow man, but we all possess the innate ability to do some good, if even in the smallest of ways. Some people choose to show their kindness, others don't, but I am sure that the world would turn a lot easier if everyone just did their best and tried to help those around them.

It may sound like wishful thinking but Father showed me that by helping, rather than merely standing by and judging, he could actually make a difference in someone's life, and through a little kindness, he could help revive in a person the dignity and self-worth that was being eroded on a daily basis.

The gossiping women in the shop soon snapped me out of my ideals and they showed me the other side of human nature when they approached Father and opportunistically asked him for the same 'offer' that Mrs. Shields had received.

To his credit, Father maintained the charade, and made good on his promise.

Oh, the trials of a shopkeeper...

CHAPTER 6

MICHAEL THE ELDER

My first few weeks of full-time employment quickly rolled into months and it was not long before my bitter memories of dour schooldays went the way of the dinosaurs. My days were now spent firmly within the bosom of my family and I relished each and every moment. Business was not too shabby either and Father, Michael and I went about our day's work with great drive and passion. Michael and I often spoke about ways to improve the shop and we were always amazed when Father backed our ideas and gave them a go, admittedly with varying degrees of success.

The three of us became a proper little team and I know it meant a lot to Father to have us in and around the place, particularly as my mother's health had begun to dip during that period. Mother had inexplicably started to feel weak on occasion, often struggling for breath, yet things only came to a head one day when she succumbed to a dizzy spell she had in the sitting room whilst straightening out the house.

Mother of course attempted to dismiss it, but we as a family were naturally concerned and Father in particular seemed most drawn by the whole affair. At night-time I began to hear voices seeping through the thin wall of my parents' bedroom. Michael would often come into the room I shared with Edward and we would press our ears up against the wall to improve reception. Those nocturnal conversations were somewhat of a recent occurrence, as previously, the entire Soap household had all been Olympic-standard sleepers. Now, however, things had changed and we knew from our eavesdropping that Mother was having great difficulty finding slumber.

At night I would listen intently as she tossed and turned, and I longed to be by her side each time she endured a fit of coughing, but daren't for fear of giving the game away and revealing that I was secretly listening. Father, of course, had all angles covered and we knew that he tended to her as best he could, be it fetching glasses of water or just fussing over her generally.

I recall one specific night, when Michael and I overheard my parents talking about family matters, and as always we were consumed with interest as we fastened our ears to the wall. Edward, as usual, remained buried beneath his duvet, indifferent to the world and all its problems and from where Michael and I were standing he cut a very casual figure indeed.

Poor Edward was still as torn away as any tearaway before or since and my parents, despite Mother's health concerns, would still voice their opinion with one another and share concerns for his future. It had been crystal-clear from day one that Edward had little interest in school, yet an increasing panache for disobedience and mitching off lessons had blotted his copybook further, while flippant calls to leave school altogether became all the more frequent.

My mother seemed to favour the idea as a means of keeping a closer eye on him, but Father appeared to be much more sceptical as he again questioned whether the shop would be big enough to provide full-time employment for his three boys, who would one day become men.

They frequently spoke long and hard on the topic and on that particular night, I could sense that they were both getting quite animated before emotions finally settled back down to neutrality. Michael and I listened on in silence as the argument ran its course, although in truth looking back I'm not certain that two loving parents trying to work out the best course of action for their problematic child can truly constitute being called an argument.

To me, Edward was just a little different in his mindset from the rest of us and given his status as my younger brother I often saw him as a little rebel who sometimes made me laugh when I heard him giving lip. My parents would always give out to him for answering back or using bad language, but I never did, mainly because I knew that deep down Edward was just fighting the same battles that we all struggle with while growing into adulthood.

I was proud of myself for having such a grown-up view of the situation, yet also a little ashamed, as I knew it was I, myself, who had introduced him to many of his choice words. Perhaps, as a result, I knew that I could hardly reach for the moral high ground on the matter, so I just accepted his ways and tried to understand his train of thought without judgement.

My parents' nightly news bulletins would yield some very interesting topics, yet it was Edward who more often than not grabbed the headlines. I was shocked as well as disappointed when I heard that he had been caught stealing coins from a jar that my mother had set aside for utilities, and talk of him bullying smaller boys on our street greatly troubled me. Michael and I had always looked out for Edward as best we could, but he always seemed intent on placing a distance between us, a distance summed up as Michael and I strained up against the wall to hear, while Edward lay across the room either sound asleep or lost in his own disinterest.

The next morning, after another secret summit, my parents went about life as if the previous night's conversation had belonged to them alone. Mother did what her energy allowed her to do around the house, while Father busied himself further, trying to imitate our Lord by being everywhere at once.

My parents to their credit were simply trying to shield us from upset and instead of polluting the shop's air with worry, they instead chose to confine it to their little bedroom. They showed great strength and consideration as heads of our household, and my brothers and I always knew that if it came down to it, they would walk through the fires of hell for any one of us.

Michael and I continued to eavesdrop as the debates continued long and hard into sleepless nights, and for every "It'll do the boy good," my mother offered, my father countered with "The shop cannot provide a future for all of them, Angela".

They eventually settled on the only real solution that was available to them and even though it was becoming something of a Soap family tradition for underperforming schoolboys, it was decided that Edward, at fourteen years of age, was to leave school to take up full-time employment within the shop. Subsequent rumours of expulsion from school were never confirmed to me, but whatever their reasoning, I accepted that my parents knew best when it came to rearing their children.

Despite already knowing, Michael and I acted really surprised and somewhat taken aback when it was announced over dinner one evening that Edward would be joining us on the shop floor. In all honesty I was less than enthused by the decision, as Edward, in spite of all the love and goodwill afforded to him over the years, had never once shown the slightest interest in the family business.

Father, Michael and I continued to complement each other on the shop floor and we worked collectively and without complaint to ensure that the business maintained its high standards, yet now, despite his small stature, Edward's presence felt like an elephant in the room. Often staff would outnumber customers and regularly we began to feel like we were tripping over one another.

Edward didn't exactly pull up any trees when it came to work, but the truth was that there was very little for him to do, yet rather than accept his good fortune and realise his position, he began to pass comment and criticise every decision that was made without his consultation. Given Edward's age and lackadaisical attitude to life, his views were always taken with a pinch of salt, and more often than not, he would cause more problems than he solved. Tensions on occasion simmered without boil, but I always got the impression that an argument was brewing beneath the surface.

I know Michael, at nineteen years old, felt particularly disillusioned by the whole affair. He had been working tirelessly within the shop, yet still he understood that his efforts could not be reflected in his pay packet, as the business simply did not make enough money to adequately decorate all of the outstretched hands. We received little more than an allowance as it was, yet Father now had to include Edward on the payroll leaving things even tighter than before. Granted, we were doing a respectable trade but we were restricted greatly by the size of our little shop and as ours was a corner house on a busy road, any sort of expansion was just pie in the sky.

I know my father was of the same mind and he constantly worried that his boys would struggle to make a life for themselves as they grew older and gained dependants of their own. I know this to be true as Michael and I repeatedly overheard him admit as much to Mother, as we continued to cling to my bedroom wall like strips of wallpaper.

Father also worried that he had somehow failed his boys by not being able to provide proper employment for them, and one night in particular he asked Mother if things would be different if he had pushed himself further to achieve more. He wondered if there was something he could have done differently that would have discouraged his sons from feeling the need to cling onto a branch that clearly could not support their collective weight. Indeed, he became so emotional that my mother, in spite of her poor health, found herself coaxing him back from the brink of distress. I could not tell if my father was crying, but I did get the feeling that a tear could at any minute seep through the bedroom wall.

My parents' room went quiet a short time later and our home fell strangely silent. Prompted by this I whispered over to Michael, and I asked him what he thought all this could mean. My less-than-probing question went without reply however and Michael simply turned and walked out of Edward's and my bedroom and silently retreated back to his own room across the landing. The next morning, when I had him alone in the yard, I again tried to broach the subject but he said he didn't want to talk about it and over the next few days he grew quieter with each passing second.

It was all of two weeks later before I learned the true extent of Michael's feelings and while sitting around the dinner table one evening he unexpectedly and quite shockingly announced to the family that he was going to live in America.

Such an outlandish notion caused me to smile from ear to ear and I sat with bated breath as I waited for a punchline that never came.

"Sure Michael lives here," I thought, innocently.

The practicalities alone made it beyond contemplation, not to mention the fact that not one member of our family would be able to locate America on a map. Even with the benefit of a compass and a week off work we would struggle to locate Galway, such was the great depth at which our family's roots were embedded into the Dublin soil.

I looked to my parents, expecting my eyes to be met with faces struggling to restrain wild laughter, but all my eyes met with was a knowing look from two people who had already resigned themselves to their son's decision. Michael, it turns out, had discussed his thoughts with my parents at length and unbeknownst to me, a bold choice had already been made. My eyes welled up as I listened to what, for me, was frankly an unacceptable explanation for my brother's impending departure and tears managed to escape despite my noble struggle to contain them.

"There's just no way the shop can provide livings for three young men, let alone secure the futures of three middle-aged men with families of their own," Father explained.

"He's right, and as I'm the eldest it's up to me to make way. I'm going to try my luck in Chicago," said my brother in a forthright manner.

Michael added that work was plentiful in America and that he was going to be one of many thousands of Irish people over there. He said that he, along with three of his old school pals, had come to the decision to emigrate, and now with his mind made up, he was not for turning.

I wanted someone to put a stop to this madness. Michael wanted to be one of thousands in America, but I wanted him to be one of five here in Dublin. I didn't want our family to be broken up, and I said as much but my pleading fell on deaf ears and I was simply told by all parties concerned that, "It was for the best". I was to lose my hero, my best friend, and I was losing him not through death or misfortune, but through something as avoidable as geography.

You see Michael was always a chap of real substance; that much was clear from the outset of our lives. He was a strong character, the type who would take a hit for his family and think nothing of placing our needs above his own, but I still feared for him, as he had no formal skills or education to speak of. I worried that he would end up labouring on building sites, carrying out back-breaking work for a pittance, beneath skies as changeable as the most indecisive of minds.

Father as always had his 'practicalities' hat on and he was more than a little distressed as to how Michael was going to pay for his fare to the United States, not to mention all of the other costs associated with such a bold move. The modest wage Michael earned from the shop would barely stretch to the bus into town so a ticket to America was out of the question as things stood.

With the news out in the open, secret conversations were no longer confined to my parents' bedroom and Father became quite vocal with his opinions on the whole situation. Although he supported Michael in his decision, he was unable to support his move financially as the business simply did not generate enough income to fund such an expense. Father even emptied out his savings for what they were worth, and he gave them to Michael who gratefully accepted, having seen a degree of desperation in Father's eyes. A number of times, I heard Michael reassure him that he "had done more than enough".

As with many, and I dare say most, Irish households, it was the Mammy who provided the solution and she did so when she joined us for dinner a few nights later. Over the previous couple of weeks, Mother's presence at the dinner table had become sporadic as her coughing and lack of sleep had sadly taken its toll on her, so it was with great excitement that we sat around the table as a family of five again.

As Father pulled a chair out from the table and helped Mother sit down, we noticed that she was holding a pocket-sized book, which had a large white envelope wedged inside it. Easing herself down onto her seat, Mother then placed the book on the table in front her and as she did so the familiar insignia of Stepaside Credit Union revealed itself. With a proud smile on her face, Mother opened the envelope and produced, what looked to be, all the money in the world.

As Mathematics has never been a strong point, I cannot say for sure how much was there, but all who witnessed it were dumbstruck at the amount of notes revealed.

"Oh such wonderful silence," said Mother, smiling softly. "I would have brought this money out sooner, had I known it would deliver such peace and quiet".

Mother went on to explain that she had prudently squirrelled away a portion of the wages she had received for cleaning up the mess that others were either too proud or too lazy to do for themselves, and that her countless bicycle journeys to Murnaghan's pub were only now paying a dividend.

"You take this money Michael, put it along with the money your father gave you and book your ticket son," Mother said as she handed the money over to a clearly perplexed Michael.

It was obvious that Mother's revelation was also news to my father as his eyes near bore a hole through the paper notes. Sensing his shock she placed her hand gently on to my father's wrist, and for a brief second he didn't react as Michael picked up the money. Then as if awakening from a deep unconsciousness, he repositioned his hands and placed them firmly on top of Mother's.

"I hope you are not mad at me for keeping such a secret?" Mother asked.

"I'll only be mad if you haven't any more secrets like this one!" said Father jokingly.

I remember that moment as if it was yesterday and I felt so happy and proud to be part of such a family, but I was almost afraid to open my eyes to its true consequence as, sadly, it proved to be the last time that my family ever sat down together as one.

The work ethic and decency my parents showed towards Michael has remained with me to this day, and even though they would miss him so terribly, they both did all that they possibly could to enable him to leave their side. I guess that is what parenting is all about.

Some people have such a great desire to have children and to surround themselves with family, that often their judgement becomes clouded. They begin to see the family unit as the be-all and end-all, yet often individuals can only flourish and thrive when outside the family circle.

I strongly believe that parents should never dictate to their children, rather they should let nature take its course and allow each child to branch out in whatever direction they choose. If that direction is leading them far from home, a parent should realise that to truly guide and nurture a child, they must allow them to follow their own path in life and make their own decisions. Each child is of course different, but as a parent, your role is forever the same.

The next few days passed by in a blur, as having bought a ticket for a transatlantic voyage by sea, Michael hurriedly prepared to set sail. Having said his goodbyes around town, he packed his case with the few possessions he had and then anxiously awaited the clock's tick.

By way of 'something to remember me by' Michael gave me his favourite pullover, a navy blue jumper with red detail down the side, as he knew that I had always admired it. When Michael handed it to me he told me that it didn't fit him anymore, but in truth it still fitted him like a glove. Keeping that knowledge to myself I accepted it graciously, having made a conscious decision to go along with the pretence for both our sakes. Thanking Michael, I took hold of the jumper and I treasured it for many years, long enough in fact for it to become more hole than jumper.

When the fateful departure day finally came, Mother kissed Michael goodbye at the shop's door rather than seeing him off at the boat, as she insisted that someone must look after the place; but it did not take a genius to work out her motives for staying behind. With his bag in hand, Michael said goodbye to a few neighbours who had gathered to wave him off, he then joined Father, Edward and I as we crammed into the van and set off for the port.

Before he set sail I hugged Michael, and wished him well as I tried to fight back tears in an ever-losing battle. Edward offered up a hug of sorts, but their goodbye was perhaps best summed up by the simple handshake that followed. Michael and Edward may not have been the best of friends, but they were brothers after all and that still counts for something.

Father also embraced Michael before warmly shaking him by the hand, adding with a wink, "Get on that boat, before they go off without ya".

I often envied the sailors I saw in Dublin, going off on their travels around the world, but I did not envy Michael his journey. Quite how he made each step onto that boat I will never know, as fear and sadness would surely have gotten the better of me.

Father, Edward and I watched in silence as the official checked his ticket, and on approval Michael turned and waved before stepping on board. We returned the wave with as much enthusiasm as we could muster, and with that simple gesture he was gone from our lives. My brother, my best friend, would now sadly take on the much lesser role of 'long distance pen pal'.

Father, Edward and I then made our way back through the port and as we did so we were oblivious to the entire goings on around us. Father to his credit tried to make light of the moment but his words fell on deaf ears.

"After years of importing, us Soaps are now exporting. We're going international, eh boys!" Father said, unsuccessfully attempting to raise spirits.

On any other day I probably would have laughed, but that day, the realisation of the truth brought sorrow not joy to my face.

Michael, as we all expected, blossomed into a fine man and he is as he always was, a credit to our family. Not long after he arrived in America he found work with one of the big railway companies and after serving his time he progressed to become a train driver. He met and fell in love with an American girl named Una McNally, whose family, as the name suggests, were of Irish descent and it wasn't long before news of their engagement reached us by post.

Any far-fetched notions we in Stepaside had of travelling over to Chicago for the wedding quickly evaporated, as the shop's needs outweighed our own and Michael, to his credit, understood without fuss. He later sent us on a photograph of himself and his bride, and on receipt Father made sure it found a home for itself, pride of place, on top of the mantelpiece in the sitting room. Reminding us all that even though Michael was not with us in body, he was still very much at home in spirit.

Dearest Conor, the island of Ireland has always had a long and often unwanted relationship with emigration and I can barely think of one household that has not been affected by it in one way or the other. For such a small country we seem to have scattered ourselves to the four corners of the globe and Irish people have set up home in places as far-flung as their desire for work would fling them.

Our country periodically succumbs to harsh times and whether it is through famine or recession, it is repeatedly forced to give up another one of its lost generations. Through necessity, we, the Irish have been forced to brave strange new shores or follow well-trodden paths so often now that it has become almost second nature to us as a people. I truly hope that one day we can put an end to this endless cycle of peaks and troughs, and I long for the day that Ireland can provide a home for all who wish to live here. Because I'll tell you what, if and when we can master that one thing, there is no better place on earth in which to rear a family or indeed rest your tired head.

CHAPTER 7

WITH A LITTLE HELP FROM MY FRIENDS

WITH MICHAEL NOW RESIDING BENEATH THE Stars and Stripes, I found myself shuffling around Dublin with a sense of loneliness that took even me by surprise. After all, it was because of Michael's kindness and decency that I had come to depend on him so much and he really was like a one-man army to me in terms of love, support and guidance.

For several weeks after Michael's departure I regret to say that I retreated back into myself in a way I didn't think possible, and I found myself spending more and more time inside the confines of the shop. Although they never said as much during that period, my parents must have been sick of the sight of me wallowing around feeling sorry for myself and it is fair to say that I cut a pretty pathetic figure. Mercifully however, in my hour of great need, my spirits were restored quickly by my two old school mates, who valiantly formed a cavalry between them and set about rescuing a fallen comrade.

Donal Ryan and Peter Carty were two chaps I befriended during my primary school years, and any time not spent with Michael or taken up by the shop's demands, was invariably spent with that pair of scallywags. Rather rudely but always to their faces, I would refer to them as 'my number 10' as their physical appearance always put me in mind of that figure. Donal was tall and lanky, with a quiff of red hair that you could light a candle off, and he looked like a number one. Whereas Peter back then was always what you would call on the broader side of hefty, a lad whose puppy fat had doggedly turned mongrel, so he formed a serviceable zero for my point of reference.

Peter of course was not fat in comparison to children these days and on a side note, I must say that I despair when I see youngsters waddle down the street today. You simply didn't see that back then because we had neither the access nor the inclination to destroy our bodies with fast food, and besides, we were always too busy playing games or generally just running about the place. Nowadays, all you see is advertisements on television for video games that play tennis or football, and these games usually come with quite a considerable price tag. Heaven only knows why parents would pay such a sum when the real life games are free to play by all who choose to play them, not to mention the fact that God in his infinite wisdom will even throw some fresh air into the bargain.

We did not have computer games or those DVD things when I was young and I happen to think that we were all the better for it. We had to make our own fun and if we didn't make any for ourselves we simply went without. I am aware, of course, that I am talking about a different era, a simpler time, and I realise that it was a lot safer to play out on the streets back then.

It goes without saying that crime occurred when I was a lad and that sadly the world has always been a violent place, but the difference is that we were never truly exposed to such things, and as a result we were allowed to grow up and live our lives in blissful ignorance. Today, 24-hour news channels and whatnot constantly drive the message home to people that the world is a dangerous place, but surely for every problem this solves, it creates another one. Children now are almost forced to roam in packs or gangs, as society has deemed it too unsafe to go about on your own or even in pockets of two and three. Consequently, many of today's children are prisoners in their own homes, while watchful parents act as overzealous prison wardens. I dare say that a written application may be required in some cases to merely step into the back garden unaccompanied, thus proving that the world has gone mad and with no end in sight.

For Donal, Peter and me, our play and imagination were not restricted to a computer desk or television set and we found all our joys in the outdoor environs of Stepaside. Good old Mother Nature herself offered us up an unrelenting list of endeavours in which to partake to keep us occupied and we were grateful to her because of it. We would play football most days and conkers when they were in season. Although primitive by today's standards, the lads and I had a great love for that game, even though at times it gave us more pain than pleasure.

To start with, we would gather up as many of the horse chestnuts as we could from beneath the old tree at the end of our road and we would then set to work. I would always supply the screwdriver needed to bore a hole through the conker, while Donal would supply the bad language every time he stabbed his finger in the process. Peter was an expert knot-tier, in so much as he could tie a half decent knot, and together we contested matches with as much enjoyment and aggression as I'm sure the games inventor had intended. I would always have to turn my face away as I extended my hand out to dangle my conker from the shoestring, as I knew that any second one misplaced hit from my opponent would result in my knuckles taking an almighty pounding. If I was feeling brave enough I would risk a peek, only to see Donal or Peter sprint towards me with a chestnut swinging like a wrecking ball, primed to collide into mine. In the end if your nerves, conker and knuckles remained intact while your challenger's conker lay in pieces, you were victorious. It was a simple game for a much simpler time.

I wonder whether these games are even played anymore in the schoolyards or streets up and down the country, but I half suspect that the health and safety mob of today will have put a stop to it. Their killjoy decision will no doubt be taken from a foolish rulebook of pedantic nonsense and would have centred around the overly cautious belief, that a hundred-year-old or more tree may suddenly now topple over due to global warming or whatnot, and squash the little fun seekers below.

I wonder are we now reaching a point where trees will soon have cordons placed around them, so that children or even the young at heart will be unable to satisfy their need to climb something that is just screaming out to be climbed. Will we then see fences built in front of our oceans, or perhaps a tax on skipping in an attempt to nullify one's little wants? Perhaps even the placing of a love levy on the happily married. Who knows?

Similar concerns no doubt festered in the minds of overly pernickety people when I was young, but thankfully we were decades away from the self-serving 'do-gooders' of today, who are ruining the world in their never-ending quest to wrap the planet in cotton wool. Were these notions for the common good, I would pass no comment, but I suspect that these issues are being raised by people with the view of somehow feathering their own nests. Nests they probably keep at ground level, for fear that their old foe gravity will get up to its usual trick.

Thankfully, during our teenage years, Donal, Peter and I had no concerns for such matters and our play was without limits but I do recall on one occasion when our longing for adventure made us come a cropper.

During a lively kickabout, Donal had suggested that we should camp outside in his parents' back garden one night. Peter and I quickly agreed, not even letting the noticeable lack of a tent dissuade us. Our better judgement was no doubt influenced by the fact that young boys and old boys for that matter tend to think of themselves as brave Tarzan-type figures, impervious to the elements and the dangers that lurk in life's jungle. This is presumably a result of being told about how cavemen survived as hunter-gatherers, and how armed with just a spear they had the responsibility of fending for their families' lives.

In the minds of young Donal, Peter and I, it was clear that if it came down to it, we could comfortably wrestle a grizzly bear or even tackle a wild boar if required, yet the reality is that most young men would struggle to face down their own ineptitude. For the wild young cavemen of Stepaside, hunting and gathering would most likely yield only the pitiful return of a handful of berries or perhaps just a small animal that had died previously from natural causes. But we remained undeterred.

With innocence still very much of mind, I met up with the other two brave souls at Donal's parents' house, the Ryans, and we set about fashioning a tent out of three old bed sheets and some frayed washing line. We laboured for the best part of an hour until our new base was erected and I'm not ashamed to say that it looked dreadful. Although to be fair a blue sheet, a yellow sheet, a stained white sheet and an orange washing line, are materials rarely used when building a structure of any sort of stability.

Before we ventured into the 'tent', Mr. and Mrs. Ryan decided that to give us even half a chance of making it through the night, we were to have our tea inside at their kitchen table. The two lads and I duly wolfed down the beans and toast that Mrs. Ryan prepared for us and wasting no time, we then stepped back out to face the elements. Peter confided in us that he was concerned about the stability of the tent and its ability to withstand the fierce Irish wind, should it pick up during the night.

"One stiff breeze from the Irish Sea and that thing will end up in Longford," said Peter, pointing at our makeshift home.

"Well if the beans kick in, a stiff gust from me will send us in the opposite direction and we'll end up in England," Donal added crudely, as we all bundled beneath the sheets.

"Ah, it already smells in here. I should have taken my passport for when we land in England," I added, shamefully proud of my ability to join in with the coarseness.

We all laughed as we settled in for the night and I was surprised but grateful, that no one had bothered to point out the fact that I didn't even have a passport.

Father had loaned me a little old-fashioned oil lamp and from under its dim light we sat and talked about everything and anything. Tall tales were told by one and all, yet it was not long before we fell into a stunned silence as Donal produced a small hip flask from beneath his pillow. Having twisted off the lid, Donal told us that he had taken the flask from his grandad's sock drawer, the revelation of which left Peter and me amazed by his cheek.

"What is it?" Peter asked.

"Whiskey," Donal whispered mysteriously.

I curiously brought my nose towards the top of the flask but before I got to within a hair's breadth of it, the aroma hit me like a stream train, causing me to recoil in horror.

"This is what John Wayne drinks, so it must be good stuff," said Donal, as he took a big swig from the flask, before suddenly erupting into a fit of coughing.

Taken aback, I was worried that Donal would cough up a lung or dislodge his Adam's apple, so I took the flask from him and began to pat his back aggressively in order to defeat the all-encompassing cough.

When Donal regained his composure and settled himself back down, I foolishly chose to ignore the warning signs and set about the flask with great gusto. Cautiously at first, I let the pungent liquid kiss my lips before taking a mouthful, which I instantly regretted, as it led to my chest going on fire. As I gasped for breath, Peter suddenly snatched the hip flask from me and before I had a chance to warn him, he greedily drank more than his fair share with surprisingly little or no fuss. In fact Donal and I probably would have been quite impressed by this, had we not been so consumed with trying not to die. After a few moments or so, I began to come around to myself and Donal and I looked across at each other without speaking, with the relief of two soldiers who had survived to the end of a war.

Our peaceful moment, however, did not last long as the sudden sound of Peter's gut wrenching banished away the silence and dragged us unwillingly into a scene of almost biblical carnage. The noise inside that tent became deafening, and arms and legs flayed about in a fit of panic as three dazed and confused souls searched for the exit.

When Donal and I hit the fresh air we were met by Mr. and Mrs. Ryan, who had come outside to see what all the noise was about. I have to say that despite our obvious distress, the Ryans looked very amused by it all and it appeared to me as though they were struggling to hold in laughter. Seconds later however, all eyes were on Peter, as he finally freed himself from the tent and emerged drenched in his own vomit, still foolishly holding onto the hip flask. Mr. and Mrs. Ryan's mood changed instantly on its reveal, and they turned quickly around to Donal, giving him a good clip around the ear for this trouble.

What should have been our first night beneath the stars, ended up being spent beneath the ceiling of Donal's bedroom, as the sight of three crestfallen teenagers eventually managed to sway the Ryans into leniency and forgiveness.

"I can't believe John Wayne drinks that stuff. You'd think he'd have more sense than that," Donal exclaimed from the comfort of his bed.

"Yeah, wouldn't ya, what with him being on the telly and all?" said Peter, as he lay beside me on Donal's bedroom floor.

"That's probably why he's always on a horse, he's probably not able to walk half of the time," Donal said, looking down from his perch.

"You'd wonder how he manages to shoot straight," I mused without reply.

Donal, Peter and I let that thought inhabit our minds before we drifted off to sleep, safely tucked up under a roof that was thankfully not dependent on the stability of a washing line.

Young Conor, in life your family members come predetermined whereas you alone are responsible for choosing your friends and as a result you sink or swim on the quality of your own judgement of character. While you must ensure that you choose wisely by selecting people who will bring fun and enjoyment to your life, it is more important to choose friends that will retain your best interests at heart. I was very fortunate on that score, and all of those vital traits were perfectly wrapped up in that pair of roustabouts who would prove to be lifelong friends.

I hope that you grow up to be surrounded by only the very best of friends. I'm sure that you will. Anyone would be lucky to have you in their life and even after all my years, I consider myself blessed to have been able to meet you. Looking at you, lying in your cot, I can see that you already have a kind face and a cheeky little smile and you recognise me each time you see me, you really do. I'm sure of it.

So much so, that the other day I allowed myself the nice little thought that perhaps you see me as your first real friend. I would really love if that were the case, and I would be deeply proud and honoured if you do.

CHAPTER 8

MOTHER

WE IRISH MEN ARE A STRANGE breed indeed and we have a reputation all around the world as rebels, fighters, storytellers and hard drinkers. A quick history lesson is enough to prove the first two traits to be accurate, whereas equally our gift for storytelling is simply unrivalled, with Beckett, Joyce and Wilde all battling each other for a place at the very top of the literary tree.

As for the nation's reputation as hard drinkers, we can, by and large, always ensure a podium finish. Granted, I wouldn't win too many individual medals in that regard, but I do know quite a number of people who could have had gold draped around their necks as they wobbled unsteadily beneath the tricolour.

Of course such traits could be construed as a sweeping generalisation, yet there is one facet to the Irish male that is set in stone and defines him more than any other aspect of his character. By which, of course, I am referring to his infinite and abiding love for his mammy.

An Irishman would cross the deserts barefoot, just to make his mammy a cup of tea. Likewise he would gladly retrieve a chocolate biscuit from the summit of Mount Everest, if she happened to fancy a little something to go with it. I dare say he would even swim the world's oceans in pursuit of the rarest of fish, on the off-chance that his mother might have a midnight craving for a scant piece of seafood.

I myself was no different in that regard and I always appreciated the sacrifices that Mother made to ensure that she did only her very best for her family. I too have tried to do my best in life and I do so as much for her sake as my own, as I know that Mother always took great pride in me no matter how small my achievements were.

As the only female in the Soap household Mother rarely complained, despite the fact that the poor woman was surrounded on a daily basis by male voices, male smells and the dreaded male indifference to focus. Instead, she held it all together with the quiet dignity that resides only inside a woman's soul.

Perhaps the best word to describe my mother would be 'busy' as she constantly kept herself occupied with various jobs and chores, and no sooner was one job completed than another was put to task. Her only break was a quick pause for a cup of tea during her morning rituals and that was when I would always seize the moment to have a good chat with her. My, how I loved the simplest thing of just being able to sit at the kitchen table and talk with my mammy.

During mealtimes my seat was always to the left of hers, but during our little chats I would sit directly opposite so I could look at her and she would radiate warmth that would rival the temperature of the cup of tea I was holding. Mother and I would sit and talk about life in general and she would even take the time to humour me as I regaled her with my tales of adolescent woe. Such was her interest in her family, Mother would sit and patiently listen as I droned on about something that usually didn't even affect me, and she never once questioned why I felt the need to complain.

You see I was always something of a puzzled chap and if I thought something didn't make sense I would question everything about it until it sat right with me. Even now I rarely make it through the day without encountering something that leaves me shaking my head in bewilderment. If I attempt to make a phone call to a council office or utility company, I end up speaking to a computer and being told to key in more numbers than an accountant, when all I want to do is speak to a human being. We really have lost the simple ways of life and the worrying thing is that we know full well who has stolen them from us, big corporations, yet collectively we do nothing about it.

My mother, however, would always provide a receptive ear and a silver lining in my cloud of problems. She would some-times teasingly call me 'Mona Soap' when I was moaning about something and each time she did I would smile without fail, as my concerns for the world were temporarily lifted.

As time went on, however, our little chats were forced to change location as poor Mother's health began to worsen further. For a long time she had tried her best to ignore her ailments but before long her days were spent mostly confined to her bedroom. During breaks in work, some official some not, I would pop upstairs to check in on her and several times a day I would boil the kettle and make us some tea. When I entered her room, through a door which was always open, I was routinely greeted by the sight of my mother's smile beaming towards me. Mother rarely closed her bedroom door during the day and she once confided in me that had she done so, she would have felt completely cut off from the rest of the world. I tried my best to remind her just how important she still was to everyone and I hope that my words brought a degree of comfort to her, as well as the realisation that she was still very much the centre of our world.

As I gave her the teacup, Mother would give me an appreciative smile in return and I always felt that I was coming off better in the trade. I would then perch myself at the edge of the bed and tell her all about the goings-on of the day and having made a conscious effort to be the bearer of only good tidings, I always kept the chat light and airy. Mother's illness had altered my priorities and I refocused onto what really mattered which was, of course, family and the health and well-being of those within its circle.

My memories of those chats are among my happiest. Each time I made sure to spend only quality time with her, rather than using the opportunity to unburden myself of complaints and I soaked up all she had to say and the views she held on the world. In the three months she was bedridden, Mother did not call me 'Mona Soap' a single time. She had no need to.

Of course, light has a very nasty habit of changing to dark and early one morning before my eyelids properly parted, I was startled awake by the most heartbreaking of sounds. Through a thin wall and slightly dated wallpaper, I heard mother convulsing in a fit of coughing. I immediately ran to her room, where I found Father struggling to comfort her as she sat upright on the bed. He was holding her shoulders forward and Mother was clearly in great discomfort. Father held a handkerchief over Mother's mouth as she was overcome with coughing, and I could see shiny beads of sweat forming uniformly on the brows of both my parents.

I was greatly taken aback at the level of distress in the room and standing just inside the doorway, I froze as if welded to the floor. I didn't know what to do and I was frightened that any move I made could somehow manage to make things even worse. Suddenly, I felt warm breath on the back of my neck, and without turning I could hear gentle sobs coming from behind me. I knew it was Edward, but my gaze was fixed straight ahead. Mother eventually stopped coughing but, bereft of strength, she then slumped back against the pillows. Father unceremoniously discarded Mother's handkerchief to the floor, before helping her settle into whatever comfort he could find for her. I watched on in silence as Father held her hand and gently moved her hair away from her eyes. Several moments passed and the only communication used came in the form of a reassuring wink from Father, which he sent spinning in the direction of Edward and I.

Mother eventually managed to fall asleep and the relief on Father's face echoed that of my own. Father then ever so gingerly got up from the bed and began to quietly tidy around the room, removing a glass of water from my mother's bedside locker before bending down to retrieve her banished handkerchief from the floor. He froze without explanation.

"Da?" Edward said from over my shoulder.

"Go get Dr. Agnew," said Father, without turning to face us.

Edward hesitated.

"Now son!" Father quietly, but forcefully, ordered.

The breath ceased on the back of my neck and the sound of feet running down the stairs filled the unsettled air. Father turned around to me and I saw his eyes glisten with tears. Not knowing what to do, my gaze drifted down, seeking comfort in the floor, but my eyes stopped halfway when I saw Mother's handkerchief rest in Father's hand. The plain white cotton was now speckled red and such was the tremble of Father's hand that it swayed uncontrollably from side to side.

I couldn't move. I couldn't speak. No young boy wants or needs to see his parents in such a state of vulnerability, as they are his strength, his champions. Father slowly walked over to embrace me, and inches from the door frame we both shed an unwanted tear as we clung on to one another. Unbeknownst to him, I also wept for the final loss of my innocence.

When Dr. Agnew, our family doctor, arrived a short time later, Edward and I were ushered out of the room. Curious to hear what was happening I took up a familiar pose of having my ear pressed against the wall. Edward, for what must have been the first time in his life, also took up position beside me, and his very presence made me worry all the more.

Dr. Agnew remained in the room for what felt like a lifetime, so Edward and I took it in turns as posted sentinel. During my downtime I lay in something of a daze, until out of the corner of my eye I saw Edward peel himself from the wall, before turning to address me.

"I think Ma needs a cup of tea," said Edward.

"What are you on about? Is she awake?" I quizzed.

"The doctor just said that Ma has tea-bag-a low-sis," Edward explained.

"What's that?" I asked.

"Something to do with tea I'd say. Maybe she's low in tea," guessed Edward.

God young Conor when I think of it now, perhaps my innocence was not lost after all, because I leapt out of bed and ran to the kitchen to boil the kettle!

As I prepared the tea, duly assisted by Edward, Father joined us in the kitchen having shown the departing Dr. Agnew to the front door. He quietly told us that he needed to speak with us and we immediately dropped what we were doing at his request. Father told us that Mother was very poorly indeed and he went on to explain at some considerable length, that she had a thing called Tuberculosis. Soon it became abundantly clear that the combination of Edward's youthful ears, scant vocabulary and historical layers of wallpaper had led to a muddling up of the doctor's heartbreaking diagnosis.

Father suggested that we should pray to God and ask him for his help, so that night as I lay in bed while sleep ceaselessly evaded me, I prayed without pause until my eyes ushered in the morning's light.

In the days that followed, Father, Edward and I kept a bedside vigil and Mother had some better days than others, but for the most part we just sat and watched her sleep. One morning, however, when she defied her condition and her shortness of breath, she spoke softly and asked for Michael.

"Michael's coming, don't you worry," Father reassured her.

Father's words were tinged with doubt, but I knew that he had at least sent Michael a letter in the post. In it, he gave details of Mother's condition and he also suggested for Michael to make the journey home from America, if at all possible. I often think about how hard it must have been for my father to write that letter and how hard it must have been for Michael to have to read it so many miles away.

Although such a suggestion may seem simple by today's standards, America was like the dark side of the moon to the average man in the street during the 1950s and 60s. It took an age to get there by boat and the fare alone was out of most people's reach. More often than not when someone made the brave decision to leave Ireland for the United States, the Atlantic Ocean seemed to grow wider and wider even before they stepped boldly aboard the boat.

Several agonising weeks passed without word from America, while at home above the shop we just made Mother as comfortable as we possibly could. Father, Edward and I managed to keep the business going by taking turns tending to its needs and I must say that my younger brother really rose to the challenges imposed on our family at that time. Edward worked twice as hard as I had ever seen him do before and although that wasn't saying much, considering his previous efforts, he really did throw himself into all he was tasked with and a lot more besides.

Each morning, keen eyes were cast in the direction of the letterbox, as we waited in hope for the postman to bring word of Michael's return. Some mornings the postman didn't see fit to even grace us with his presence, and the mornings he did he merely unloaded a glut of bills, which served only to add further weight to our ever-increasing family load.

I spoke to Mother each day and she replied whenever she could. I tried to reassure her that she would be okay and that she would be up and about in no time, and selfishly I did this as much for my own morale as hers. My words were spoken with more optimism than certainty, but when the chips are down hope is sometimes your only emotional ally. On occasions when Mother managed to summon the strength to reply, she would simply sigh, "I'll get there, Joseph".

On the saddest of mornings I entered Mother's room in order to exchange her bedside jug of water for a fresh one. Father had prepared some food for Mother and he was attentively sitting next to her in case she needed help or assistance with it. Not wanting to disturb them, I quickly took the old jug downstairs and as I did so, I couldn't help but notice that precious little had been poured from its lip.

As I descended the stairs I heard the letterbox on the front door open and then slam shut, and its distinctive sound prompted me to run like the dickens into the hallway, in the hope of word from America. I took the bottom corner like Sterling Moss, somehow only spilling a drop or two of water and immediately I saw a solitary letter resting upon the doormat.

Having abandoned the water jug on the side table I picked the envelope up, and I was immediately transfixed by all the stamps and markings that decorated its outer face. I hurriedly searched for clues amongst what seemed to be a million squiggles until I eventually made out the words 'United States of America' in faded green ink, and my eyes lit up like a firecracker.

Back then a handwritten letter, which may have taken mere minutes to write, could take many weeks to arrive and the suspense was as thrilling as it was frustrating. Nowadays, with the speed of modern technology, such anticipation, which was built up out of the necessity to wait, has become redundant but my goodness was there excitement when something you craved finally arrived in the door.

This letter was different. With no time to waste I sprinted up the stairs and burst through my parents' bedroom door. Father snapped his head back as he braced himself to give out to me for causing such a rumpus, but as he did so he saw that I was waving a letter as though it were a full house at Bingo. Father quickly rose from his chair and I handed him the envelope in silence.

He proceeded to open the letter and he did so as though it were made of glass. Knowing its importance he took time to peel back the top right-hand corner, before gently running his finger along the inside of the envelope. Finally freeing the letter and exposing it for the first time to the Irish sunshine, which was by now peeking through the bedroom window, Father unfolded the paper with due precision.

Standing with his back turned to my mother, Father read the letter quietly to himself and as his eyes moved from left to right and back again, I watched as his heart sank before me.

"Is it Michael?" asked Mother, in a near whimper.

"Yes pet. Michael is coming home. He's coming home to see you," Father reassured, having taken a moment's pause.

Mother nodded her head twice as if to seal her approval, but she was unable to complement her actions with either words of elation or relief. Father and I collected up the breakfast tray, its contents barely touched, and we prepared to leave Mother's side in order to allow her to rest some more.

"You'll be up and about in no time and we'll all be there to greet Michael when he arrives," Father said, as he headed for the door.

"I'll get there, Danny. I'll get there," said Mother, as my father and I slowly left the room.

Soon after, Father brought Edward and I together on the shop floor and he informed us that Michael would not be coming home, as he simply could not afford the fare. Indeed, were Michael to sell all of his few belongings, he would barely muster up a tiny portion of what was needed to grant his poor mother her dying wish.

Like Father's letter, I wondered what heartache and anguish Michael must have gone through as he sat to spell out such sad words. In our heart of hearts I suspect that we always knew that Michael would not be returning but we allowed the fantasy to take hold regardless, as much to appease Mother as to delude ourselves with wishful thinking.

It now became apparent that the goodbye Mother and Michael shared before he left for America was to be their final time together. I wondered if somehow Mother, ever the realist, knew that when she kissed her boy goodbye at the shop that day, she was doing so for the very last time.

It is heartbreaking for me to think that Mother remained behind while the rest of us left for the port to see Michael off, because she could not bear to see her son set sail out of her life forever. I don't know this for certain, but as her son I am as qualified as anyone to make the assumption. Although knowing my mother I wouldn't rule out the possibility that she wanted to spare Michael further upset and heartache.

Later that day the arrival of Dr. Agnew made me sense the worst. Father had gone upstairs to check on Mother only to then quickly return back down, from where he bellowed for Edward or I to fetch the doctor. My worst fears were realised later that very evening and thoughts previously unthinkable became reality as the Soap family lost the guidance of its true shining light.

My mother, Mrs. Angela Soap, passed away shortly after 8pm on 19th May 1958, surrounded by her family, Dr. Agnew, and our parish priest Father Fitzgibbon from Our Lady of the Wayside. She was forty-two years old.

As confusion and sorrow swamped my mind I wanted to ask Father Fitzgibbon why God had not answered the many impassioned pleas that I had offered up to him as I begged him and tried in vain to convince him not to take my mother from me. However, I am ashamed to say that I lacked the courage needed to pose such questions. Perhaps I was too afraid of what the answers might be, and like the many others who were affected by my mother's passing, I simply held onto my silence.

Mother's funeral was as dark a day as I can remember and rain clouds hung over our heavy hearts as we helped her into the next world. I was grateful in a way that God had sent the dark clouds as the rain helped disguise my tears and despite trying to stay strong for Father and Edward, I simply could not hold back my emotions. A huge crowd turned out that day and I spoke to each one in turn. Lost in amongst them Father looked so fragile and when the opportunity permitted he would take Edward's and my hands and hold onto us as though we were the most important things left in his world, which I suspect we were.

I remember watching as Mother's coffin was lowered gently into the ground. I knew that at that moment she would be really scared, so I closed my eyes and tried to reassure her that she would be okay. I only hope that she heard me, and that she drew strength from it.

Standing at the graveside, Father, Edward and I watched as the last of the mourners made their way to the gate, and as we stood in solidarity with one another we began to feel the full magnitude of our loss. I held my father's right arm, Edward his left and we each waited for someone to speak words that never came. We simply bowed our heads and headed towards the cemetery gate.

When Father, Edward and I passed through the gate we faced into yet another challenge. A get-together for family and friends in Murnaghan's had been arranged and although it was the last thing that the three of us felt like going to, unity was now very much the order of the day, and we would face it as one.

Young Conor, I miss my mother to this very day and it deeply saddens me that she missed out on a long and happy life. Her untimely passing will never allow us to know what she would have made of being a grandmother or indeed a great-grand-mother, but I think I can speak with good authority and say that she would have relished every second of it. I can at least take solace from knowing that she is watching over us and it pleases me that after all these years, she has not missed a single smile or frown on my face.

I would dearly love to be able to sit down with her once more at our old kitchen table, for a good old catch-up and a spot of tea. I have so many things I would like to talk to her about that I would struggle to even know where to begin, but I know in my heart of hearts that she would show great patience and understanding while I decided.

CHAPTER 9

COPING

A SMALL PRIVATE GATHERING HAD BEEN arranged in Murnaghan's pub and in an Irish tradition as long-standing as breathing in and out, family and friends joined together in order to give the dearly departed a right good send-off.

It is an unusual thing to do really and I have even heard it said that it is an undignified way to honour the dead but in fact I couldn't disagree more. Through the benefit of experience I see it as a way of snapping a grieving family back into life and as trying as those times are, it is important for people to remember that it is not they who have died. The bereaved still belong amongst the living and that well-trodden phrase 'life goes on' becomes crucial as without it said time and time again, the family have little chance of ever finding peace or indeed the strength to carry on.

The tragic loss of my mother not only brought with it an unbelievable sadness, but it also caused Father, Edward and

I to question all that we knew to be true in our lives. Our whole world was now spinning off its axis and without the steadying hand of my mother we faced a future devoid of belief, hope and certainty. The pain housed beneath our roof seemed never-ending and although some relief was gained while busy, the real defeats came after dark when the night-time left us to wallow in all we had lost.

This burning sense of grief was perhaps understandably felt most by Father and following the initial devastating blow of Mother's passing, he sank further and further into the depths of despair. In fact such was his grief that I cried as much for his troubles as I did for my own. With consideration in mind, I tried my very best to understand what my father was going through but I lacked the years of life and the experience which they yield to offer him any meaningful advice or solutions to his pain.

However, this little nation of ours and its people did my thinking for me and as always on the auld green sod, any liquid stronger than water was tasked to heal all wounds. With the religious ceremony now completed we headed on to 'the afters' part of the funeral, which saw the pub replace the church as venue of choice and wine not limited to that of a mere sip from the priest's chalice.

Such occasions usually start in much the same way, with long silences dotted in between rambling conversations as people mundanely discuss the weather of the day. Rain during the funeral will prompt a random old lady to say, "The heavens have opened to welcome the departed", whereas if the sun happened to split the trees, a wizened old man will no doubt offer up, "The Lord has smiled down from above". Cynics may dismiss such notions as having a 'glass half full' outlook on life, but that sort of positivity is vital on such days. In its presence, it is best to just smile and nod agreeably and to park cynicism where it belongs, which is in the hearts and minds of naysayers.

The chat and banter in the room will gradually build and the rate of increase will more often than not rise in tandem with the barman's profits. Stories told about the fallen are ones you will have heard a million times before, but for one last time they enthral as though you were hearing them for the very first time. In such circumstances, it is important to remember that if someone cares enough to tell you a story, then the very least you can do is listen to it and try to draw something new from its message.

By the time darkness descended outside Murnaghan's it was like Sodom and Gomorrah on Saint Patrick's Day. Tongues were loosened, beer was flowing and the fiddler's elbow was going in and out like the pistons in a steam engine. It was almost as if people had shamefully forgotten the real reason they were there in the first place, yet at the back of all my concerns I remained sure that my mother's spirit drifted in and around each conversation.

Of course, there is always one table which is quieter than the rest and given the absence of both my mother and eldest brother, that particular distinction fell upon the table that

Father, Edward and I cowered behind. I tried my best to relive stories of Mother with all those who came over and attempted to console me, but it was as if my mind had forbidden me to even speak her name. I just couldn't bring myself to talk about Mother and I found myself forcibly changing the subject whenever someone started saying "I remember the time".

I hated to hear my mother being spoken about in the past tense, like she hadn't lived for a thousand years, after all it was only days previous that her fingers held mine as I said goodnight to her. How could a life just stop like that? How could God allow a life's story to end practically midway and years from a fitting and proper conclusion? How could God take away a young man's mother, when he faced so many years ahead without the one person nature had appointed to help and cradle him through all that life could throw at him?

I sat with Father and I watched as he sought comfort in his pint of porter and the small glass of whiskey that stood to attention at its side. I held a glass of lemonade conspicuously in front of me and having made a very conscious decision not to touch a drop of alcohol, I spurned every opportunity to dishonestly relocate some of Father's whiskey to my own glass when he wasn't looking. In all truth, I had no interest in food or drink and I merely raised my glass to my lips in order to break up the statuesque pose I found myself sharing with the world.

Everyone and anyone who was there took their turn to approach Father and each placed a drink down in front of him so his drinks without fail were always two abreast on the table. The small snug area we were sitting in offered us the all the privacy of a Hollywood red carpet, yet as a family we were afraid to leave it as the lounge area to our immediate right swirled with Mother's name. Likewise, the exit door to our left brought us home to an emptiness that we dreaded above all else.

I watched as Father picked up each glass and I studied every mouthful hoping to see a flash of emotion in his eyes as the black and amber rivers flowed into his mouth and gradually washed away his senses. However, all I witnessed was a man who would struggle to even describe the taste of what he was drinking.

Edward sat sheepishly beside us and I noted that on more than one occasion he discreetly helped himself to a drop or two of Father's whiskey whenever the chance arose. I decided to take leave from my duties as big brother as quite frankly the last thing he needed was to be told off or punished for a youthful indiscretion.

The night continued in predictable fashion and as the midnight hour came and went, the bar's patrons sluggishly rose from their seats and headed for the door, in what looked like a scene from an old Hammer Horror film. When Father, Edward and I finally waved the last of our goodbyes, I must say that the peace and quiet that rushed the empty pub came as a great relief to us.

We remained behind in our now familiar silence and watched as the barman tidied up the empty glasses, of which there were many. I knew that the barman was hoping we would leave as the night had clearly run its course, but he respectfully kept his distance as I think he saw us as a little family who was just struggling to cope amid broken hearts and desolation. Whenever I caught the barman's eye I would nod my head in appreciation, as Edward and I continued to sit as we waited for Father's prompt to call it a night.

A further hour or so later we watched the barman polish a brass nameplate behind the bar for what must have been the third time, while he watched us in its reflection in the hope that Father would polish off the last of his whiskey. When the moment felt right I decided to ask Father if he was ready to go home.

To my surprise he instantly corrected his slouched position in the chair and sat up straight with his back pushed in against the seat. He then raised his two arms like giant cranes and placed them tightly around our shoulders.

"Come on boys, let's go home," said Father, preparing to rise.

The three of us stood up together and I felt the partial weight of my father as he laboured a little to stand up. As we made our way to the door our show of unity got broken up, when Father veered off in the opposite direction and walked back towards the barman.

"Bottle of whiskey," Father asked of the barman.

"I'm sorry Mr. Soap, but we don't sell bottles," he replied truthfully and much to my relief.

Unperturbed, Father paused for a moment as though trying to get his mind in focus, before he turned unceremoniously around and walked back towards the table we had just left. I think everyone feared another prolonged sit-down, but what Father did next made me long for the much more dignified moments of before.

When Father reached the table, he picked up the empty lemonade bottle which I had left behind me and he brought it without explanation over to the by now confused-looking barman.

"Fill that up," Father said strictly.

The barman agreed to my father's demands and he proceeded to fill the bottle to the brim with Jameson, which had been Father's sole tipple of choice for the latter part of the evening. He then handed it back to my father, who in turn paid the hastily totted charge.

I then watched as Father's eyes searched across the floor, until he saw a discarded bottle cap, which he bent down to retrieve before applying it firmly onto his makeshift whiskey bottle. The barman looked towards my direction by way of apology, but I just glared back at him.

I wish to this day that I lived in a world where that barman had shown as much concern for my father's overall well-being as he did for his own inflated profits. Being a barman is of course a noble occupation but ultimately and when push came to shove, that man showed no duty of care whatsoever towards a weak, vulnerable man and I just hate to think it was greed that clouded his better judgement.

When we eventually hit the night air our walk home proved to be slow and laboured, but we at least all managed to make it home in one piece. Edward and I helped Father onto a chair in the kitchen before placing the kettle onto the stove, even though Father had already spurned our offer of a sobering cup of tea. With a dismissive wave of his hand, Father then retrieved his prized bottle of whiskey from his jacket pocket and began to drink directly from it.

A short time later, a worn-looking Edward retired to bed, but I remained with Father until he eventually tilted the bottle skyward to release the last drop from it depths. Crestfallen, I made one final attempt to coax him to his bed but I had to content myself with the feat of getting him safely onto the sofa in the sitting room instead. Exhausted, I curled myself onto an armchair and after much fidgeting I managed to drift off to sleep, mere moments after Father finally found some peace by closing his eyes to the world.

I regret to say that the business began to suffer over the weeks that followed, and it did so through no fault of its own, as its once solid pillars began to crumble in the face of unprecedented hardship. The bricks and mortar of our little shop were being let down and betrayed by the frailty of the human spirit and broken hearts began to weaken the foundations on which it stood. The shelves slowly started to become bare as supply trips to the dock became a daily step too far for Father and it became an achievement in itself if he even made it there once or twice a week. Understandably, it didn't take long for the customers to dwindle in numbers and the lack of demand soon met perfectly with the lack of produce on offer.

The shop went on to labour its way through several months of constant struggle and at the end of one particularly disappointing week, the respite of a Saturday evening mercifully rolled around once more. I divvied up that week's meagre takings and I handed the cash bag over to Father for him to place in the safe which he kept hidden in the hot press upstairs. Clearly unsteady in both hand and mind Father took the bag from me and headed upstairs, while I went out to the backyard to tidy up before finally clocking off for the day.

Just when I had the yard tidied and looking the best it could, the back gate flew open and in barged Edward without so much as a 'hello' in my direction. I readied myself to chastise him for not helping out yet again, but my words fell short when his sheer aggression became all the more apparent.

Edward kicked over two wooden pallets that were clearly harming no one and he then sent an old bucket crashing against the far wall. Without knowing why, I saw that rage had taken hold of him and all I could do was stand back and stare, as I noticed the black eye and cuts on his face and hands. The anger quickly subsided within Edward before disappearing off to possess another susceptible soul, leaving my brother deflated and slumped down against the wall.

Slowly and tentatively, I approached him and asked what on earth had happened. After a few moments of coaxing, he told me that some local lads had teased him in the street, so he reacted by punching one of them in retaliation, only for the others to then set about him like a pack of rabid dogs.

"Why did they tease you?" I asked with the most genuine of interest.

"Because of Ma," said Edward, amid welling tears.

"What did they say?" I asked softly, leaning closer into him.

"They teased me, saying that I haven't got a mother anymore, and that Ma left for heaven without me because she didn't love me anymore. I tried to tell them that that wasn't true, but I just snapped and hit the one who was teasing me the most," Edward said, with hurt and annoyance laced in each word.

I listened to what Edward had to say for himself and I paid my respects to the severity of his words, by allowing them linger in the air.

"Look Joseph, I know you're a 'holy Joe' and you're going to give out to me and tell me that I shouldn't have hit anyone. I know you're going to say that Ma would be disgusted at me for fighting, so you may as well just say it now and be done with it," added Edward, as tears suddenly got the better of him.

"Go on say it!" reaffirmed Edward, leaving no time for reply.

"Did you hit him hard?" I responded, having considered his words carefully.

"I knocked him to the ground," said Edward sheepishly, but with a hint of pride.

I paused for further thought, before putting my arm around him for what must have been the first time since our primary school days and I told him what I thought our mother would have made of all that palaver.

"Knowing Mother she'd be disgusted all right, disgusted that you didn't pick him up and hit him back down again for saying that!" I said with a smile and a look towards the heavens.

Edward and I both laughed and we shared a nice little moment together, before we got up and headed back inside.

Poor Edward was neither use nor ornament with regards to the shop, yet strangely I found my attitude softening towards him and I came to accept that he was forever destined to fall short of the demands and responsibilities of running a family business.

I walked ahead of Edward when we went into the house, as I wanted to spare Father the further upset of seeing his youngest son with a head like a bruised peach. When I reached the upstairs I saw that Father was nowhere to be seen so I informed the trailing Edward that the coast was clear, following which he ran past me and chased into the bathroom in order to clean himself up.

With Edward now out of sight I entered the kitchen to see if Father had made an attempt at rustling us up some dinner, but I found only an empty room. I did, however, notice that the bag containing that week's takings now lay sideways on the kitchen table, and on examination it appeared to be light a day or two's earnings.

Now I am in no way suggesting that Father stole that money as it was his after all, but my issue with the whole situation was that such an act was so out of character for my father, that it set alarm bells ringing in my mind. It was just not what I had come to expect, not least from the man I knew before my mother's death, and I was now concerned that Father's mind was being corrupted by the same grief that I knew was crippling his heart.

Father had been drinking to frightening excess, and every drop he drank led to the needs of his family losing further pace with the rest of his troubled life. His new love affair with alcohol had already caused him to ease off on his working responsibilities, leaving me with little option but to seize the wheel and attempt to steer our little family boat through choppy waters.

My father was a good and kind-hearted man, the best you can ever imagine, but when I was left to pick up the slack left in the trail of his drinking, I regrettably began to question his emotional strength and moral backbone. That is something which I am ashamed to admit even all these years later but it is honestly how I felt during that period, as I increasingly struggled to understand why he just did not stop drinking. I also questioned without answer why he chose to spend so much of his time in the pub, rather than at home with two sons who needed his guidance much more than the pub needed his custom.

If I had taken leave of my senses, I would probably have questioned his love for Edward and me, as his problems with drink only arose after the death of Mother, but thankfully I never came close to that conclusion. I know now of course that once alcohol gets its claws into someone, they are faced with a lifelong battle to free themselves from its clutches and, unquestionably, it is not just a simple choice to stop drinking. In an ideal world, the first appearance of a loved one's tear would give those afflicted the strength needed to banish the controlling evils of alcohol, but unfortunately we do not live in an ideal world.

So, young Conor, there I was a young man with the weight of the world upon my slender shoulders with no one to turn to to help lessen the burden. If I could build a time machine and go back to that moment I would love to tell my younger self to stop fretting and panicking. I'd also go to great lengths to point out the simple quirk of life that things have a habit of working themselves out for the best, but only if we stay calm and unrushed in our surroundings.

Without knowing it then, I was destined to live a life filled with love and companionship and all I needed to do was wait just a little while longer…

Patience, Joseph Soap, patience.

CHAPTER 10

WALLFLOWER BOY

As the Soap family continued to unravel at the seams I was left with little option but to go from apprentice to sorcerer, as Father had by now made Murnaghan's his second home. Surprisingly, and in spite of what was probably good for me, I actually found myself enjoying my new role as acting head shopkeeper and I quickly embraced all the responsibilities that went with having such a focal position.

The business itself, however, continued to wane for several months and our once regular stream of customers understandably showed an indifference towards our shop that I would have happily forgiven, if only they had made the first move towards reconciliation. With truthfulness and hindsight combined it is little wonder that our regulars went elsewhere in search of their groceries, and our little shop now faced crisis from outside as well as from within.

The bloom, if not the root, of our ever-increasing list of problems may have stemmed from Father's new-found indifference but when a new foe arrived on our patch, we could do little about the immediate stranglehold it placed on our industry.

You see the late 1950s saw the ominous arrival of large supermarket chains into Ireland and consumers were immediately attracted by their scale. So much so, that they were even prepared to bypass the convenience of the established local shops, which led to loss of business in the town centres that were traditionally the heartbeat of the community. Local values were easily cast aside in search of a bargain but as far as I could see, the only 'bargain' on offer was produce of a similar or poorer quality to our own, sold by faceless entities who cared little for the needs of the individual.

That era, in my view, brought about the beginning of the loss of the human touch within the shopping experience and it led to a sad turn of events best summed up in a way I still struggle to believe, namely the introduction of the self-service checkout.

I was out and about with your father the first time I saw one of those contraptions and its very sight, as well as its pointless wizardry, caused me to stop dead in my tracks. Perplexed beyond words, I stood and shook my head in complete amazement at what I was witnessing, so much so, that a young girl working there came up to me and asked if I was okay.

"Am I okay?" I replied in bewilderment. "That jumped-up washing machine is going to do you out of a job!" I informed the girl.

The machine of choice in my day was the van we used to transport our stock and from an age slightly younger than what was right, Father had intermittently begun to teach me how to drive the old Bedford, as he knew that one day I would literally be handed the keys. I was and remain thankful for Father's foresight in teaching me how to drive before Mother's death, as without that consideration our little business would have floundered. Of that I have no doubt.

Now, as a fully licensed driver, I was able to cover all aspects of a shopkeeper's duties and what I lacked in experience, I more than made up for in passion and effort. During that period I lived for little else as every minute was committed to turning around the shop's fortunes and I became a workaholic long before the term was even coined. Indeed, the only people who saw me outside of the shop were the dockers and traders, when I collected my latest stockpile. Most of those men knew me from my trips accompanying Father over the years and that familiarity made it much easier for them to accept me as a young trader in my own right. Equally, I knew that they were aware of my family's troubles and it is to their eternal credit and decency that they never once tried to rip me off or take advantage of my situation.

Slowly but surely, business began to pick up and each returning customer merely steeled my determination and belief that I could make a right good go of the shop and steer it back onto a positive course.

As I toiled away amid the demands of the business, the other members of the Soap family blissfully went about their lives in complete ignorance of the harsh realities of their surroundings. Edward was up to his old tricks, while Father partook in his new ones and the pair of them showed a shameful lack of interest in the shop. I knew that Edward never had his sights trained on the shop so that was to be expected from him, but it was Father's disinterest that really hit home with me. He had loved the shop as though it was in some way a living, breathing part of our family and he had dedicated his life to it, yet now he looked upon it as a mere inconvenience. To him, our family home had become somewhere which simply provided a roof over his head while he slept, just as Murnaghan's sheltered him while he was awake. My father was lost to grief and his little shop provided no solution to his great despair.

During this period, I was faced with a one-sided choice, when due to work commitments and the pressures involved, I found myself forced to choose between my family's livelihood and my friends. My pals Donal and Peter had begun to branch out socially in search of both booze and girls, and they would regularly attend the local dances which took place every weekend in and around Stepaside.

I myself was rarely seen outside the shop and I must say that I felt as though my friendship with the two lads suffered as a result of my hectic work schedule. I just didn't have the time to spend with Donal and Peter as hard work occupied my days, while the quest for a peaceful night's sleep filled my moonlit hours. Both lads tried their best to coax me into their social scene, but time and time again I would repeatedly let them down with genuine excuses and the odd tall tale.

In all honesty, I didn't care very much for alcohol or dancing so I never really felt as though I was missing out on those things. And although I have always held a keen interest in the fairer sex, I knew nothing of women so I missed them as much as I missed walking on the surface of the moon.

I did, however, feel that I was missing out on some laughs and companionship and often the longing for the simple things in life proves to be the most painful. It looked to me that everyone bar me graced the Dublin dances and, undeterred by my absence, Donal and Peter bopped their way into adulthood as my life seemingly froze in time. Even that little scamp Edward got in on the act and attended the dances by claiming to be older than his sixteen years. I continued to watch from afar while everyone else seemed to revel in the untold pleasures of leaving their adolescence behind them and rather than leaving a trail of empty pint glasses and broken hearts in my wake, I made do with stewed tea and a lonely heart.

You will not know this young Conor but there was a very famous term used to describe the shy girls who attended such dances. They were known as 'Wallflower Girls'. This term, rightly or otherwise, was used in reference to their timid and often nervous demeanour, as they stood back on the sidelines while the other more brazen girls jived away to their hearts' content on the dance floor. I don't mind admitting to being worried that I would end up tethered to similar walls and left hopelessly behind on the margins of society. In fact I lost many a night's sleep worrying that I was destined to become the first ever Wallflower Boy!

It was at one of those very dances that Donal met his future wife Shelia and such was his excitement, he was shouting it from the rooftops. I recall opening up the shop one morning and, with only the fruit and vegetables to keep me company, I prepared as best I could for the day ahead. As I raised the blinds the morning sunlight engulfed the shop and my latest stint walking the shop floor started on the stroke of eight o'clock. As I pottered about the shop, my attention was suddenly turned towards the door, when the little bell that hung above it rang out to herald the arrival of an early bird. I threw my head around to happily see Donal walking in and I noticed instantly that he was smiling from ear to ear. He quickly told me that he couldn't wait for his news to travel along the grapevine, and he excitedly began to tell me all about the beautiful redhead he had met the previous night.

Just as I was settling in to Donal's story the shop's door swung open again and in walked the dreaded Mrs. Kirwin and her curious daughter Deborah, who barged straight past Donal without so much as a by your leave. Confronting me directly, Mrs. Kirwin proceeded to interrogate me as to what particular type of potato happened to be in season. Clueless to her questions I managed to hazard a guess of some description and I brazenly spoke with authority only found in the world's leading experts or, in my case, those with the most fanciful of unenlightened minds.

Donal and I stole a quick glance when Mrs. Kirwin's head was turned and he smiled knowingly having guessed correctly that I hadn't the slightest clue what I was talking about. I figured, as the Kirwins were clearly in the dark themselves on such matters, I was in no danger of being caught out so I carried on regardless, with tales of Maris Piper and King Edward. I was mid-fib when the doorbell beckoned again and another customer walked in holding an empty shopping bag, which needed to be filled. Sensing my time was not my own, Donal made his excuses and left before I had even half a chance to ask him his girl's name. It was only later when things died down a little that I felt bad for not being able to provide a proper audience for a story that Donal obviously wanted to share.

While I was delighted for my friend's upturn in all things romantic, I felt that I saw little of Donal as it was but the arrival of Sheila, whose name I later established, now only compounded matters. Indeed, we barely saw each other in the many months that followed. I, of course, could never blame Donal for that but I admit that it did add further weight to my mounting feelings of isolation.

Donal and Sheila quickly became engaged as was the want of people in those days, as strong desires both mental and physical helped chase many a young courting couple up the aisle. You see the church dictated that sex (ask your father) was for married couples only and even then it was solely for means of procreation. This was at a time when religion still held Ireland in a chokehold and the entire nation firmly believed that the fear of God was matched only by the scolding delivered from an angry priest's tongue. Thankfully, this grip on youth and young love seems to have loosened somewhat, although in the interests of parity, perhaps it has loosened too much.

I only learned news of Donal's engagement by overhearing people talk about it in the shop, and at first I was disappointed that he had not come in to tell me in person. I worried that perhaps he now saw me as a bit-part player in his old life rather than a leading light in his new one and not for the first time in my life, I felt as though I was losing my best friend. I had, after all, already lost my mother through death, my older brother through emigration and I increasingly feared that I was slowly losing my father to alcohol. The question of whether I ever really had Edward in the first place, was another day's worry.

The feeling of being left behind is something that can strike at any age, but I feel that it affects young people to an even greater extent. Often they are more susceptible due to the insecurity within themselves, as life may not yet have taught them the inner strength needed to really embrace change and identify the positives it can bring.

But life is a funny old thing and each and every day provides a blank canvas on which it can work its magic. Some days are better than others, of course, but each one never fails to amaze and surprise me. If only people who live their lives beneath a cloud of constant disappointment could manage to weather the storm, either through belief or good fortune, they would see that things can turn around in an instant, often bringing sunshine that can illuminate the soul.

That is something I tried to remember as I continued to work practically every hour God sent and although the work was hard, I constantly tried to remind myself that I was fortunate to have something which made all my efforts worthwhile: our little shop.

Thankfully, life and indeed people have a habit of picking you up just when you are at your lowest ebb and my dear friends Donal and Peter certainly came through for me in that regard, I'm embarrassed to say, just when I was beginning to doubt that they ever would. At close of business one evening, Donal and Peter entered the shop and I was as surprised as I was delighted to see them. With the shop's sign turned to 'Closed' I suspect they knew we would not be interrupted by customers with potato quizzes or the like, so to their credit, they wisely seized that moment to come and make my day.

As it was a Saturday evening, I quizzed their casual attire, leading Peter to tell me that they had left their dancing shoes at home in order to spend an evening in my company. I told them both that they were most welcome and before long, the laughter was in full flow as we put the world's wrongs to right. Donal went on to tell me that he and Sheila had set a date for their wedding and, out of the blue, he asked me to be his best man. Quite taken aback, at first I just smiled in acceptance but Donal and I soon shook hands, so as to seal the deal. It meant so much.

That night Donal, Peter and I sat for hours and we talked about things that made us laugh in the past and things that we hoped might make us smile in the future. I was told all about Sheila and of the lovely times she and Donal had spent together and from the enthusiasm in his eyes it was clear that he had found the kind of wonderful girl that he richly deserved. I was so very pleased for him.

Looking back on that period now, I realise that even though I had cut myself off from life to the point where I had all but abandoned my friends, they still stubbornly refused to give up on me or the friendship we shared. Joseph Soap, the Wallflower Boy, had been prised from the wall and I am truly grateful that they both thought I was worth the effort.

Donal's engagement and subsequent wedding proved to be a turning point in both of our lives and little did I know at the time, as the old saying goes: 'One wedding leads to another...'

CHAPTER 11

AUDREY HEALY

ONE'S WEDDING DAY IS OFTEN BILLED as the most important day of a person's life and for Donal's sake I truly hope that his big day more than lived up to expectations. From my own selfish point of view there is one thing that I can say with an absolute certainty, and that is that Donal's wedding day hands down proved to be the most important day of my life.

The butterflies in my belly woke me shortly after 6am and I immediately resumed my panicking exactly where I had left it the previous night. The thoughts of standing up and making a best man speech in front of a room full of people had alarmed me from the moment my initial joy abated. As a naturally shy person I had always felt that my role as a shopkeeper had forced me to outwardly project myself slightly more than I was comfortable with, but this role was to be on a different scale all together. I was to be centre of attention, for a few moments at least, and I was well aware that one slip of the tongue could cause irreparable damage and cast a dark cloud over my best friend's big day.

Fretting to no end that morning I hid underneath the bedclothes and I gave more than a second thought to staying safely tucked up for the day. Thankfully common sense eventually intervened and reminded me that sooner rather than later someone would come and get me, so I rose from my bed and set about casting fear to one side in an effort to give the day a right good go.

Scrubbed and polished up as best I could I left my house that morning knowing nothing of the life's joy that the day was about to bring me and as I walked the short distance down past Saint Patrick's Park towards Donal's house, I placed my crumpled-up speech into the pocket of my rented suit. When I got there, Donal was already suited and booted and if he was nervous he was doing a great job in disguising it. On his father's instructions he necked a drop of whiskey to 'clear away the cobwebs' while I feigned my enforced sip by merely touching the 'uisce beatha' against my lips, before kissing it back into the glass.

Donal's neighbours turned out in force to see us away before we set off amid fanfare, on foot towards Our Lady of the Wayside, which was just up the road. Donal seemed quite calm about the upcoming ceremony yet he appeared somewhat preoccupied with another upcoming event and with the church's steeple coming into view, he aired his concerns about how he was going to consummate the marriage later on that evening. Perhaps wisely we both agreed that my advice on such matters would purely be guesswork and we quickly concluded that there was little point in the blind leading the blind, so for better or worse we changed the topic in order to save both our blushes.

We reached the church gate in little or no time and once through we strolled up the pathway, which curved up a gentle hill. From there we took up position in front of the church and we nervously faced back down towards the gate, in order to greet the guests.

Donal stood chatting to a never-ending procession of aunties and uncles, while I stood idly by against the church's huge wooden door. Although weather-beaten to within an inch of its life I noticed that the old church door had surprisingly polished hinges and by way of adding further contrast to it, it now sported me slumped up against it, looking as though I were somehow propping up the entire building. As I leaned back against the church door with my cold hands buried deep in my pockets I must have cut the figure of a chap waiting for a bus, rather than one who was about to have his heart lifted into the heavens.

Donal, perhaps reacting to my apparent lack of interest turned and asked me to straighten myself up and he implored me to at least try to look half clued-in to the day's proceedings. I apologised and explained that I was just nervous about my speech and Donal to his credit tried to reassure me.

"Some best man I am," I said, pointing out that it was me who was meant to reassure the groom were nerves to make an appearance.

As Donal and I stood our ground he smiled and waved politely at well-wishers, while I scanned the crowd in hope of a familiar face or two. After drawing a blank I realised that I knew no one there so I was left to ponder whether that was a good or bad thing, when it came to making my speech.

Standing perplexed in the shadow of the church's towering spire I was brought back to reality by what remains my very definition of perfection, as the most beautiful girl I had ever seen came walking gracefully through the church gate. My gaze remained fixed on the beautiful brunette walking up the pathway and whilst under her spell I reasoned to myself that no man, either past or present, could possibly have witnessed a more flawless young lady. Her long dark hair was perfectly tied up, which highlighted her pale skin, full lips and the blue eyes that reeled me in immediately. She was wearing a striking red and black dress and as I watched it flow in the soft autumn breeze I repositioned my jaw, which had dropped ever so slightly open.

I knew instantly that I had to meet her so I turned to Donal and asked him a question, a question so pure and delicate that it could have been taken from Shakespearean romance.

"Who's your one in the red?" I asked without a blink.

Donal informed me that the beautiful girl was in fact his cousin Audrey Healy and without warning he then, somewhat mischievously, beckoned her over.

Well, blind panic set in that instant and my face turned a colour reminiscent of the approaching dress. Tensed up like a statue, my perspiration could have irrigated the Sahara desert a dozen times over. Such reactions were perhaps understandable; after all I was seconds away from meeting the love of my life and each time I recount that moment, I find myself tingling with the same nervous excitement.

"Calm yourself Joseph!" I whispered to myself.

Donal's wave had caught her eye and Audrey Healy walked straight from my dreams, into the centre of my world. At first Donal and Audrey exchanged small pleasantries while I stood there silently, looking like a crow staring into an empty packet of crisps. I didn't know what to say to her as shyness had robbed me of words so I decided to hedge my bets and wait for her to speak to me.

Audrey was clearly unaware of my train of thought and several uncomfortable moments passed before she readied herself to enter the church. I believe Donal could sense that I was about to let slip the chance of a lifetime so he kindly, if somewhat belatedly, introduced Audrey and me.

Audrey offered her hand to me and I took it as gently as I could and in a single heartbeat I knew that I never wanted to let it go. The very second she spoke to me the weight of the world lifted from my shoulders and miraculously words began to flow from my mouth in a way that caught everyone, including myself, by surprise.

We were annoyingly interrupted however by a portly lady with a camera, who seemed hell-bent on having her photograph taken with Donal. Perhaps out of obligation Donal agreed to the snap and once completed, he then cheekily asked the lady if she would mind taking a photograph of "Joseph and Audrey". I smiled at the very idea of it before posing for a photograph which I still treasure to this day. It is a picture that captures perfectly the very moment that love proved its existence to me and it shows that even for modest guys like me its captivating magic is attainable.

With the photographs taken and the portly lady satisfied and now nowhere to be seen Donal made something of an indiscreet exit, leaving Audrey and me alone in each other's company. We spoke politely about the day and the great style that was on show and before long Audrey kindly asked whether I was feeling nervous about giving my speech. In hope of looking macho I briefly contemplated dismissing the very notion out of hand, but instead I chose to just tell the truth and I confided in her that I was in fact quite a bit nervous.

"You'll be brilliant, I know you will," Audrey said, before gently tapping my forearm in confirmation.

I instantly believed her words to be true and her kind reassurance gave me the sense of belief in myself that I so badly needed. I knew then that come the moment of truth Audrey's face would be the only one I would see amongst the crowd and just like when speaking to her in person, the world that surrounded us held no fears for me.

Soon, the church bells beckoned everyone to the pews and Audrey and I said our goodbyes, before leaving for our respective places. The ceremony went without a hitch (by that I mean problem, not marital) and for me its highlight was undoubtedly when Audrey was called upon to do a reading.

She read out a letter from Saint Paul to the Corinthians, doing so beautifully I may add, and I positively hung on her every word. Usually on its utterance I would spare a near-blasphemous thought for Saint Paul's overworked postman as, to my youthful ears, Saint Paul seemingly wrote a new letter to the Corinthians every week. This time, however, pleasing both myself and no doubt the Lord, my attention was solely on Audrey's reading. While speaking to me outside she had not mentioned that she was tasked with a reading and I thought it a wonderful thing that she was more concerned with my nerves for public speaking than her own. In many ways that little gesture summed her up to perfection.

After the ceremony we headed towards the Glenview Inn where the reception would take place in its function room, and I must say that I was giddy with excitement. I knew that Audrey would be there so I spent my time wisely by thinking up things to say to her, just in case the cat got my tongue. Once there, everyone spent an hour or so happily chatting away before the meal commenced whereas I cut the figure of a man who was present in body rather than soul as my mind raced, and my eyes searched the room for Audrey.

"Maybe she isn't coming to the afters part. What if she could only make it to the ceremony? What if I never see her again?" I fretted to myself.

A bell soon rang out to signal the commencement of dinner prompting Donal, groomsman Peter and I to take up our positions at the top table. I was properly worried now and I took my seat amid thoughts that surely I hadn't found love, just to have it taken from me.

Moments later and to my greatest relief Audrey walked into the function room accompanied by an older couple, who I presumed were her parents. It later transpired that after the church they had decided to stop somewhere for a cup of tea, before making their way to the reception. Although I rued the fact that such plans had not come up in our conversation, I was so very glad to see her nonetheless.

As Audrey took her place at the table directly in front of mine, I found myself waving at her like a right ninny. Surprisingly, however, my lack of decorum proved fruitful as Audrey very kindly returned the wave, albeit in a much more dignified fashion.

Worryingly, it didn't take long for my old doubts to creep back in and even with Audrey at an arm's reach, I found myself no longer immune from uncertainty. In fact such were my nerves that I hardly even touched my dinner throughout save for the small fort I made, out of mashed potatoes. Gravy doubled for a moat as I tried to convince myself that by building up a vegetable wall of defence, I would somehow be able to shield myself from the hordes that had now gathered to consume my every word.

As damn luck would have it the place settings had positioned Audrey with her back turned to me, but as the speeches got underway I watched as she manoeuvred her chair to face the top table, which I took to be a good sign.

After exchanging bashful looks with me for a moment or two Audrey leaned slightly in towards me and asked in a delicate whisper, if I was still nervous about my speech. I mouthed silently that I was, which prompted her to bite down gently onto her bottom lip before flashing me a sympathetic smile for my predicament. She then assured me that I would be great and with that, it was time for me to stand up and begin:

"Eh, Ladies and Gentlemen…"

Now I'm not saying that my speech was perfect; it wasn't, by any stretch of the imagination, but the congregation didn't boo me, so I classed it as a victory of sorts. At the end I noticed that Audrey clapped the loudest out of anyone in the room and she silently gestured to me a big "well done" as all those around her settled back into their seats, following the final toast to the bride and groom.

When the food was cleared away and the tables moved back against the wall, I was left feeling like a new man. With formalities out of the way I sat and chatted to Donal and Sheila who congratulated me on my speech, while I again congratulated them on their nuptials and pleasant banter complemented the mood of the day perfectly.

I later rose in order to buy the bride and groom a drink to celebrate and I made my way to the unfamiliar setting of the bar. With drinks in hand, I made my way back to the table and en route I delighted in bumping into Audrey, as she walked across the edge of the empty dance floor. Thrillingly, I could tell that she was almost as glad to see me as I was her, and we both passed comment as to the relief we felt following our bouts of public speaking. Brave as a lion, I offered to buy her a drink, which she accepted, before kindly agreeing to meet me at the bar when I returned from giving Donal and Sheila their tipples of choice.

Amid great haste I quickly deposited the drinks with the newlyweds and returned to the bar, where I was relieved to see Audrey standing waiting for me. I bought her a tonic water and lime as requested and even though I already had a drink back at the table I got myself another one, just so I wouldn't look odd. Chancing my arm further, I boldly asked Audrey if she would care to take a seat and on her kind agreement, I proudly escorted her back to my table.

I was grinning like a Cheshire cat as I walked the most beautiful girl in Ireland back to my table and although I didn't quite know how or indeed why it was all happening, I certainly wasn't going to question my good fortune. Donal and Sheila had been joined by Paul and his parents, Mr. and Mrs. Carty, who on my return collectively shuffled around in their seats to make room for Audrey and me. As they did so, I watched as one by one they all shared a disbelieving look with one another but as I could hardly believe it myself, I could hardly blame them.

Audrey and I sat and chatted for hours and we did so as if no one else in the world existed. I pursued her romantically with the freedom of a man who believed he had no chance in the first place. Simply put, I felt like a king when I was with her. The fact that a girl like Audrey would even speak to a bit of scruff like me amazed me, let alone the fact that she was clearly interested in my opinions and all I had to say. I loved every word she used, every sentence she spoke and the twinkle in her eyes made me lean in closer to her in anticipation, whenever she paused to sip from her drink.

Love at first sight had been followed up by its very confirmation and at that moment I truly believed, as I believe now, that I was the luckiest man alive. As the night played out Audrey and I tenderly held hands underneath the table and I, for one, dreaded the thought of ever being anywhere else. Had it not been for Audrey's visibly disapproving parents arriving at our side attempting to whisk her away at the end of the night, we would probably have remained sat at that table. Certainly until guests from a future wedding demanded that we vacate their seats.

Mr. and Mrs. Healy and I exchanged a couple of awkward hellos before Audrey somewhat reluctantly rose to her feet and manoeuvred to join them. Jolted into action and determined to ensure that she and I were not going to end up as ships passing in the night, I tentatively asked her if she would care to meet up with me again sometime. Miraculously, Audrey agreed to this and right there and then we put plans in place to meet up the following week.

Audrey was then finally and somewhat unceremoniously shepherded away by her two rather stern-looking parents and as she was led towards the door, we exchanged as many as three waves goodbye. I remained standing long after the door had swung closed behind her. Eventually retaking my seat and left to review the day in my own mind, I really couldn't quite believe what had just happened to me. After all it had been a day that had started out in the throes of worry, yet by the end of it I found myself perched on cloud nine. I guess love can do strange things to a man.

Young Conor, be prepared for when love hits you because when it does, its lightning bolt will knock you for six. It is a feeling matched by no other and once you have experienced it you will never be the same again. I was a changed man from that day, thoroughly for the better, and I suddenly found myself with a pronounced spring in my step and a new-found glint in my eye. The world of course would still lay down its challenges for me that much was unavoidable but with love now circulating in the air around me, I drew strength and great comfort from the fact that I would not be facing them alone.

CHAPTER 12

JOHN, PAUL, GEORGES, RINGO AND EDWARD

DO YOU KNOW THAT I AM firmly of the mind that my younger brother Edward was always destined to become one of life's great wallies? He was and indeed still is a guy who cuts so many corners, it is little wonder he has found himself constantly going around in circles.

Right from an early age Edward rarely extended himself in terms of effort, yet, for some reason, he found the inclination to stretch the patience of all those around him, often to near breaking point. As we Soap boys all grew up beneath the pitched roof of our little shop Father and Mother gave Edward every possible opportunity they could, certainly every one afforded to Michael and I, but he forever failed to accept guidance or even see sense.

As the youngest member of our family, Edward, if anything, received more time and attention than us but as his older brothers, we thankfully had the maturity to understand our parents' predicament. It is after all, a natural part of life to fawn over the youngest in a brood and I must say that, on reflection, I am proud that Michael and I didn't add further weight to the troublesome load our parents were carrying, by throwing the proverbial rattle from the pram.

Any extra attention Edward received was of course borne out of necessity rather than favouritism, as right from the very beginning, it was clear that he was something of a wayward soul. My parents always did their very best for Edward and by constantly trying to save him from himself they at least deviated him slightly from the hopeless path he had set off on. Were repeated attempts not made to keep him on the straight and narrow, I honestly believe that he would have careered off into heartbreak and tragedy, rather than into the relative safety of the near-professional idleness in which he now resides.

You see Edward was always an enemy of hard work. They simply never went hand in hand, nor saw eye to eye and his contempt for it goes a long way in explaining why people invariably roll their eyes up at the very mention of his name. It is after all an indisputable fact of life that hard work will always improve your chances of success and even if reward evades your grasp, you can rest assured that by at least trying your best you will have gained the respect of those who witnessed your efforts. This, of course, was lost on Edward and he cared not a jot for the opinions of others; instead he chose to live in a world where only one opinion mattered: his own.

Over the years, I have often wondered if his puzzling ways affected my parents more than they ever let on. They never really spoke about it to me, at least not to any great length, but knowing my parents, when it came to Edward, I suspect that there was more than a tinge of sadness behind their seemingly calm exteriors. My parents wished only happiness for all three of their boys, so to see Edward shoot himself in the foot time and time again, as he lived a life without focus, must have brought them heartache and frustration in equal measure.

A parent's unequivocal love for their child is a birthright enjoyed by all children, and I must say that I have always felt that Edward both knew and exploited this to his personal gain. I dare say, he even knew that despite our often-strained relationship, Michael and I also loved him dearly, a fact which further enabled him to piggyback his way past hard work.

If there is one thing I know for sure about my dear brother, it is that he never once looked upon our little shop as a suitable theatre for his self-styled persona of 'lovable rogue'. To anyone on the outside of poor Edward's brain his talents were virtually non-existent, but in his own mind's eye he was the be-all and end-all. He thought he was streets ahead of everyone else and that if he just continued on his merry way, sooner rather than later the world would sit up and take notice of his charms. Much like common sense, fame and fortune would elude Edward his entire life, but as a young man prone to impression, he was at least prepared to chase it to the ends of the earth.

Well, to England at least...

The morning after Donal's wedding I prepared a hearty breakfast for Father and Edward, with the view of sitting them down and telling them that I was in love. I, of course, wanted the whole world to hear, but I thought it only fit and proper to give my family first opportunity to congratulate me on finding happiness. Such was my excitement I celebrated the boiling of the kettle as though it were a win on the pools, and I practically skipped for joy whilst retrieving some toast from beneath the grill.

As I prepared to dish out the full Irish, a rather worse for wear-looking Father arrived into the kitchen, followed in tow by the consistently inconsistent Edward. Father had been unable to attend Donal's wedding due to work and drinking commitments, while Edward's absence was due in no small part to a lack of an invitation.

When we all sat down to our fatty feast, Father and Edward both seemed surprisingly keen to hear how Donal's big day had gone, and in particular, they quizzed me as to the success or failure of my speech. More than eager to recount the day, I talked them through the entire proceedings, and while adding detail for detail's sake I primed myself to unveil my greatest ever news. However, just as my account was placing me outside of the church door, Edward blurted out, without so much as a by your leave, that he and some friends were leaving Ireland and heading for the bright lights of Liverpool.

Silence descended on the room and I noted that Father's head moved gently from side to side, while a look of dejection formed on his face as he quietly contemplated the prospect of yet another loss to our family.

I, too, was upset, but for very different reasons, as it wasn't so much the content of Edward's announcement but rather its timing, that annoyed me. Granted, he was unaware of the news I was about to break but as my brother, he should have sensed the new-found passion and excitement in my words, and ceased from self-absorbingly cutting short my tale mid-flow. I didn't even get a chance to mention Audrey's name, let alone talk them through my finest hour, as Edward simply flung into conversation the fact that he was leaving because he was "sick of this place".

I am ashamed to say that neither sadness nor lament entered my mind, as rightly or wrongly, in my eyes at least, this was not on the same scale as the departure of Michael. Michael's decision was after all based on practicality and necessity and he had shown great bravery in putting his family's needs above and beyond those of his own. As the elder statesman of the Soap brood, he opted to make a personal sacrifice for the common good, as he knew that our little shop was bound to get pulled under by the weight of three young men clinging for life.

Edward's sole reason for upping sticks was simply his desire to follow a flight of fancy. You see in the 1960s, England was the epicentre of all that was new and exciting in the world. The great cultural change that was sweeping across Britain had not yet managed to cross the Irish Sea, so for countless numbers impatient for change, its lure proved too hard to resist.

When The Beatles arrived on the scene the pace of change quickened even further and almost overnight old were discarded for new when it came to music, clothes and attitudes. Miniskirts left nothing to the imagination and hemlines encroached onto necklines as they seemingly reached for the heavens, and this and a lot more besides would reel young people in from the four corners.

Young women flocked there as they wanted the freedom to express themselves without a dour Irish society casting a disapproving eye upon their exposed knees, while young men couldn't quite believe their luck at seeing pretty girls who weren't covered by four layers of lambswool clothing. Change is of course aimed at the young, but even then the very idea of such notions were as foreign to me, as the land from which they came.

Also in England at that time, Manchester to be precise, a less fazed sort of young Irishman named George Best was capturing the world's imagination both on and off the soccer pitch. Having blazed a trail across the Irish Sea, countless bums were raised from seats as he jinked between defences and his riding of ferocious tackles proved to be an inspiration to all those who feared a bully's wrath. Even those who had to make do with listening to his displays on the wireless could visualise the action, as spellbound radio commentators struggled to do justice to moves often described as magical.

Young Mr. Best was of course fantasy, very much the exception and not the rule, and to compare him to the vast majority of young Irishmen in England at that time is a most unfair comparison. In the harsh reality of mere mortals, life was a struggle across the water, and for anyone not blessed with the considerable talents of 'the Belfast boy', hard work had to take precedence over enjoyment.

Manual, unskilled jobs were relatively easy to find, as the Irish community, staying true to form, tended to inhabit building sites and chainless gangs in every major town and city in England. We, as a nation, always seem to get drawn to the shovel as soon as we land on foreign soil, and it is almost as though we are on a never-ending quest to visit strange lands, only to then take instruction from the locals as to how best dig it up. The perception in Britain is that if a hole needs to be dug, the Irish will charge towards it, but I suspect that we do so only because we are running away from something that pains us a lot more than the hard work itself: the fear of having no work at all.

Nowadays, young Irish people tend to bypass England altogether and Australia now seems to be the destination of choice. Quite why that's the case I will never know, when you consider that there are parts of Macclesfield that we still haven't dug up. Obviously I appreciate that the weather may play a part in their decision, but the 'Land Down Under' should not expect to see me anytime soon because at my age, I will be 'Down Under' soon enough!

When Edward left for England, he did so without the emotional family escort which had been afforded to Michael, but that was a choice all of his own making. Rather than keeping

Father and I abreast of his travel arrangements, or even how he intended to fund such a venture Edward discreetly and without warning cleared out his belongings and left without fanfare, less than three days after he made his announcement.

I remember wondering at the time if Edward perhaps felt that Father and I wouldn't care that he was leaving, or that maybe he felt that we would be glad to see the back of him. Well if that were the case then my brother was very much mistaken, and by thinking such a thing, he was doing a great disservice to the people who loved him the most.

Out of a deep and underlying love for Edward, we as his family would have done what all families do in times of great unrest or crisis, we would have put on a show. I know for sure that Father and I would have been supportive when push came to shove and we would have waded in with words of encouragement, to convince ourselves as much as Edward that, at just gone eighteen years old, he was doing the right thing. Family is family after all and blood is much thicker than the waters of the Irish Sea, but unfortunately my brother never give us the chance to prove that to him.

We didn't hear a dicky bird from Edward for several months, until out of the blue we received a letter from him, saying that he had settled and was doing well. Time would prove that the 'doing well' part was something of an exaggeration but at least we now knew that he was safe and that he had the wherewithal and presence of mind to put a stamp on a letter and post it.

Through acquaintances, Father and I later found out that Edwards's views, as per usual, did not tally with those of the general consensus and rather than 'doing well' he was merely getting by, while bouncing between the bedsit he called home and the pubs that saw the brunt of his wages from the various jobs, which he routinely won and lost.

Of course, Edward had no excuse for such a life really, as back then most jobs permitted people to learn on the job and work their way up. Nowadays the likes of Edward would have no chance whatsoever, as young people seemingly need to have a college degree, in order to make a cup of coffee in one of those fancy tearooms you see dotted all over the place. Society today really has a tendency to overcomplicate things and seems intent on bamboozling the everyday man in the street with superficial nonsense.

My own, often tested, sensibilities were rattled to their core a couple of weeks back in an encounter I had with a customer, as I was helping out in the shop. Whilst serving a rather studious-looking young man, I made the mistake of commenting on the rather desperate weather we happened to be having for the time of year. It was a fairly innocent and innocuous thing to say really, as small as talk can be, yet incredibly by way of reply the young man quite matter-of-factly informed me that it had rained 1150 millimetres since last year.

Now I am not an expert on the metric system by any stretch of the imagination, in fact I have let the whole thing wash over me with the bliss that only total ignorance can provide on such matters, but out of politeness I decided to hazard a guess as to what that amount might be in inches.

"Is that about eighty-five inches?" I asked politely.

"It hasn't rained eighty-five inches since Noah was commissioned to build the ark!" the young pup cheekily replied, before laughing obnoxiously at my expense.

Quite how he knew that 1150 of those milli-things had fallen is anyone's guess, as was the fact that he felt the need to share such a pointless piece of information with me. The poor deluded soul had somehow gotten it into his head that I wanted, or perhaps even needed, to hear this ill-perceived golden titbit, when in actual fact I was more dumbfounded by his arrogance than I was by his supposed words of wisdom.

I mean why in the name of all things holy did he, or even those like him, feel the need to measure water in units of length in the first place?

1150 millimetres... of water!

I mean what next? A kilogram of air? Or maybe even a centimetre of sound?

But I digress.

My brother Edward still lives in England, Leeds in fact, where he has done so for the best part of fifty years. There he has lived out the most predictable of fates, by squandering the little money he ever earned on cheap beer, second-rate horses and third-rate women. It would, of course, be remiss of me to suggest that Edward has been a failure in life, when I too have not exactly placed myself amongst the supposed elite, but I can honestly say that I have at least tried my best along the way. And perhaps it is an achievement in itself, to have done one's best.

Michael and Edward chose very different paths for themselves in life and in terms of both attitude and geography; they literally went in opposite directions. Whether or not Edward's dream turned into a nightmare only he can honestly say, but it is perhaps obvious to all those looking on, that he never quite managed to become the 'fifth Beatle' and like so many before him, he ended up more Pete Best than George.

Edward Soap, the boy without direction, grew into a man forever lost and in doing so he became the second of my two brothers whose life now touches mine only from a distance. We speak on occasion, once a year or so, and when we do, I always make a point of wishing him well.

He is still my brother after all.

CHAPTER 13

COURTING

Audrey and I had arranged to meet up at the Fusiliers'
Arch entrance of St Stephen's Green, the week following Donal's wedding, and our first date was quite literally a walk in the
park. Sunday was my only day off work in the week, so the day
picked itself really and as it was our very first date I decided
that it was only proper to meet during daylight hours, so we
agreed to meet at one o'clock sharp in the afternoon.

I rose early that morning to wash and shave, before setting
about my clothes like a Mother Superior. I was determined
to make a good impression so I pressed my best shirt as if my
life depended on it and I guess in a funny way, it did. With
a steady hand I did not so much run the iron over it, rather
I allowed it to gently caress each strand of the material. The
tricky collar area, that bit everyone dreads, took even more
time than it should have but I was careful to iron out each
crease, for fear that one unsightly fold could negatively sway

Audrey's judgement of me. Granted it was an unlikely call to make on a trivial blemish but I convinced myself that it was a risk not worth taking.

I got into the van shortly before ten and made the short spin over to Our Lady of the Wayside for mass and a quick prayer, as I figured that a bit of divine inspiration would do me no harm at all. I nipped in for the ten o'clock service, and dressed in my finest attire you would think that I would stick out like a sore thumb, but I most certainly didn't. You see in those days, people really made an effort to dress in their 'Sunday best' when going to mass, hence the phrase, and the congregation in general really was a pleasure to behold.

This, of course, sits in total contrast with today, as people nowadays don't even bother to turn up let alone make an effort to look respectful, and those who do muster the strength to tear themselves away from their beds in order to praise our Lord, rarely if ever wear a smart coat or even a tie.

Shining like a new penny I sat and I prayed for my family and friends, as I always did, but this time I also selfishly asked God to keep me from getting tongue-tied on my big date with Audrey. Obviously that request was not going to be very high on the Lord's list of priorities, but nothing ventured, nothing gained. There was always a chance, albeit a small one, that he would bestow a blessing on me out of pity, and I was not above pity when it came to winning favour with Audrey.

After a rather pleasant service I got back into the van and

headed into town, leaving myself with more than enough time to cover any eventuality that may crop up, and I drove the streets of the city until I found a suitable parking spot close to St Stephen's Green. With no end of time to kill, I strolled around Grafton Street and I watched with faint curiosity as people went about their business.

Such was my eagerness to see Audrey I soon took up position at the Fusiliers' Arch, and found myself standing outside the park's gate a full hour earlier than was expected. To keep nerves at bay I began pacing the footpath but it was not long before worry set in and I began to fear the worst and in a public display of agitation, a shallow trench was almost worn into the paving.

"What if something unfortunate has happened and Audrey is unable to make it?" I fretted to myself.

I would have no way of knowing and hell be damned if I was leaving, for fear of missing her, if for argument's sake she was only running late. Wisely I decided to give her every opportunity, and to cover all angles I prudently decided to set a time limit as to how long I would wait for her, should the requirement arise.

"Right, it's gone half past twelve now, she's due at one… I'll give her till eight o'clock. Nine to be safe," I reasoned, as I prepared mentally for a possible lengthy stint.

Those stretched timelines seemed more than reasonable to me but truth be told I'd have slept on a park bench overnight if it meant that I got to see Audrey.

I'll admit only to you, young Conor, that I became extremely anxious at that point, as without mobile phones, making arrangements back then was often a complicated affair and you needed the forward-thinking of a town planner in order to get anything done. Best-laid plans were often changed at the last minute and as a note tied to a pigeon's leg was the closest thing we had to instant communication, people were often left high and dry.

I tried my best to resist the notion that Audrey might change her mind altogether, because if I allowed myself to believe that she was not coming, and then per chance she arrived, she would find me sitting in a pool of my own tears. But deep down I knew she would come, as not only did I believe Audrey to be a girl of her word, but I also felt the strong reassuring hand of destiny on my shoulder.

It was shortly before one o'clock when, to my great relief, I saw her walking down Grafton Street. Eager to get her attention, I waved excitedly over to her and while she waited until it was safe to cross the road, she enthusiastically waved back to me. I quietly cursed each and every passing car that was keeping her from me, and I was even half tempted to burst out onto the road in order to hold back the traffic, as though I were some sort of 20th century Moses.

Thankfully, the urge to behave like a raving lunatic was quelled from within, and I simply and without fuss, walked to the edge of the footpath to greet her. Graciously, a male driver, obeying the unwritten rule of the road that permits pretty girls to pass as and when they see fit, stopped his car and allowed Audrey to proceed across the road. I extended my hand out to help her step onto the path, and my pulse rate quickened for the second or so she held onto it, while steadying herself. Audrey beamed as she greeted me and I for my part combined a smile with a blush, as I warmly returned her greeting.

We both stood silent for a clumsy second or two, before I suggested that we take a stroll in the park. To my joy Audrey agreed and we made our way into St Stephen's Green, where we meandered our way around the pathways without a care in the world. Shyness, the downfall of many a humble young man, did not make an appearance I am glad to say, and inexplicably I found myself with an endless stream of words at my command.

Audrey as expected was a total delight, and she spoke eloquently with a manner and intelligence that complemented her beauty to a tee. I was totally transfixed by the girl of my dreams, but at the same time bemused as to why my every word met with the most receptive and attentive of ears. I really could not believe some of the witty things I was saying, or understand how they flowed so freely from me, but it wasn't long before I realised that being with Audrey made me feel different. I now felt ten feet tall and I found myself walking with the kind of swagger that only becomes apparent during the first tentative steps into a lifelong romance. We spoke about everything from family, friends and general interests and the more I found out about her, the more I wanted to know.

After a lap or two of the park, we sat down on the grass beside the duck pond. I would like to be able to tell you that we then romantically fed the ducks together but in truth, we didn't have so much as a slice of bread between us, so we had to make do with waving at the ducks as they floated by on the water.

A most unfortunate change in the weather forced us to take stock of our location, and a sudden burst of heavy rain sent us running towards the gate. We were laughing at our misfortune as we hastened our way out of the park, and in a moment that I remember well, Audrey took my hand as we ran back through the Fusiliers' Arch and out onto Grafton Street.

Drenched, we sought refuge from the inclement weather in the nearby Bewley's Cafe, where we sat at a table for two, beneath the old stained-glass windows that adorn the cafe's walls. While there we attempted to dry off over a pot of tea and some freshly made scones, on which I was careful not to overload the strawberry jam, in the hope of doing my best shirt a favour. Audrey and I sipped our tea at no great pace, and I must say that the conversation was as charming as our surroundings.

As darkness reduced the spectacle of the stained-glass windows my day was rounded off to perfection, when Audrey accepted my offer of a lift home. After I settled up at the till Audrey and I sheltered inside the cafe's doorway for a time until the rain subsided, before we made a quick dash to the van. As we ran hand in hand, I recall thinking that we were running towards the end of the day, a day I wished would go on forever, but I consoled myself with the knowledge that, for Audrey and me, life was only just beginning.

As we left for home, I was relieved that a day that had promised so much had well and truly delivered and not only that, but it had exceeded all expectations. The thought occurred to me as we drove home, that Audrey and I had arrived separately earlier in the day, yet here we were now, making the return journey home together. If symbolism was to play any role in our relationship then all signs pointed to a very successful first date.

When we pulled up outside of Audrey's house, we finalised plans we had made on the way home to meet up again a few days later and having confirmed a date to the pictures, we simply shook hands and said our goodbyes. On the way back to the shop, I replayed the whole day over and over again in my head, and once in the door I found it very hard to settle myself down. That night I had the greatest sleep of my life and in it, I dreamt about the most perfect girl in the world. She was my perfect girl.

The subsequent trip to the pictures, to see an aptly named film called *Never Let Go,* meant little to me in terms of cinematic enjoyment, indeed I can barely remember anything about the film, other than it starred a great favourite of mine in Peter Sellers. Throughout its showing I sat in complete silence, not out of respect for traditional picture house rules, but out of pure disbelief. Why, I thought, should I concern myself with fantasy, when I was blessed with an actual leading lady of my very own?

Audrey was as pretty as any film actress, more so in fact, and no romance ever committed to film has come close to conveying the love I felt for her. We held hands throughout the showing and I just longed for the credits to roll, so I could talk with her again.

After the pictures I walked Audrey home, and as we prepared to part company outside her front gate she leaned gently in towards me and kissed me so tenderly on the lips. If my hand hadn't been resting on the garden railing in an attempt to look cool, I would have floated off into the night sky, but I quickly steadied myself and returned the kiss as best I could.

That, in all truth, was my first ever kiss, and a historic moment in the life of yours truly. It lasted barely a second but it felt as though it ran for a lifetime. When Audrey stepped back, parting our lips, I immediately longed to kiss her again but I perhaps rightly chose to enjoy the moment, rather than pushing my luck. I briefly contemplated saying, "Thank you", but thought better of it.

Fortunately, our romance continued to blossom over the weeks and months that followed and Audrey and I spent as much time together as we possibly could, given the constraints of the shop. It was such a wonderful time, with each day new and exciting and I felt as though my world was opening up to endless possibilities.

The 1960s was of course the great era of the Showbands in Ireland and each week the various halls and theatres across the nation were packed to the rafters. Great entertainers like Joe Dolan and Dickie Rock performed to great acclaim, and quite how Brendan Bowyer never gave Elvis Presley a run for his money on the international stage, I will never know.

Audrey and I soon began to mingle in amongst that crowd and it was there I tried my best to fit in on the dance floor, but in all honesty I never once felt comfortable. Although I have always had a love of music, I much prefer it on the wireless in the comfort of my home, yet there I was bopping away for the whole world to see. Without alcohol fuelling a man's legs, he runs the risk of looking quite laboured and cumbersome on the dance floor, so to the casual observer I must have looked like a fish up a tree.

Audrey on the other hand was a natural and male admirers swooned as she glided across the floor, yet for whatever reason she only had eyes for me. On occasion, Audrey would let out a little giggle when I executed moves which few would call dancing, but to her credit she always seemed to appreciate the fact that I was at least giving it a go. So much so that my advice to any young couple starting out in a relationship is to act as though you are cocooned inside a little bubble. Savour every moment you have together, laugh as much as you can and float through life as though you are lost in a world of possibility.

Audrey really was a great beauty and I knew that people must have been thinking that I was punching well above my weight, but I didn't care for one second, as after all they were absolutely right. This was the girl of both my and everyone else's dreams, and I came to the conclusion that if she was going to sell herself short with anyone, she may as well do so with me.

After a couple of months of blissful courtship, Audrey and I both agreed that the time had come to finally meet our respective families and arrangements were duly made on both sides. I had, of course, already told Audrey all about my father and two brothers and I even recall a conversation in particular, where we spoke at length about the terrible loss of my mother. Audrey listened intently and offered me a sympathetic ear to poor Mother's plight and we somehow managed to grow closer as vulnerability reared its head in our relationship for the very first time.

Audrey too had spoken about her family and she often detailed with great affection stories of her two sisters Maeve and Laura, and of her parents Cyril and Marjorie Healy, whom I had met only briefly at Donal's wedding. That night I had pegged Mr. and Mrs. Healy as being quite stern-looking, yet in truth I had barely spoken to them long enough to gauge an honest opinion, but now, by the sound of Audrey's loving description of them, I was in for something of a treat...

CHAPTER 14

THE OUTLAWS: THE GOOD, THE BAD AND THE GRAPEFRUIT

Although I try not to speak ill of the dead, I must share with you my honest belief that both Cyril and Marjorie Healy were truly dreadful people. I am almost ashamed to admit that here today but my feelings on this matter have not diminished in the slightest over the years, and I stand firm on my opinion. I do not utter these words lightly and if I come across as belligerent on this matter, then I further rue the day that Mr. and Mrs. Healy entered my life.

The Healys were one of those terrible couples that you feel truly deserved each other and their only redeeming trait in life was the fact that they agreed to marry one another, thus saving two other poor souls from what equated to a lifelong tethering to a hollow old tree. Looking at the pair of them together you wondered if they even liked each other, let alone questioned whether love played any part in their marriage.

It crossed my mind on more than one occasion that maybe the two of them were just too stubborn to admit defeat and call off a marriage, which was obviously lifeless and bereft of any sort of romance. They were individually bad, collectively desperate and I dare say that a highly motivated caveman, with two sticks and all the time in the world, would fall short in creating a spark of fire that would ignite passion in those two people, or even guilt them into trying to look happy.

Cyril Healy was a small man in stature with grey hair and a complexion equally devoid of colour. He had ears that he never really grew into and an attitude that stank to high heaven. His personality was, at best, wanting and he never willingly stretched the corners of his mouth upwards to face the sky. Simply put, he was not a man who gave away a smile too easily, and perhaps the best way to describe him is by saying that although I did not know how old he was, I somehow knew that he looked his age.

His wife Marjorie was the sort of woman who turned her nose up at the world; so much so, that it acted like a sundial you could set your watch to. She was a heavy-set 'lady' with short brown hair, glasses and the personality of an over-ripened grapefruit. Mr. Healy's other half was neither better nor worse than he was and she was famed locally for being forever at his side, which observers always felt was to ensure that they had all angles covered to judge and further annoy people. Her social skills peaked at "hello" and it was always downhill after there, as she displayed all the warmth of a winter's day to whoever had the misfortune of crossing paths with her.

Quite how two such people managed to create a girl like Audrey I will never know but maybe she was a sign from God that, on occasion, the apple does indeed fall far from the tree. Audrey possessed kindness of heart, consideration, decency and a beautiful free spirit that, when added to the rest of her personality, made up the perfect girl. Her parents on the other hand sapped the energy from whatever room they were in, while at the same time giving out a look of disinterest and contempt to anyone who stood at the base of their imaginary pedestal upon which they had elevated themselves.

The Healys owned and ran a decent-sized hardware shop in Stepaside and because of this they both thought that they were very much to the manor born but in reality, they had both come from extremely humble backgrounds. With very selective memories, they now held notions so far above their station that they both could have gotten part-time work with NASA, were it to ever open up a Dublin branch.

The Healys had, in their own minds, made the great leap from working class to middle class, yet now they found themselves stuck in limbo as they lacked the financial means and social graces to kick on and join what they perceived to be the 'upper class', which they no doubt craved to be part of. So deluded were they, that they failed to notice that Ireland is not a country built on a class system, and while we have always been an island of 'the haves and the have-nots', notions of 'Lord and Lady Muck' only appear in the form of teasing, should a friend happen to buy a fancy new coat or some other item deemed a non-essential frippery.

In what was to be the official unveiling of yours truly, Audrey had arranged for me to go around to her parent's house for Sunday dinner so, eager to impress, I arrived sharply, adorned in my Sunday best. As I walked into the house for the first time I was still oblivious to the true ways of her parents, and had I known the sort of people I was about to encounter, I would have concealed a wooden stake and some garlic about my person, for defence.

God love me, I had a preconceived idea of the Healys in my mind's eye from what Audrey had told me about them and foolishly, as I entered, I had them pre-pegged as being salt of the earth. It didn't take me too long to alter my view however, and tellingly, my opinion, unlike Audrey's, was untainted by the innocence of bias.

Audrey and I made our way into the living room where we found the waiting Mr. and Mrs. Healy, and on arrival I was not so much welcomed into the room, as acknowledged. I was offered neither a hand to shake nor cheek to kiss and there was certainly no danger of them troubling the kettle into action for a cup of tea.

"So this is young Soap is it?" Mr. Healy bluntly enquired, from the depths of his armchair.

"It is indeed. Pleased to meet you, Mr. Healy," I said, while extending out a hand that was not met; in fact it barely grabbed his attention.

"You can call him Cyril, silly," offered Audrey, nudging me gently on the arm.

"Let's just stick with Mr. Healy, shall we?" Mr. Healy interjected, quite matter-of-factly.

Now, I had not expected her father to greet me with outstretched arms, but I had not expected such a show of passive aggression either. Audrey, for her part, was so keen to introduce me to her mother that she may have assumed that her father was just teasing, but the glare I received directly from him as I made my way over to meet his wife confirmed to me that he was as serious as a hole in the bottom of a lifeboat.

Mrs. Healy also remained seated throughout my introduction and when the moment came to meet her she offered me only a smirk, in lieu of a smile. Rather than call her by any sort of title, I decided to play it safe with a simple "hello" as I half suspected that anything short of "your Highness" would have seen me hung, drawn and quartered at her behest.

With introductions complete I sat myself down awkwardly on the sofa, while Audrey excitedly told her parents all about me. I must say that her enthusiasm for me was most evident and her kind words helped lighten my mood to no end. She told them every little detail she knew about me, from working in the shop, to my musical tastes and I was amazed how she had taken the time to remember even the smallest points of note.

Audrey was however fighting a winless battle in trying to gain me favour in the eyes of her parents and I clearly saw her energy levels drain when she realised that her endeavours had not even prompted her parents to ask a single question or pass comment as she spoke. The silence was deafening when Audrey finished speaking and such was the awkwardness, I would have attempted to hide in the bottom of a teacup, had I been offered one in the first place.

The dour silence was eventually broken by the sound of Mr. Healy's newspaper rising to meet the base of his nose, quickly followed by Mrs. Healy's knitting needles, which began to click in perfect timing with the brass clock on the mantelpiece. With little option for much else, Audrey and I sat and chatted to one another for a while before eventually making my excuses to leave, and I could tell that she was a little crestfallen as a result of my big introduction turning into something of a non-event.

She need not have worried, however, as that day still proved to be a memorable one for me, albeit for all the wrong reasons.

"Joseph is heading off now. He has some work to do in the shop," said Audrey, as she finally admitted defeat.

"Eh, nice meeting you Mr. and Mrs. Healy," I lied.

"Yes it must be very time-consuming, running a shop when your father is stuck in the pub all day," Mr. Healy said from behind his newspaper.

"I beg your pardon Mr. Healy?"

I stood with Audrey by the living room door, my exit now on hold, and I stared at the back of his paper which he continued to hold aloft.

"I'm sorry, did you say something Mr. Healy?" I demanded, but my question again fell on deaf ears.

I took a pace forward.

Sensing trouble, Audrey quickly grabbed my forearm and ushered me outside, where she calmed me down as best she could. Her beautiful blue eyes were filling up at the upset of it all and she apologised what must have been a million times. It was, of course, not her fault and I tried to reassure her that it was just the natural reaction of protective parents, even though I didn't believe that for one second. With my rage finally suppressed, we decided to let sleeping dogs lie and rather than dwell on the past, Audrey and I chose to look forward to our next milestone, which was dinner at my house the following Sunday, where she would meet my father for the very first time.

Father's drinking was still taking priority over his work but when he could, he would help out in the shop, and without his contribution, scattered as it was, it would have been impossible for me to run the business on my own. Father had agreed to meet Audrey over Sunday dinner and he even said that he would "cook his famous roast chicken to welcome the girl"; chicken which was famous only for its dryness, but no one ever had the heart to tell him. In the week leading up to the meal, Father assured me that he would not let me down, and I would have had no trouble in believing him whatsoever had he not been drunk a skunk while telling me.

When the Sabbath rolled around again, I found myself quietly confident of a pleasant day ahead, no more so than when I watched Father select the finest vegetables from stock before setting about preparing the dinner, as though he were a chef on trial for a job at a fancy restaurant.

Yet when Audrey knocked on the door at twelve noon sharp, Father was nowhere to be seen.

I had happily left Father toiling away in the kitchen, while I went for a wash and shave, but by the time I got back he was gone. I also noticed that some money was missing from the small tin we used for storing loose change, a tin usually kept above the stove, but now lying open on its side on the kitchen table. I really was so bitterly disappointed and even as the son of an alcoholic, I felt genuinely let down by this show of heartlessness.

In no time at all, there was a knock at the front door and I made the short walk downstairs to let Audrey in and as I did, I spent my last remaining seconds in the empty house, trying to figure out an excuse for my father's absence.

At the base of the stairs I opened the door and there, pretty as a picture, stood Audrey. I greeted her with a kiss before inviting her inside, and as she stepped into the hallway she commented favourably on the smell of food coming from upstairs. After making light of such praise, I began to close the door behind her, but before the door's lock had a chance to meet with its receiver, a foot darted in from outside and wedged coarsely in between the narrowing gap.

Startled by its abruptness I spun around quickly, only to see a hand now clinging to the inside of the door, soon followed by a flustered face, which I recognised immediately.

"Not so quick, son. You almost took my head off!" said an out-of-breath Father.

I was so overjoyed to see him, and I will confess to being disappointed in myself for ever doubting him.

Father introduced himself to Audrey while shaking her warmly by the hand. He explained that he had nipped out to get some stuffing as he had forgotten to buy some for the dinner, and he went to further pains to explain his puffing and panting, by pointing out that he had practically run home to be there in time to meet her.

"Chicken is not chicken without a bit of Paxo, and if you are going to do something, then do it right," Father said, in between draws of breath, as we all made our way upstairs for a cup of tea and a chat before dinner.

That afternoon was a joy to behold, and Father seemed to come alive as he sat and chatted to Audrey and for the first time in ever such a long time, I recognised the wonderful man I once knew. He was warm, funny and charming throughout and right from the outset, he was clearly taken with Audrey as they spoke without pause until finally we sat down to eat.

During dinner, Father mischievously mentioned on more than one occasion that I had been something of a whiny baby, so in an attempt to save face in front of Audrey I told her that I had plenty to whine about back then, but she didn't believe me for a second.

"How could you have anything to complain about with a Father like this, Joseph?" Audrey laughed.

"Oh she's a keeper son, she's a keeper!" said Father, pursing his lips theatrically.

We really had a lovely day together and it sat in total contrast to the debacle that was tea with the Healys. Even the dinner was an unexpected triumph and I noticed that Audrey made a point of complimenting Father as she made her way around her plate.

"The stuffing is delicious, Mr. Soap. The whole meal is a credit to you," said Audrey politely.

"Mr. Soap was my father, dear, you go ahead and call me Danny," Father said, while clearly delighted with such culinary praise.

The evening was rounded off with yet more tea and on its last boil, the poor kettle made a sound that was a cross between a whistle and a sigh of relief. At the end of the night while saying their goodbyes, Father and Audrey embraced each other like long-lost friends, while I readied the van to drive her back home.

Audrey spoke fondly of my father on the way back to her house and on reaching our destination she thanked me for a lovely day. For fear of bumping into Mr. and Mrs. Healy, I shamefully spurned the offer of walking Audrey to her door, as I knew that such an encounter would only serve to dampen what had been a real day to remember. Instead, I made my excuses and watched from the van, until she was safely inside.

On my way home I felt really proud of Father and all he had done to make the day a success, and whether he would admit it or not, I knew that his efforts were as much for my benefit as they were for Audrey's, which made me all the more thankful.

When I got back home I found that Father had tidied up the dishes and the pots and pans, and he was nestled down in his armchair, reading a newspaper. I sat down opposite him and thanked him sincerely for everything, but he modestly brushed aside my "silly talk" by telling me that he thought that Audrey was terrific.

"You should look after that girl, son," said Father, holding his gaze to highlight the importance of what he was saying.

I promised Father that I would do just that, before taking the opportunity to speak with him about Mr. Healy, sparing him the comment passed about his drinking. I told him what had happened the previous week and Father looked genuinely annoyed for my situation. He told me that he knew of Mr. Healy, but added that he did not know him personally.

"Has he still got that wife of his?" enquired Father.

"Yes," I replied. "Mrs. Healy."

"Good, well he is suffering enough," Father joked.

"Listen, son, you don't let that oaf spoil things between you and your girl. If he doesn't want you around his house or his daughter, then all the more reason to go back around and show him that you won't be intimidated," Father elaborated.

I took my father's words of wisdom to heart and with them ringing in my ears I went around to Audrey's house a few days later. There I found Audrey home alone, and my relief must have been evident as she tried to reason that her father was probably just being protective of her and that with time he would warm to me as much as she had. Audrey then explained her father's absence by telling me that he was doing some work in his hardware shop and she suggested that I go and purchase something small, like a paintbrush, so as to seize the opportunity to speak with him on a one-to-one basis.

I was hesitant at first until I remembered that Father and I had some shelving in the shop that had seen a better day, so I decided to kill two birds with one stone and get it mended. That shelving had been there for many years and no doubt had several more years of good service still left in it, but in an effort to win Mr. Healy over and make things easier for Audrey and me, it would be replaced.

Heeding Audrey's suggestion I returned home and took the measurements of the shelving, before making my way gingerly to 'Healy's Hardware' for some supplies and a spot of confrontation. On my arrival into the shop, Mr. Healy was standing behind the till chatting to his assistant. I walked slowly up to the counter and said "Hello" to Mr. Healy, and following a moment's strained silence, he responded to me as if he were laying eyes on me for the first time.

"Yes?" asked Mr. Healy

"How are you today Mr. Healy?" I enquired to deaf ears.

"Was there something you wanted?" he asked abruptly.

Slightly flustered and taken aback, I told him that I was looking for some lengths of timber, a saw, screws and a new screwdriver, as I had a bit of a job to do in the shop. As soon as I passed my measurements across the counter, Mr. Healy instructed his assistant to gather the items, before turning his back to me as he feigned interest in a box of masonry nails that were housed on a countertop behind him.

Silently acknowledging his rudeness and in an attempt to save face, I told the back of his head that I would move my van closer to the door, in order to load up the materials.

"I don't want that battered old van parked outside my shop. I'm not having people think that I've fallen on hard times. It's bad enough that it's seen outside my home," Mr. Healy said, having spun around to issue his barbed comment. "Get it loaded around the side and then get it shifted!"

1... 2... 3... 4... I silently counted to ten.

The shop assistant gathered the supplies and brought them over to Mr. Healy where he checked each one carefully, to note the price. As he did so, I wagered to myself that each lifeless object he held probably had more of a personality than he did.

When satisfied, I paid Mr. Healy what he was due and he in return passed me my change without eye contact or comment. Summoning up as much dignity as I could muster I gathered up my purchases and thanked him for his service, before leaving the shop in a flustered state, which I hope was not too obvious.

I was due to visit Audrey again the next day, but such was my dread of another run-in with Mr. Healy, I found myself contemplating whether to go or not. At home I again confided my concerns with Father and he was quick to offer me his own unique brand of advice on the matter.

"Son, you are a Soap, and we don't take that sort of rubbish from anyone. Get back round there and plant the Soap flag right in the centre of the little sod's living room!" advised Father.

I again decided to take Father's words on board, and even though this time there was a fair chance that they may get me killed, I headed back around to Audrey's the following day.

When I reached the Healys' house I knocked on the door, which was in turn answered by the ray of sunshine that was Mrs. Healy herself.

"Hello, Mrs. Healy, I've come to see Audrey," I pleasantly explained.

"Audrey is in the living room," replied Mrs. Healy, practically mid-turn as she walked away from the door.

Unperturbed, I closed the front door behind me and walked unaccompanied to the living room door, where I knocked gently before entering. Audrey was sitting on the sofa at the far end of the room and I went over to embrace her outstretched arms, before sitting down cosily beside her. Audrey was very keen to know how I had gotten on in her father's shop the previous day, but I didn't have the heart to tell her the whole story as I knew it would upset her, so I just glossed over a few details and told her that it went fine.

"Did Daddy give you the 'friends and family' discount?" she cheerily asked.

In response, I told Audrey that no discount had been applied to my order, and that this was the first time I had even heard of such a reduction. I added that I hadn't expected a discount, and if anything, I would have been embarrassed if one had been given. Audrey seemed very surprised at the apparent lack of a concession and even offered to speak with her father about it but I repeatedly told her there was no need.

Audrey and I then spent a very pleasant afternoon chatting on the sofa and occasionally listening to the wireless, and our company was only parted when she offered to make us some tea, which I accepted. She left the living room for the kitchen, before returning all of fifteen minutes later with two cups of tea and some biscuits neatly balanced on a tray. She then carefully rested the tray upon a side table, before squeezing herself back down snugly beside me. Just as I reached for my cup, and I dare say a biscuit or two, the living room door swung open and in stepped a furious looking Mr. Healy, who quickly fired a distasteful glare in my direction.

"You want a discount, do ya boy? Well here's your discount!" he raged with contempt, as he sent some small change crashing to the floor in front of me, some of which ricocheted off my shoes.

"I wouldn't want you crying poverty and blaming me. Heaven forbid you caught TB or something!" Mr. Healy said spitefully, as he closed the door behind him.

Furious, I jumped up and attempted to follow him out the door. Audrey, too, rose to her feet and tried to bring calm to what must have been an upsetting situation for her also and with her arm wrapped tightly around my waist, she somehow managed to keep me from following him. After a prolonged hug, littered with a reassuring kiss or two, I settled down some-what, even retaking my seat, but I soon found more unrest for myself, leading me to cut short my visit and head for home.

It was of course not Audrey's fault. She was only doing her best to mend bridges, but for the good of all those concerned, I knew I had to leave that house, and quickly, in order to put as much distance between myself and Mr. Healy as I possibly could.

Alone that night, I steeled myself with the conviction that 'if a blaggard like Cyril Healy wanted a fight, then he damn well had one on his hands now', and I resolutely promised myself that I would do all in my power to prevent him from making waves in Audrey's and my happiness.

Young Conor, I have no way of knowing if Cyril Healy was referring to my mother when he mentioned TB, a dis-ease which in those days was often mistakenly thought to be caused by poverty and a lack of cleanliness, but knowing the man he was, I believe that his words were cold, calculated and well thought out.

I pray that your time on this earth is not spent in the com-pany of such people, but if you do happen to encounter their like, please have the good sense to limit the opportunities they have to make you fall foul of their ways. Time, after all, should be spent in the company of good and decent people, not those who merely sap your energy and drain your enthusiasm.

I do so hope that God (or whoever was responsible for their creation) had the good sense to break the mould when Cyril and Marjorie Healy were made, as just like a bicycle without a saddle or fish aroma perfume, there is little demand for such hurtful and unpleasant creations.

CHAPTER 15

A DECENT PROPOSAL

I KNEW THAT I WANTED TO spend my life with Audrey from
the moment I saw her walk up the church pathway and as our
courtship went from strength to strength, I became more and
more convinced of it with each passing day. For that to happen,
I would have to make my feelings known to her as for all of
Audrey's gifts and charms she was not a clairvoyant, so it was
down to me to pluck up the courage and ask her to marry me.
Daunting as that was to me, I knew it was something that I
longed to do and something that I needed to do, but like many
things in life, the timing had to be perfect.

As a man new to romance, I thought long and hard about
how best to approach such a thing and my brain was racked
to its limits, trying to come up with an appropriate setting in
which to lay my love on the line. Audrey and I had known
each other less than a year, yet I could barely remember a time
without her. She filled my mind during every waking moment

and such was her indelible imprint on my life, that she also loomed large in each night's dream.

If I had the means necessary, I would have wined and dined Audrey in only the finest of establishments and spoiled her like she deserved to be spoiled, but practicalities, the modest man's foe, kept my dreams closer to reality. A wallet light of notes would hinder any notions of an elaborate proposal, so I was left facing the prospect of having to make a little go a long way.

At least I knew that I could just about stretch to a ring if I broke up my piggy bank and further excavated a few well-pressed notes from beneath my mattress. The latter option, of course, is another practice of yesteryear that is frowned upon by today's generation, who claim that it's not safe to keep one's money under a mattress. I half suspect that those views are just the health and safety brigade on the march again, who perhaps fear that well-off people, with fortunes hidden beneath their bedsprings, will topple off and do themselves a mischief. If that is the case then they need not worry about me, as with my meagre few bob, I am much closer to the safety of the ground than I am to the dizzy heights of the ceiling.

People naively say that the banks are a much safer bet but I'd sooner trust myself with my own money than the faceless bankers in pinstriped suits, some of who would be more appropriately attired if they were dressed in a striped prison uniform.

When I decided to air my plan in public for the first time,

I rightly chose Father as my first port of call and over tea one night, I just dropped my proposal plans in mid-conversation. Father, to his eternal credit, was brilliant and he did nothing but support and encourage me in my decision and it even looked as though my news had rekindled something lost inside him. He told me that his years spent married to my mother had been his greatest and that any man who is lucky enough to find love should realise his good fortune, seize it immediately and then hang on to it for dear life.

I firmly believe that Father was a romantic at heart, but as life had seemingly conspired against him and robbed him of his one great love, he had all but retired any such notions for himself. Yet from the look in his eyes it was clear that he still believed in the joy that love can bring to the lives of others.

When I told Father of my precarious financial situation he understandably greeted the news with little or no surprise, as our finances went hand in hand with each other's. Our little shop provided a decent life for us and by its very nature it never failed to put food on the table, but by the same token we were not exactly awash with riches either. Undeterred, we set about trying to prove that romance was not solely for those of means, rather it was something which was freely available to all those who believed in its existence.

If you exclude the letter I popped in the post to Michael, I chose Donal as my second confidant. When I shared my plan with him, I was delighted not only by his positive reaction, but also by his offer to help me in any way needed. I was very grateful to him for his kind offer and it wasn't long before I held him to his word as I was soon faced with the daunting trip to purchase an engagement ring. Donal agreed to come along for a bit of moral support and as he had previously managed to get engaged himself, I had him very much pegged as a leading expert in the field.

When the day came to purchase the ring, we went along to Midas Jewellers in Stepaside. I was relieved to have Donal by my side throughout, not only for advice on choosing the ring, but also to act as a credible witness to daylight robbery at its most blatant. Simply put, the cost of the rings available was just extortionate. We are talking about the little village of Stepaside in 1960s Ireland here, yet the folks at Midas were plucking their prices from the far end of the skies.

As a general rule of thumb, a man should spend around a month's salary on an engagement ring, but at the prices quoted, and with my weekly wage, it looked as though Audrey might have to make do with a ring from a barmbrack.

"A carat is how much?" I said in the throes of disbelief. "If I sold carrots at that price, I'd have been out of business a long time ago!" I added, somewhat unnecessarily.

By way of haggling, I eventually managed to talk some sense into the jeweller and I agreed to purchase a much more modest ring from him, at a price that would at least enable me to sleep at night. I paid the man his due, before taking my shiny new purchase home in a grip so tight that I almost caved the box in. When I arrived home, I showed the ring to Father and he looked at it for a second or two, before taking his spectacles from his chest pocket for closer inspection.

"Aye, that'll do the job son. She might say no to you, but she won't say no to this," said Father with a smile.

I took the ring and placed it under my mattress, towards the side to avoid discomfort, and following the mass exodus of my life's savings earlier that morning, I was secretly relieved to have something to put back under there.

With the blessing and backing of both my father and Donal in place (and Michael's pending), I now needed only the blessing of Mr. Healy to complete the circle. Given my relationship, or lack thereof, with him I thought long and hard about how best to broach the subject, as well as considering whether or not to even bother.

I have always prided myself as being something of a traditionalist and were the day ever to arise I envisioned myself asking the would-be father of the bride for permission to take his daughter's hand in marriage. But this was different. I knew that Mr. Healy would go out of his way to cause problems for me and the only 'hand' I was likely to receive from him, would be his own bouncing off the side of my face at great speed.

I discussed the matter with Father and he offered to go and speak with Mr. Healy, but I just thought that that was a step too far and would serve only to fuel the fire, so I graciously declined. We continued to speak at length until we both arrived at the same conclusion, which was that Mr. Healy would almost certainly attempt to throw a spanner in the works and we reasoned that the prospect of him offering his blessing was practically non-existent. So it was with great regret that I decided to propose to Audrey without her father's permission.

I must admit that I was pained slightly by the whole affair and I felt as though Mr. Healy's failings as a human being were in some way robbing me of a rite of passage. It may seem like a tired old tradition, irrelevant in today's society, but the same could be said of all the old customs and practices. If we were to pick and choose which traditions to uphold, sooner rather than later they would all fall foul of the whims of a fickle society and what previously meant so much to so many, would be lost forever without any hope of resurrection.

So, with Mr. Healy out of the picture, the wheels were set in motion and our scaled-back operation was now in full flow, with all ideas and suggestions for the proposal welcome. Father told me all about a romantic day he and Mother had spent at Howth during the early days of their courtship. He described what he labelled as "a perfect day" and his enthusiasm for detail transported me back to a time long before my first breath.

Through a mile-wide grin, he spoke of how they walked along the rugged coastline for hours on end, before resting on an old stone bollard near the door of the Howth harbour lighthouse. There they feasted on some fish and chips, as they watched the boats pass by at a gentle pace that was fitting of such an occasion. I saw the joy in my father's eyes as he relived and played out his Red Letter Day and I hung on his every word as he brought my mother back to life, if only for a few precious seconds.

From passing, I knew that Howth harbour lighthouse stood proudly at the end of the pier and all things being equal, I imagined that there would be no better place on earth in which to propose to one's girl (depending on the weather, of course). It was simple, it was romantic and it would allow me to follow in the footsteps of the happiest couple I have ever known.

I decided that the following Sunday was to be D-Day and during that preceding week, I coyly suggested to Audrey that, come the weekend, we should take a spin out to Howth. I knew from conversation that Audrey had a great love of the sea and as expected she jumped at the chance of a day's trip away, especially as it came with the promise of a nice coastal walk and some freshly caught fish and chips (the fish that is, not the chips).

When the day finally came around, I picked Audrey up from her house at half past ten in the morning and after stopping briefly for Mass, we went off in search of some coastal adventure. Whilst in the van, I must have checked my jacket pocket all of twenty times to ensure that the little box was still buried deep inside, and in case Audrey smelled a rat or twigged my motives, I just passed my constant fidgeting off as a persistent itch.

When we arrived at Howth, we were delighted to find that the day was being rocked gently by a crisp sea breeze, which was perfect weather for a good stroll, as it prompted people to share a warming embrace or two as they went along. Audrey and I were no different and we cuddled in close as we set off and as always I felt lucky just to be able to hold her hand as I showed her off proudly to the rest of the world.

We ambled along the seafront, before following a well-trodden route up a hill walkway and our adventure went wherever the pathway led us. I confessed my great love for Audrey on more than one occasion along the way, as if to somehow sow the seed of what was to come, and thankfully she saw fit to respond in kind. The beauty of the rugged terrain was matched only by the girl who was gracing it and as we paused to take in the view from above the harbour, I again checked the ring using the subtlety of a reassuring nod from a wise old man.

Once we had conquered the hill, we made our way back down towards the harbour, where fish and chips were the order of the day. We bought two generous portions in a chip shop facing onto the water and I then suggested that we stroll over to the harbour lighthouse to eat. The warmth from the fish and chips made us all the cosier as we went along the way and the inviting smell they gave off was incentive enough for us to quicken our pace.

The lighthouse grew taller and taller as we made our way along the wonderful pier that hugs the harbour, until finally we stood beneath its towering old stone walls. Almost directly across from its door, towards the edge of the pier, stood the stone bollard that Father had spoken of and as I gazed upon the scene that he and Mother would have savoured, I could almost see the two of them sitting there, lost to the world.

During the years in which the lighthouse was active, the bollard would have spent its working days having rope wrapped around it, tethering boats to land, but now in its retirement, it was to act as an accommodating seat for our backsides. Audrey and I perched ourselves cosily on top of the bollard and we greedily tucked into our fish and chips, as we basked in the beautiful view before us. As well as my parents I also tried to envisage the countless other courting couples over the years who must have shared a special moment there too, and I wagered that if said couples were even half as in love as Audrey and I, then that old stone must have hosted a lot of happy bottoms in its day.

When we finished our food, I walked over to a rubbish bin to dispose of the empty wrappings and as I did so I discreetly moved the engagement ring from jacket to trouser pocket. In my head, I quickly went through my well-rehearsed proposal lines for one last time, before steadying myself and returning to Audrey, who had remained seated upon the bollard. When I sat back down Audrey threw her arm around me, just as the pier embraced the still waters, and she thanked me warmly for a lovely day. The time was right.

Seizing my chance, I took Audrey's hand gently in mine and held it as I manoeuvred myself down onto one knee. At first Audrey looked indifferent and a bit confused, as I moved into position. Perhaps she thought I had spotted a fallen chip beside her feet. However, when I produced the box from my pocket, her face froze as she immediately sensed its importance. As I steadied myself on one knee, which is easier said than done on cobbles, I opened the box to reveal the ring and as I did so, Audrey's eyes lit up as brightly as the lighthouse's guiding light.

My mind was racing a mile a minute and best-laid plans leaped from my head into the bottom of the sea, as I suddenly forgot words I had learned off by heart. Stage fright deprived me of my lines at the worst possible moment, leaving Audrey hanging in an air of expectation and, left with little option, I just start talking, all the time silently hoping for the best.

"Audrey I'm not going to beat around the bush here and I've never been one to mince words or to skate around a subject. You know me well enough by now. I always shoot from the hip. I'm not going to drag this out for any reason, I'm just going to get straight to the point, and the point is this. Well, the point is that I'm not going to dilly-dally about here. I'm just going to ask you straight out, and of course feel free to tell me if I'm rabbiting on, but..." I said without pause.

"You *are* rabbiting on, Joseph, ya' big eejit!" laughed Audrey.

Audrey's eyes looked at me with both affection and patience, just as one would fawn over a baby dear learning how to walk. I could tell that she didn't know whether to laugh or cry but considerate to the last she just bit gently down on her bottom lip, so as to suppress her emotions further.

I must say, that I wouldn't have blamed her for laughing. After all, there I was trying to win my dream girl's hand in marriage, with the meandering words of a babbling madman.

By way of encouragement, Audrey gently touched the side of my face, which I must say reassured me to no end and made me believe that all was not lost just yet.

I paused for a second to draw breath, and much to my relief I managed to compose myself long enough to string a few words into a serviceable sentence or two. I told Audrey that I loved her so much and that I had to pinch myself each day just to prove to myself that my life was not all one big dream.

On bended knee, I gazed up at my girl and spoke softly:

"Audrey Healy, will you marry me?

"Yes…yes… of course I will. Now get up, silly, and give me a kiss," Audrey sobbed happily, as I hurriedly placed the ring on her finger.

As we embraced, we were serenaded by a chorus of applause from a small group of onlookers who appeared as if from nowhere and we waved over to them, as though we were film stars on a red carpet. It was such a joyous moment and I felt happiness that before, I daren't even believe possible.

When the tears were finally wiped away, Audrey and I left our makeshift throne and we walked around the back of the old lighthouse, so we could take in the view from the other side. We both wanted to prolong the feeling, the feeling of invincibility and hand in hand we walked around to gaze over at the beautiful sight that is Ireland's Eye, the small island adjacent to Howth itself. Audrey and I drank in the scenery and we held one another without the need to share a single word.

When dark clouds indicated that it was time to go, we drove

back to Stepaside right away and en route to Audrey's house, we stopped off to tell Father our good news; news at which he hugged us both in congratulations. Audrey took great pride in showing off her engagement ring and to my delight she repeatedly told Father how much she loved it. He wanted to know every detail of the proposal and after hearing the day's tale from start to finish, he simply said, "Well done, you pair".

Understandably, Audrey was keen to break the news to her parents and sisters, so following a celebratory cup of tea with Father, we made our way around to the Healys'. When I pulled the van up outside her house Audrey got out and practically ran to the front door with excitement. I followed up behind, but it must be said that I did not quite show the same level of enthusiasm as my bride-to-be.

When I walked into the living room I saw Audrey hugging her clearly shocked mother, before moving on to her father who by now, had a face like thunder. Audrey's enthusiasm was clearly not catching on, but I recognised that her parents were at least trying to suppress the rage that was painfully evident to all in the room, with the thankful exception of the delirious girl smiling from ear to ear. Audrey, oblivious to any tension, was clearly thrilled and the look of joy and excitement on her face was all the reassurance I needed to know, that I, and indeed we, were doing the right thing.

"Where are Maeve and Laura?" Audrey enquired, as to the whereabouts of her two sisters.

Without even waiting for a response from her parents,

Audrey ran out the living room door and raced up the stairs in search of her younger siblings. The silence in the room she had left behind spoke volumes, and it was only interrupted by wild screams of delight, as three celebrating sisters were heard overhead.

"Marjorie, could you excuse us for a moment?" Mr. Healy calmly asked of his wife.

"Certainly," replied Mrs. Healy, before leaving the room without so much as a polite nod in my direction.

"Here we go," I thought, as I braced myself for an onslaught of abuse.

Mrs. Healy closed the door aggressively behind her and I was left standing in the front room alone with her husband, whose complexion had by now morphed from its usual grey, into a shade of red I had not known previously.

"What the hell do you think you're doing, you little shit?" growled Mr. Healy

"Making your daughter happy," I replied.

"You didn't even have the decency to ask me for my daughter's hand in marriage! I should have expected nothing more from the likes of you!" said Mr. Healy, while stepping in close to my face.

"I didn't ask you because I didn't think you were familiar with the word 'decency', Mr. Healy, but now that I know you are, I'll be sure to remember for again," I offered back, as I stood firm.

I could see that he was taken aback by my stance and he had

just cause, as I had a new found inner strength that was matched only by the self-belief his daughter's love had instilled within me. I wanted Audrey more than anything and I sure as hell was prepared to fight for her. If Mr. Healy didn't know that before, then he damn well knew it now.

"Over my dead body, will this sham of a wedding go ahead," said Mr. Healy.

"I would hope for Audrey's sake Mr. Healy, that it doesn't come to that but the wedding will go ahead, make no mistake about that," I said bluntly.

As the anger boiled on Mr. Healy's face and his head prepared to pop from his shoulders, the door flew open and we were both swamped by all three of the Healy sisters, who started hugging and kissing everyone and everything in sight. As singing and dancing erupted in the room, Mr. Healy was left with little option other than to retreat back into his armchair from where he pretended that all was well, while simmering quietly with rage.

Neighbours, on hearing the commotion, soon added further weight to the numbers in the living room and as a full-blown party ensued, Mr. Healy continued to hold the facade that all was rosy in the garden. A display for which, it has to be said, he deserved an Academy Award.

Young Conor, for all Mr. Healy's huffing and puffing he was unable to cast a shadow over a wonderful day, a day that having listened to the advice of my own father, had proved to be a 'perfect day' of my very own.

Audrey Healy, the girl of my dreams, had agreed to become

my wife and that night, as I prepared to leave for home, I promised her that I would love her always.

I have kept that promise.

CHAPTER 16

WEDDING BELLS

THREE WEEKS SHY OF A FULL year passed before our wedding day wheeled around, and any initial nerves I woke up to on that momentous morning were quickly displaced by sadness at the realisation that my brother Michael would not be by my side at the altar.

In the lead-up to the wedding, Father had informed me that he had received word from Michael through the post, stating, with regret, that he would be unable to make it home for my big day. In what I was told was barely legible writing, Michael revealed that his wife Una was heavily pregnant with their first child and this coupled with the associated financial constraints, made travelling all but impossible. Father said that Michael signed off the letter by adding his best wishes but it was hardly the same as receiving them in person, and although his reasoning was perfectly understandable, I am afraid to say that his message of goodwill counted for little in his absence.

I would have so loved for Michael to have been there and to have acted as my best man but I resigned myself to the fact that, sometimes in life, things just don't work out the way we want them to. Following initial disappointment, I remembered my own rule that family comes first and as Michael was about to have a little family of his own, I eventually penned him a letter in response. In it, I wished both him and Una well for the upcoming birth as well as promising that they would have my prayers for the remainder of the pregnancy and beyond. I finished off the letter by telling him that I would be thinking of him, as well as Mother, during my wedding day and while signing off with sincerity, I assured him of a special mention in my speech.

With best man duties now up for grabs I decided to move from older to younger brother and while again obeying the strict code of family first, I drafted in Edward as a ready-made replacement; the knock-on effect of which promoted Donal from usher to groomsman.

My alarm clock bell had sounded hours before its church counterpart and Father, Edward, Donal and I readied ourselves amid energy not felt in the house since the time not long past, when Mother and Michael would walk its carpets with us. With everyone adequately suited and booted we attached flowers to our lapels, smeared on a touch of Brylcreem and by way of finishing up we dabbed on a splash of Old Spice to seal the deal. I must say that we all shined up like new pennies, although perhaps that is taking liberty with the truth, because at best we probably looked like pennies that had not been long in circulation.

As I made one final check in the mirror before leaving, Father took me aside and asked me to come down with him to the shop. Bless poor Father but I presumed that he was going to offer me some kind advice on married life, so to humour him I descended the stairs out of politeness, rather than to quench a non-existent thirst for sacred marital knowledge.

Father led the way downstairs and on reaching the base of the steps we both took the sharp turn left, which leads towards the adjoining door into the shop. As we passed through I noticed that the shop's lights were switched on, which was most unusual while the shop lay idle, and I readied to query Father as to whether on not he had been secretly working on today of all days.

With the first syllable of my question perched on the tip of my tongue, the shock of a lifetime brought me and my senses to a shuddering halt as there, as if by magic, stood Michael. He was a vision to behold.

Standing there like an everyday customer, albeit a very excited-looking one, Michael stood grinning on the far side of the counter, a counter which I practically hurdled over to shake his hand and embrace him. Dumbfounded, I tried to ask Michael how he had made it home but he brushed my ramblings away, saying that he would explain later. When I turned around to Father, I saw that Edward and Donal had also arrived down in the shop and it became clear that I had been the only one who was minus a clue as to the plans that had been afoot all along.

It later transpired that Father had used some of the money he had received from a small but prudent insurance policy on poor Mother's life, to fund Michael's (and indeed Edward's) trip home. I am sure that the benefit he felt from reuniting his family for such a special occasion outweighed all notions of extravagance in Father's eyes and standing on the shop floor, surrounded by his three boys, it was clear that he deemed it to be the best money he had ever spent. As well as being a truly wonderful gesture, it also made a dream of mine come true and I felt it fitting that Mother's hand was also at play in amongst it all, albeit in the most tragic and heartbreaking of circumstances.

Father, I am told, had collected Michael from the port at an ungodly hour the previous night and then brought him 'cloak and dagger' to hide out at a friend's house just around the corner from the shop. This was of course a wise decision, as trying to conceal him in among the apples and pears in the shop would have proved entirely fruitless, if you'll excuse the pun.

With no time to wait and the church bells not far off ringing, I released Michael from my grasp and in the highest of spirits we all set off for Our Lady of the Wayside, where I was to marry the girl of my dreams. En route, I posed a question in my own mind, which wondered whether any one man deserved to have such luck, but I wisely decided to leave that musing for someone with thoughts on a much higher plane than my own.

When we reached the church, the other guests made as much fuss of Michael as they did of me but I was more than happy to share the spotlight with my big brother, as he always was the star of the family in my eyes. Michael's appearance had brought with it a calming reassurance, which served to completely banish any lingering butterflies I had left in my belly. An added tingle of excitement now coursed through my veins and I shook every hand offered to me with great gusto as I made my way up toward the altar, where I joined my awaiting brothers. I positioned myself right beside Edward and knowing my dear brother as I do, I prudently used the opportunity to ask him if he had the wedding rings in his possession.

Worryingly, Edward's face suddenly contorted into a look of bewilderment and he hastily began to tap his trouser pockets before moving his search north, to the inside pockets of his rented suit jacket.

"I don't have them Joseph," said Edward, straight as a die.

"What do you mean you don't have them?" I asked in a panic.

"I'm sorry Joseph, but I haven't got them," he reaffirmed.

"I only gave them to you this morning! What the hell have you done with them?"

Now, I always knew that Edward was lackadaisical at the best of times, but this was incompetence on an entirely different scale, even for him!

I stood aghast at the foot of the altar, my blood pressure at near boiling point and it was only the presence of God himself that saved Edward from a torrent of bad language. As I held my tongue, the look on my brother's face slowly began to change and it was only when a hint of mischief peeked its way through, that I knew he was hiding something. I only hoped it was the ring!

Suddenly, Edward's expression broke into something of a smirk and I must say that it was one which I immediately wanted to wipe from his face. When prompted further, Edward confessed that he was only teasing me, yet he then inexplicably pointed out that, in spite of his over-the-top remonstrating and play-acting, he actually didn't have the rings in his possession. Thankfully, however, he hinted that he at least knew where they were.

Just as I was about to drag the truth out of him, Edward revealed that he had given the wedding rings over to someone else or "a safer pair of hands" as he put it. In response, I shook my head in total bemusement at his indiscipline before demanding through gritted teeth that he divulge, immediately, who the hell he had given them to.

You see, with a chap like Edward, you wouldn't be surprised if he had tied the rings around a stray cat's collar, or even absentmindedly hidden them someplace so remote that Sherlock Holmes and Watson would have to work weekends and nights to stand any hope of retrieving them.

"Joseph, the best man should always hold the rings," said Edward, in a knowing tone.

With further explanation, he then took a pace to the side, leaving Michael to formally step forward whilst holding the two rings in the palm of his outstretched hand. After a second or two's pause my gaze averted back over to Edward, and before I could even attempt to protest, he pointed out that Michael, as the eldest brother, was the more fitting choice for best man.

"Besides, I think Ma would have liked it," added Edward with considered thought.

Breaking the habit of a lifetime, poor Edward was actually right in what he was saying. Michael had always been my first choice but I hadn't dared believe it possible for fear of getting my hopes up, but thankfully the heavens aligned and Michael was able to fulfil the role he was born to play.

Of course, the Good Lord still had a further treat in store for me, as Audrey Healy, the most beautiful girl in the world, would soon be arriving at the church. And it was with His grace and her will, that she would become my wife. At that moment, I felt as though everything in my life was coming up roses and as I waited for Audrey's arrival, I quietly counted my many blessings.

When the church organ bellowed into life, I ran my eyes down along the aisle, towards the big opened double doors of the church, which I noted were resplendent in sunshine. Seconds later, Audrey appeared and her perfect silhouette cast a shapely shadow down onto the aisle. A much less shapely shadow was also being cast beside Audrey's, in the form of an austere-looking Mr. Healy, but I quickly and wisely diverted my eyes away from his repugnant patch of darkened carpet.

Audrey began to slowly walk down the aisle and her beauty was enhanced with each step she took towards me. When she reached the altar, I gently took her hand and I spoke the truest words I have ever spoken, by telling her that she looked beautiful.

"So do you," said Audrey, provoking childish sniggers from both of my brothers.

Father Fitzgibbon, started the ceremony with a few welcoming words and he did a great job in putting everyone at ease before presiding over a wonderful service. When the rings were exchanged, I was pleased that I managed to place the band onto Audrey's finger without too much of a palaver and when her turn came, my sweaty hand ensured that the ring slid on a treat.

"I do."

"I do."

On the priest's prompt, I kissed Audrey on the lips and as I did so a roar of approval flew around the church, as our guests made their feelings on the matter known. It was a simple act, within a brief little ceremony, but its importance and meaning would form the cornerstone of my life from that day to this.

When Father Fitzgibbon ended the Mass, we walked down the aisle to a chorus of congratulations, before taking residence outside the church door to receive our guests. When all hands were shaken and all cheeks garnished with a kiss, myself and the rest of the bridal party waited back to have some photographs taken, while our guests made their way to the reception, which was to be held in the function room above Murnaghan's.

The images captured that day are of precious seconds in my life and I truly cherish each one of them and the feeling of warmth which they continually evoke in my heart. I gaze upon them almost on a weekly basis and as I do so, I remember something different about the moment each one was taken. I remember with fondness the jokes made by my brothers and many protests made by my father at the photographer's constant command to "Face the camera please, Mr. Soap!"

"Which Mr. Soap? There's four of us!" Father exclaimed, before raucously laughing at his own joke.

My lasting memory, when faced with the full glare of the camera, is of holding Audrey's hand whenever the photographer (Audrey's Uncle Kevin) broke for adjustments and we did so discreetly and without fuss, in order to avoid a telling-off for not maintaining our positions. Standing there, collectively as one, we radiated love and looking now at all those smiling faces, I doubt whether a happier group of people has ever been captured on film.

When we reached the reception, I was really delighted with the effort that everyone had made, as the function room was tastefully decked out with some nice flowers and decorations and, although quite small by today's standards, it was a room filled to the brim with joy and elation.

Mr. and Mrs. Healy had both put on brave faces in the lead-up to the wedding and they had clearly made a concerted effort not to burst the blissful bubble on which Audrey had floated since the engagement. Mr. Healy, by way of a wedding present, had even seen fit to pay for the reception, but I was under no illusion that his generous gift was with his daughter's feelings in mind, as opposed to doing me any favours. Their attitude towards me had not changed in the slightest and I am convinced that, had Mr. Healy gotten his way, he would have forbidden the wait staff from moistening my dinner with even the paltriest drop of gravy.

I have no doubt that it pained Mr. Healy considerably to hand over the money, but to his credit the reception was a great success and personally, I could not have wished for anything more. Regardless of the fact that my feelings barely registered with him, I really did appreciate his gesture, which is why I am ashamed to say that during the dinner, I laughed heartily as he grappled for some water when a rogue piece of veg appeared to go down the wrong way.

My relationship with the Healys was never exactly one to write home about, and it peaked with an acknowledgment during Mr. Healy's speech, when he went through the motions of welcoming me into the family. He spoke insincerely about how well he and I had always gotten along with one another and he even gushed that I "felt like a son to him", which prompted a not-so-subtle cough and knowing snigger from Father.

"I'll give him one thing. He'd make a better politician than he will father-in-law," Father mockingly whispered in my ear.

The reality, of course, was that Mr. and Mrs. Healy welcomed me into their family with all the enthusiasm of a knowing cow walking through the doors of an abattoir. They didn't like me and I didn't like them, yet we both shared an undying love for Audrey which would keep us entwined in each other's lives, whether we liked it or not.

When it was his turn, Father got up and said a few words. He did a pretty good job in telling some funny stories before going on to speak lovingly about Mother and of how proud she would have been of me. I so deeply missed my mother's presence that day and I know she would have revelled in being the mother of the groom and all the fussing that went with it. I felt her spirit that day and I knew she was guiding me throughout by providing me with that extra reassurance that only a mother can give during times of great importance.

As Father concluded his speech, he thanked everyone for coming, but I noticed that he failed to mention both Mr. and Mrs. Healy by name. Perhaps he didn't trust himself not to turn the air blue.

When my own turn came to speak, I kept up the pretence by thanking the Healys for their generosity "not only for today, but from day one", to which Father nudged my leg jokingly under the table. The charade continued when, as is tradition, I handed Mrs. Healy a bunch of flowers and as I did so I dartingly pecked her on the cheek, for show. I'm sorry to say that her coarsely applied rouge make-up did little to lessen my ordeal, while her pungent scent only served to remind me of parsnips that were on the turn.

The one obvious part of my speech that rang true was when I spoke about my beautiful bride and I recounted in detail the story of how we first met, before then thanking Donal for playing Cupid. I delighted in telling a room filled with just about everyone I knew, how much I truly loved Audrey and how happy she had made me by becoming my wife. In that respect, I was of course preaching to the converted as every man and his dog knew only too well of my great love for Audrey, with the game no doubt given away by the joy peppered on my face anytime I was with her.

In stark contrast to the often-vulgar best man speeches of today, Michael gave a short, very dignified speech and his kind words proved only to confirm that he was the perfect choice. He did me proud.

When the speeches were finally put to bed, it was time for the dancing to get up and running and for our first dance together as husband and wife, we chose Elvis Presley's 'Can't Help Falling in Love' and never has a truer song been sung. Audrey really was a wonderful girl and I couldn't help but love everything about her. So much so that, as I shuffled my two left feet around the dance floor, she made me feel as though I were Fred Astaire and I can pay her no better compliment than that.

When the dancing really caught fire, I made a discreet manoeuvre off to one side and I handed the floor over to Audrey and her by-now wild sisters. As I made a hasty retreat, I noticed that Father, Michael and Edward were all sitting around a table at the rear of the room so I eagerly made a beeline to join them. As I approached the table and before their eyes caught mine, I noted that the topic of conversation was centred on Una's pregnancy back in the States. While Edward looked passively on, Father busily tried to reassure Michael that as this was their first child, Una would more than likely go past her due date, leaving him with plenty of time to make it home for the birth.

When I reached the table and following an impromptu game of musical chairs, I took a seat in amongst the Soap men, and no sooner had I done so, Michael suddenly and without explanation cut short the conversation.

"Ok, now that we're all here, there's something I have been meaning to tell you," he announced to quizzical looks.

My brother's cryptic words drew his three tablemates in closer, and Father, Edward and I began to curiously scan each other's puzzled faces for clues. Thankfully, we had not long to wait, as Michael, ever the enemy of suspense, cut right to the chase. He told us the most wonderful news, by announcing that Una had already given birth to a beautiful baby boy, a boy who had been born fit and well despite being some three weeks premature. Michael's eyes were awash with pride, as he told us that both Una and baby were doing well and having taken a photograph from his wallet, he then lovingly introduced us to the latest member of our family.

"Da, this is my son... your grandson... Danny Soap," said Michael, as he handed the photograph to Father.

Father took the picture in his hands and he held it as tenderly as he would the child itself. I watched as a look of innocence appeared on his face and I knew without words that the gesture meant the whole world to him. Michael went on to say that, as soon as baby Danny was able for the journey and whenever finances permitted, he would bring him home to Ireland to meet his grandad and two uncles. Edward and I both congratulated Michael and once the photograph was prised from Father's hands, we took it in turns to view the picture of little Danny. Who, unless I'm very much mistaken, bore a striking resemblance to his namesake.

The male Soap quartet was all together again and the comfort of familiarity made it a joy to behold. From my seat I could see Audrey and her sisters twirl the night away and in that moment I again took stock of my good fortune.

The evening went by in a flash of singing and dancing and it wasn't long before it was time for Audrey and me to call it a night. You see, in those days, the bride and groom would leave the reception early to head off on honeymoon and often they would do so long before the straggler guests began to pester the barman for one last drink.

Audrey and I departed Murnaghan's to a great cheer and we contently headed off towards Brittas Bay in County Wicklow where Father, as a gift, had booked us into a hotel. We set off in Mr. Healy's smart grey Volvo car, which he had loaned us for the wedding, and having waved our final waves, we drove off excitedly to spend our first night together as man and wife.

It felt like such an adventure to be heading off towards the wilds of Wicklow and if it were possible to hear a sound from a smile, then our journey was positively deafening.

We arrived at our hotel an hour or so later and as we checked in at reception, we introduced ourselves as Mr. and Mrs. Soap for the very first time. When we got to our room, the feeling of solitude it provided sat in total contrast to the jigs and reels of earlier on that evening, but with each other's company to enjoy, we simply unpacked and settled in cosily for the night.

Audrey and I retired to bed a short time later and as we cuddled in together as newlyweds, we felt as though we had taken the world's entire share of happiness and kept it all for ourselves. We had spent the most joyous day surrounded by our family and friends, and yet now at the end of it all, we were alone just us two. Before we drifted off to sleep that night, the birds and the bees paid us a visit for the very first time, and although they didn't stay for very long, it was marvellous nonetheless.

Young Conor, when your wedding day comes around, as it will one day, I want you to do your old grandad a favour. I want you to constantly look around the reception hall and take in all the faces and listen to all the stories, because you will never again get the chance to do so. A wedding truly is a once-in-a-lifetime opportunity to savour a room full of your family and friends and always be conscious that, due to the twists and turns of life, no two weddings are ever the same.

My face will sadly not be in amongst your guests, but I want you to know that I will be very much there in spirit as that is one day, I promise you, I would not miss for all the tea in China.

CHAPTER 17

TO THE HONEYMOON AND BACK

OUR HONEYMOON WAS NOTABLE FOR JUST a couple of things really, primarily that for the very first time we were completely alone together and I must say that we both revelled in the freedom we felt and the innocent joy that it brought to us.

The second notable occurrence, however, was a much more unwelcome one, as our romantic getaway was blotted by the start, middle and end of our first real argument.

By today's standards our honeymoon in County Wicklow must look poor by comparison, as Audrey and I did not sail the seven seas nor did we go to the four corners of the globe, but we did at least leave Dublin for a few days. Audrey's great love of the seaside and Father's generous gift had led us away for two whole nights to Brittas Bay, where we decided to spend our first full day of married life on the beach, beneath overcast skies.

By way of preparation we liberated two large towels from the hotel room, packed in some sandwiches which we had wrapped up from the wedding the day before, and took up the very kind offer of a flask of tea from the hotel's receptionist. Prompt as ever, we made our way down to the beach good and early, in the hope that an industrious ray of sunshine would manage to peek out from behind the threatening dark clouds.

As Audrey and I made our way there, we skipped along like two giddy school children and when we reached the sandy shore it was practically deserted, so without much fuss we dropped our belongings and discreetly changed into our swimwear before running at great pace into the sea.

The freezing cold water stung with a piercing chill, but Audrey's squeals of laughter quickly warmed my spirits as she hastily manoeuvred over to me and hugged me to keep warm. Audrey was laughing and screaming so hard that an old man out walking his dog stopped to survey the scene as if half expecting to witness a shark attack. I remember thinking him to be a very silly man because they don't even have sharks in Wicklow, perhaps due to the fact that sharks have more sense than to be in those kinds of conditions.

Audrey threw herself up for me to catch and I was left standing there, holding my new wife up above the waves, as if a determined mouse had somehow swum out to frighten her. I held her just above the surface of the water, sandwiching her perfectly between the icy waters and the chill in the air, and a right pair we must have looked.

"It's so cold, Joseph!" Audrey screeched.

"Oh, it's not too bad," I lied, unable to feel anything below my shoulders.

I started to move us around to get some warmth into us and in doing so I twirled Audrey lightly across the water. She looked as beautiful cold as she did warm, and her constant laughing was all the incentive I needed to toughen it out. Before long our bodies managed to acclimatise slightly to the biting conditions of the Irish Sea and Audrey wisely pointed out to me that "once an ice cube is frozen, you can't make it any colder!"

Now I have never been what you would call a strong swimmer but I went to great lengths (no pun intended) to exaggerate my swimming prowess for playful banter and Audrey to be fair played along to humour me.

"If I had to, I could probably swim under the whole island of Ireland and come out the other side," I said without reason.

"That's not even possible. You can't swim under an island, Joseph!" Audrey said, holding back a smile.

"You can if you practise!" I lied.

I then wagered with her that I would be able to swim full circle around the entire island in one go, before adding needlessly that I could probably do it twice, if the current was with me.

"No you couldn't, Joseph; you can barely swim the length of yourself!" Audrey said in truth.

"You have family in Donegal don't you? Maybe I could pay them a visit when I'm passing? Pop in for a cup of tea," I offered.

"I'll tell them to expect you so," jested Audrey.

Some ten minutes or so swimming and splashing around passed, before the temptation of the dry towels on the beach proved too much for Audrey, and mercifully she suggested that we get out and dry off. I was only too delighted to agree, and trembling as we went, we both chased up the beach, where we hurriedly wrapped ourselves up in the welcoming towels.

There I made a play for the flask of tea to warm us up further, while curiously Audrey instead focused her attention on her handbag. As my shivering hands twisted off the flask's cap, I wondered what was in that bag that was more important to my wife than a warm cup of tea, so I asked her as much.

"I'm putting my ring back on, silly," said Audrey, as she glanced towards her left hand.

It was at that moment that my jaw dropped open and the whites of my eyes shone so much that they could have sunk the Titanic, had it not sunk some fifty years previously. Instinctively I knew that all was not well, so I threw my gaze to my left hand in the hope of seeing my wedding ring in place, but on inspection it was nowhere to be seen. I checked my wedding finger, front and back, as if somehow that would make a difference, and in desperation I even checked the rest of my fingers on the off-chance that it may have jumped across to another, but to no avail.

Earlier, in my great haste to get into the water, I had forgotten to remove the ring, and now any hope I had of attempting a cover-up had been dashed as my startled look led to Audrey quizzing me as to its whereabouts.

"Where's your ring, Joseph?" asked Audrey candidly.

Struck dumb, I couldn't think of anything to say in response and my silence simply heightened the tension that had just that minute entered our lives. All I could do was turn my head around and gaze back upon the vast expanse of sea, which had just laid claim to my symbol of undying love.

"Oh no, Joseph you haven't!" said Audrey before she rose from the sand and sprinted like a lifeguard back into the sea.

I sat as though anchored to the beach as I watched Audrey courageously dive beneath the waves, and when she was fully submerged and out of sight I checked my left hand again in the hope of a miracle that never came.

When Audrey emerged momentarily above the water I realised with disappointment that her reappearance was due to the requirement for air, as opposed to the finding of the ring, but I supportively gave her a little wave of encouragement nonetheless. Audrey's hair was wrapped tightly around her face and she reminded me of images of a Greek goddess bathing in all her splendour.

As I watched from afar, I was taken in once again by her extraordinary beauty and elegance.

"Get your arse in here, Joseph Soap, and help me find this bloody ring!" roared Audrey, before delving back beneath the waves from whence she came.

Her words and more importantly her tone acted like smelling salts to me, prompting me to leap like a salmon, before running over to join my wife in the sea. Together we frantically searched for the ring but the piercing cold of the water only added to the panic and after twenty minutes of futile searching, Audrey decided to finally give up.

"It's too cold, I'm going back to the towels!" said Audrey, as she shivered out of the water.

"Good thinking, you're dead right pet… enough's enough. It's unfortunate but…" I said in agreement, as I began to follow Audrey.

"And where do you think you're going?" demanded Audrey.

"I thought we were getting out?" I replied.

"I'm getting out, Joseph. Don't you dare attempt to get out without finding that ring," Audrey near snarled at me.

"Oh, OK pet, I won't come out until I find it. Sure it has to be in here somewhere," I said with little or no conviction.

Suitably chastised and crestfallen I waded back into the bitterly cold water and despite the reassurances I had given to Audrey, I really didn't fancy my chances of retrieving the ring. I could have lost the damn thing at any point and I had no idea where to even start looking, so I just decided to concentrate my search on the area adjacent to our towels. There, I bravely attempted to dive to the bottom of the sea for a more in-depth search, but the salt water stung my eyes, so I wisely abandoned that idea as blinding myself would only have served to worsen an already poor situation.

With a change of approach needed I began to probe the sand and shingle with my toes, but sadly the use of the cheeks of my backside would have proved to be more of a success. I did my very best to retrace my every splash, but after a further thirty minutes or so I realised that I was fighting a losing battle. Shuddering with cold I turned towards Audrey in the hope that she would take pity on me and call me back to dry land, but all I got from her was a suggestion to "Try a little further to the left!"

I spent a further forty-five minutes in the arctic waters of County Wicklow with no success, and my skin was now a shade somewhere between yellowish white and pale blue, so I again headed towards Audrey to see if there was any sign of absolution.

"Audrey I'm like a prune in here. I'm all scaly. My legs look like a mermaid's tail," I somewhat exaggeratedly moaned.

"Good, well you can swim for longer now can't you!" Audrey said vehemently.

"But I'm not well Audrey. I'm going a funny blue colour," I said in truth, feeling sorry for myself as I got to within ten yards of dry land.

"You'll be black and blue if you come out of there without that ring, Joseph! It's your choice," Audrey said with worrying conviction.

"OK pet, I'll give it another ten minutes or so," I offered dejectedly.

Back into the water I trudged, but my continued efforts predictably went without reward. I really did feel like crying in there but I knew that my tears would only add further depth to the sea, so I just persevered as best I could. My spirits were raised briefly when I found a little hollowed-out seashell but, wisely perhaps, I decided against placing it on my finger and pretending it was my ring, as I feared that Audrey might not appreciate me making light of the situation.

I again looked over towards Audrey and this time I noticed that her face appeared to have shifted from anger to one of resigned acceptance.

"Audrey?" I said sheepishly.

"Come on out, Joseph," she sighed.

I walked over to my wife of less than one day, with my head looking down at the ground like a schoolboy reporting to a stern headmistress. When I reached her I stood for a moment with my eyes feigning interest in the damp sand in between my toes, and it was only when I could stand the silence no more, that I courageously looked my wife in the face.

"Joseph, why did you not put your ring away for safekeeping, like I did? You saw me at my handbag. What did you think I was doing?" Audrey asked surprisingly calmly.

"I thought you were making sure that the sandwiches were OK," I said weakly.

"Oh God!" Audrey proclaimed, as she succumbed to laughter.

Left with little option we were forced to admit defeat, so we packed up our things and squelched our way back to the hotel. The heavy colds Audrey and I both suffered as a consequence of our underwater expeditions made a repeat search the following day impossible, leaving yet another piece of gold forever lost to Davy Jones' Locker.

My wedding ring had cloaked my finger for less than twenty-four hours and had Audrey and I been superstitious people, we would have taken its loss as an omen to end our marriage right there and then. Thankfully and rather more sensibly we decided to chalk it down as an unfortunate bump in the road.

Young Conor, if I can give you a piece of advice, let it be this. Travel and see as much of this world as you can, and do so while you are still young enough to brush off all the bumps and bruises that come with such adventures. Remember that the Great Pyramids, the Great Barrier Reef and the Colosseum are not going to come to you, so please make sure that your passport gets a good stamping as you make your way to them. Take in everything and learn from it and never be afraid to broaden your horizons or try new things. Granted, I say this as a man who never heeded his own advice on the matter, but that doesn't mean that your auld grandad doesn't know best.

I myself have never explored countries such as Egypt, Australia or Italy nor have I ever experienced hotter climates, different languages or exotic cultures as for various reasons (mostly financial) I never quite managed to make the bold first step in the extra mile needed to get there.

Still, I harbour no regrets at my lack of travel and I delight in the fact that I have lived every minute of my life in Ireland. A country where the weather changes so often that it's prudent to take a raincoat with you when you go sunbathing, just in case.

I speak only one language and sure maybe that is all anyone really needs. Quite what I'd find to talk about with, say, an Italian person, is anyone's guess. Although I suppose I could tell them about the time I tried a mouthful of pasta, which I made at home one evening as an experiment. On second thoughts I might keep that to myself, as in all truth I found their national dish to be truly dreadful stuff and a mistake I don't plan on repeating anytime soon.

Other countries can offer so much and I imagine that they deliver more often than not, but on the same token don't be afraid to seek happiness closer to home like your granny and I did. Ireland is a great little country and it's one that has made me immensely happy throughout my life. It is a place that can offer all the joy in the world if you know where to look for it, and should your travels ever lead you to walk in my footsteps, be sure to keep an eye out for that bloody ring!

CHAPTER 18

LOVE AND MARRIAGE

WITH OUR HONEYMOON NOW A THING of the past and my wedding ring a distant memory, Audrey and I returned to Stepaside as a married couple, and in doing so, we entered into what is commonly referred to as 'the honeymoon period'. I must say that this labelling was a cause for concern, as our honeymoon had almost ended the marriage, but onwards and upwards and we knew that things could only get better.

As agreed with all concerned parties prior to the wedding, Audrey and I set up home above the shop and as she unpacked in her new home, she did so amidst the smell of freshly painted bedroom walls, which Father to his credit had done as a welcoming gift for his new daughter-in-law. Over a cup of tea, we told him what had become of my ring and it was with relief that I saw Audrey laugh as I tried to describe the extreme cold we felt, during our brief stint as human icebergs.

"If I had my way, Danny, he'd still be in there searching," said Audrey, as she cast a mischievous look in my direction.

"It's not a great start to married life, I won't lie to you. But it's the only start you'll ever have, so you may as well just accept it, laugh about it and move on," Father offered, with both wisdom and a smile.

Being a married man was, of course, all new to me, but I'm pleased to say that I took to it like a duck to water. I had always been a keen observer of people and having witnessed so many households struggling due to alcohol and gambling abuse, I had promised myself that I would learn from the mistakes of others and only do my very best for my new wife. I knew that the best way for a man to properly provide for his family was through hard work and as I had never shied away from an honest day's graft in my life, I at least felt confident that I could support Audrey and make a good life for us both.

The next morning saw the return to normality and I crept out of bed under the cover of darkness, to start my day's work. Not wanting to disturb my wife, I tiptoed out of the room and I took all of ten seconds to close the bedroom door behind me, to ensure that it didn't bang shut.

I crept into the kitchen, where I put on the kettle for my morning cup of tea and as every second is precious at that time of day, I went into the yard as it boiled. Once there, I unlocked the gate, so as to ensure a swift exit in the van when the time came. With the first of my many jobs for the day completed, I went back inside the house, in hope of seeing some steam escaping from the kettle's spout. However, when I walked into the kitchen, I was greeted by an even greater sight. There, I saw Audrey busying herself whilst standing in front of the worktop and when she turned ever so slightly, I caught a glimpse of a freshly brewed cup of tea. Which I sensed had my name on it.

"What are you doing up at this time?" I asked, as I gave her a little cuddle.

"We're a team now, Joseph, and if one of us is up, then the other is up too!" replied Audrey, as she kindly handed me a piping hot cuppa.

I was instantly glad that I was not a man who regularly availed of lazy morning lie-ins, because by the sound of things, they were going to be outlawed under my wife's new regime. Audrey, of course, was no stranger to early mornings, as from an early age, in her own family's shop, she witnessed the hard work required to run a family business. She had seen first hand the need for everyone to pull together, while at the same time learning that a family enterprise can ill afford to carry any idle passengers, if it is to thrive and be successful.

Audrey, it seemed, now saw herself as 'lady of the house' and rather than just sit back and powder her nose, she was determined to pull her own weight and contribute in any way she possibly could. She was a woman of purpose, my wife, and one who was more than a match for whatever the world could throw at her.

We sat down and had breakfast together before the demands of the day forced us to part and before tearing myself from her side, I kissed Audrey on the lips, before going about my business.

Later that morning, on my return home from the stock run, I noticed that all the items on the shelves were perfectly aligned, the floor had been swept to within an inch of its life and the countertop and till positively gleamed with efficiency. Flowers, too, for the first time, bloomed inside vases and I am ashamed to say that I initially struggled to see them as anything other than a missed opportunity to make a few bob, as boorishly I had always classed the things that grew from the ground as a matter of business rather than pleasure.

"Ah, I'm not mad on them, Audrey," I said in truth.

"Well Joseph, you'll get to like them," Audrey informed me, and in fairness I did.

It was clear from the outset that Audrey was going to have a positive influence within the house and it wasn't long before she turned her hand to the business and the accounts in particular. She had gained bookkeeping experience while working alongside her father and now she set about trying to improve and formalise the way our shop was run.

Without so much as by your leave, Audrey let it be known that the business (by which she meant Father and me) was underperforming. And in much less uncertain terms, she told us she felt as though we needed to have a fire lit beneath our backsides to get it back up and running. Worryingly, she said that she'd provide the matches. Gone were to be the scraps of paper and crumpled-up dockets that lay gathering dust every which way but loose, and in was to come a more professional and organised way of doing things, all of which would be implemented and supervised by my good lady wife.

Audrey purchased a typewriter, the very one I'm using now, and she endeavoured to get our costs and expenditure down to proper order. She immersed herself in every little detail whilst getting to know the business and she soon found room for improvement, in practically every aspect of how we did things. And to her credit she was never afraid to be vocal with her opinions.

"How you two have managed to keep this business afloat, I will never know," Audrey confessed to Father and me one night.

"It's just goods and services really. The customers want the goods and we supply the service," said Father, each word backed with a wealth of experience.

"I don't mean that, Danny. I meant that this shop is like a bucket with a hole in it," Audrey said forthrightly.

"You need a hole in a bucket Audrey, otherwise you can't put anything into it," I added.

"Yes, Joseph, but your bucket's hole is in the bottom, not the top!" Audrey replied.

It was not long before Audrey's prudent ways began to pay dividends, and we began to feel a real turnaround and difference in our overall income. We were now able to implement changes that saw the business make a steady profit, as opposed to our recent teetering between black and red, and Father and I, to be fair, were quick to acknowledge Audrey's efforts.

With the business now in full flow, our home really was a nest of activity and the gust of change that was sweeping through our lives even managed to blow away the cobwebs that had clung to the old place since Mother's passing.

Audrey also had a great passion for music, which meant that the wireless was constantly on in the background. Whenever we had a spare moment and if a good number happened to be playing, Audrey and I would have a little twirl around the kitchen, leaving Father, if present, to playfully tease us, before making his excuses to busy himself elsewhere.

I often wondered what Father must have made of all this change. Sadly I never got the chance to ask him, as almost immediately on Audrey's and my return from honeymoon, and following the demise of a promising start, he began to lapse back into his old ways by spending more and more of his time in Murnaghan's.

It was only years later, when I was in a similar position myself, that I realised that poor Father must have felt like something of a third wheel. I knew he had a great fondness for Audrey and he was thrilled to have her under his roof, but I do suspect that, as we were a newlywed couple, Father felt as though he had to give us some space so as not to get under our feet. That truly was not the case as far as Audrey and I were concerned and it transpired that Father actually gave us the very last thing either of us wanted, which was to see him slipping back into the depths of alcohol-fuelled despair.

Father was frequently absent from his duties in the shop and I would again be left to pull his weight as well as my own and before long, the toll of doing so became apparent. Audrey would see me weaken under the increased workload and try as she might to fill the void left by my father, the demands of the shop were simply never-ending. There was many a day that Audrey would openly curse the situation as she struggled to accept the weaknesses Father was showing, and she simply could not fathom how he could just drop everything on a whim and expect others to pick up the pieces.

Thankfully up until that point Audrey had no experience of alcohol abuse as for all their faults, Mr. Healy and Mrs. Healy had been teetotallers their whole lives. Although, in their particular case, perhaps a drop or two might have actually done them the power of good.

Those fortunate enough not to live beneath a cloud of alcoholism, can never truly understand what it's like to have a father who is dependent on drink. A father should be a constant in a child's life, yet alcohol can reduce his role from that of leading man to cameo appearance. The less fortunate, those left behind in its wake, can only question why booze has been chosen over them, in the battle for their father's affection.

I know that there were times when Audrey got very upset by Father's drinking and that hurt me greatly to witness. Yet at the same time, I also knew that had Father been in complete control of his demons, there was no way on earth he would ever cause a tear to fall from her eye.

The three of us eventually found a way to make it work and not because we had to, but because we wanted to. Like all families we had our ups and downs but on the whole the good times outweighed the bad. Certainly during the pleasant times there was a lot of laughter inside our four walls, enough even to banish memories of more challenging moments, and we always ensured that we made hay while the sun shone brightest.

Father and Audrey would still frequently gang up to tease me and many jibes were made at my expense with regards to my lack of imagination in the kitchen, when it was my turn to prepare dinner. Every other Sunday or so, after Mass, my wife and father would add playful scorn to my two main ingredients of 'bacon and cabbage' and deride the fact that its regularity made it as much of a Sunday staple as the Lamb of God itself.

"What's on the menu today, Joseph?" Audrey would probe needlessly.

"Do I smell something with three ingredients in it, son?" Father often quizzed mischievously.

In turn, I would point out what they already knew, which was that Ireland was reared on 'bacon and cabbage' and if they didn't like it, they should take their complaint up with their ancestors. We aren't, after all, a nation renowned for our culinary prowess but then again, do we really want to be? France is often lauded for its food, yet they eat frog's legs and snails from the garden. I mean, I can understand people eating chicken legs and such, but the French are taking things a bit too far in my opinion.

The Soap family, in our latest incarnation, went about our daily lives like all other families, amid peaks and troughs, and all in all, we were a happy and contented bunch. But time, of course, waits for no man and it wasn't long before a further blessing was lavished upon us and if married life had been an eye opener for me, what happened next ensured that my eyes wouldn't close for the best part of eighteen years...

CHAPTER 19

CHILDREN

JUST LIKE ALL OF THE VERY best news, the words that changed my life forever were shared with me over a cup of tea. As Audrey and I sat in the kitchen, having just done the washing-up after our dinner, she out of the blue asked me whether or not I wanted to have children.

"Steady on, Audrey. At least let me finish my tea!" I said in a fluster, as my cup near slipped from hand to floor.

Up until then, we had never even spoken about having children, as it was hardy appropriate for an unmarried couple to discuss such matters, but now having been pronounced man and wife, it appeared that all cards were on the table.

"Of course I do, Audrey, when the time is right I'd love to," I said truthfully.

"So what time is it now, Joseph?" asked Audrey.

"It's around seven o'clock," I guessed.

"I don't mean the actual time ya big eejit. I mean, is the time right for us to have children?" Audrey clarified, with a playful roll of the eyes.

I will admit to being surprised by the question, but I tried to answer it in a manner that was befitting of such an important subject. I told Audrey in the best possible way I could, that such matters were beyond our control and if the good Lord himself saw fit to bless us with a baby, we would then make whatever time of life we were in 'the right time'. Ever the pragmatist, I didn't want to get Audrey's hopes up, as almost certainly, there are no guarantees in life. Indeed, I knew of couples who had to wait years to conceive. I even knew of one poor couple who were never blessed at all.

"What is for us won't go by us, Audrey," I added.

"Joseph, I'm pregnant," Audrey blurted out.

Well, the news hit me like a sledgehammer, causing my Rich Tea biscuit to fall into my cup mid-dip.

"How has this happened? I mean, when?" I asked, in total shock.

"I think you know exactly how, Joseph Soap, and as for when, well Dr. Kelleher said I am about seven weeks gone," answered Audrey, before enlightening me on a visit to her family doctor earlier that day.

"I don't know what to say," I said truthfully.

"Are you pleased, Joseph?" Audrey said, searching for reassurance.

"Pleased? Oh, I'm pleased all right. I'm pleased beyond words. I just can't believe it. I can't believe I'm going to have a baby!

Well you're going to have the baby, but I'll help in any way I can, Audrey. I'm good at holding things. You know how good I am at holding things, Audrey!" I said, as the last strain of nervous shock left my system.

"Can we afford it, Joseph? Have we even got the time, with running the shop?" Audrey asked sensibly.

"We'll make more money, Audrey, and by God we'll make more time if we have to!" I reasoned in delight.

Thrilled, like never before, I immediately wanted to share the wonderful news and having instructed Audrey to cover her ears, I let out a deafening roar to beckon Father into the kitchen. Seconds later, he appeared at a pace I didn't think him capable of.

"Is there a fire, son?" panted Father.

"Audrey's pregnant, Da!" I said.

"Well holy be to God, well done you pair!" Father enthused, as he brimmed with excitement.

Over a pot of tea, the three of us sat and discussed the changes that were around the corner and Father told us at length, all the joys that parenting can bring. He also mentioned something about night feeds and tantrums but Audrey and I, whilst in celebratory mood, wisely decided to chalk such talk down as something of an irrelevance.

With Audrey now in the family way, we tailored our working day so that either Father or I would be at home at any given time, just to be on the safe side. Father, for his part, even managed to banish the booze and he now spent his time as an excited grandfather-in-waiting, as opposed to a father-inebri-ated, as had often been the case in the not-so-distant past. I was so very proud of him during this period and his actions taught me a very important lesson, that great rewards can be reaped by a person blessed with the gift of having focus in their life.

Father and I combined well in fawning over Audrey during her pregnancy and we took to the household chores with enthusiasm, which surprised even ourselves. To keep her iron levels up, Audrey would take a bottle of Guinness each night. Such a practice probably seems like lunacy nowadays, but it was par for the course back then and sure it didn't do anyone any harm. The irony of this was that Audrey now became the only drinker in the house, following Father's gallant mounting of the wagon.

In preparation for the baby's arrival, Father cleared out Michael's old bedroom, as it had been moonlighting as a makeshift storeroom and before putting brush to wall, he thoughtfully asked Audrey what colour the little one might like the room to be. Ever prudent, my wife decided on a neutral shade of yellow, before then offering to ask her own father for some discounted paint from his shop.

"Aye that's a good idea, Audrey, I hear your father is a good man for a discount," Father joked, in reference to my previous experience.

Having cottoned on to my father's teasing, Audrey wisely withdrew her offer and by way of defusing a ticking time bomb, she suggested that Father see to the paint himself. When the baby's room was finished, the walls resembled a lush field of maize and all that was left to do then was to patiently wait for the day that would change everything.

My prayers were answered when both mother and baby came through the birth unscathed and the relief I felt was immeasurable. Our son Jonathan, your father, was a grand little chap right from the very start. He weighed the same as a small bunch of bananas, but he quickly shot up, as he went about eating us out of house and home. Little Jonathan (named after Audrey's grandad) hit our home like a tornado, and if Father, Audrey and I had felt the house a bit crowded as it was, we soon got a rude awakening.

When only a year into life, baby Jonathan had more clothes than I had and he seemed to require all manner of potions and lotions, which McSweeney's chemists down the road were all too quick to supply. Luckily we had a shop which kept him in mushed-up fruit and vegetables but we rued the fact that we were unable to install a herd of milking cows out the back, to keep up with his never-ending desire for bottles.

Jonathan was not exactly the greatest sleeper in the world and during trying times I often wondered if he was crying at night just to annoy me, as though he knew I had to get up early of a morning. Nonetheless, I learned to adapt and I somehow made do with the minute or so's sleep I managed to get each night. Audrey and I would sometimes take it in turns to tend to the boy, but more often than not, her strict policy of 'one up, all up' came into play. Together, we did our best during these times and in general we did so happily as we were a little family and a right little team, albeit an extremely tired one.

Father, to be fair, also helped out at night. But only if he happened to be returning from a late-night trip to the bathroom, when he couldn't really do his usual trick of pretending not to hear Jonathan cry. A good move... if only I had thought of it first!

Audrey balanced motherhood and work to perfection and she utilised the time during Jonathan's naps, to ensure that the bookkeeping and business records were kept up to date. Father and I attended to the usual needs of the shop and once we all settled back into a routine, the whole operation ran like clockwork.

When Jonathan reached the 'terrible twos', he decided to wreak havoc during the day rather than at night and what was bad news for Audrey at least worked out well for me, in so much as I again slept uninterrupted before my day's work commenced. Little Jonathan would now expend all of his energy during the day so by the time evening fell, he was fit for nothing but sleep. I did miss spending time with him after work though and sometimes I would wake him up, to see if he wanted to play with his daddy. This, however, usually ended in disaster, with either Audrey or Jonathan (or both) screaming bloody murder. My wife's language, on such occasions, would turn the air blue and I reckon that little Jonathan would have followed suit, had he known the same choice words as his mother.

Just as our sleeping patterns had begun to return to something of normality, the good Lord saw fit to shake us from our peaceful slumber and Audrey became pregnant for the second time. Despite now having first-hand experience of the hard work involved in rearing a child, Audrey and I relished the news and we were both thrilled at the prospect of adding to our family.

Quite unlike the birth of Jonathan, the arrival of our second child was not without its complications and for the first time in my life, I was scared to the point of confusion. While tending to some ironing, all of four days past her due date, Audrey felt severe pains, which caused her to double over in agony in the kitchen. Quick as a flash, I responded to her calls and I rushed from the shop at great pace in order to ferry her to hospital, leaving Father to watch over Jonathan.

Although it was little or no distance to the hospital it felt like a journey of a million miles, as I watched my poor wife struggle in dreadful pain and discomfort. When we finally reached the hospital, Audrey was taken in to be seen straight away, leaving me outside to chew my nails down to my elbows. It was all of an hour or so later, when a kind nurse came to inform me that Audrey had gone into labour. Ominously, the nurse then insisted that I take a seat, before informing me that Audrey had suffered severe internal bleeding, as well as a number of other complications with names too long for me to remember. She added, by way of assurance, that Audrey was in the best possible hands but I was so frightened, I failed to find any positivity or solace in her words. I wanted so much to help my wife and little baby but at that moment in time, I was as helpless as they were.

The delivery room was no place for a husband in those days, so housed in the waiting room, I prayed to God and I begged him to show mercy. I wanted him to gift both my wife and baby the strength they needed to come through this, while at the same time, I also dedicated a prayer to the doctors and nurses who were working tirelessly to give them the chance of life.

What must have been a torturous six hours passed before the waiting room door swung open and in walked the nurse from before, only this time she had a smile as wide as the back doors of an ambulance. Instantly, I knew that everything was okay and the dutiful nurse merely confirmed to me that both mother and baby were fine. It was with a sigh of relief, matched only by that of a lifeguard's touch on a drowning man's shoulder, that I sat back in my seat. And while doing so, I silently and repeatedly thanked God for not forsaking us.

Baby Patricia Angela came into the world on Saint Patrick's Day and as is tradition, we tipped our cap to our patron saint. Irish people, for as long as anyone can remember, have followed the unwritten rule that sees a child born on Saint Patrick's Day christened either Patrick for a boy or Patricia for a girl. No one quite knows how it started or indeed how it will end, but it is a simple and effective way to wear one's true colours with pride and therefore it should be respected for the nice little thing that it is.

Father loved the fact that Audrey and I had included Mother's name on the birth certificate, and he simply doted on little Patricia Angela. He also seemed to enjoy the novelty of having a baby girl in the house and as the father of three bruising boys, he held on to her as though she were made of glass.

Patricia, like her brother at that age, was prone to late night/ early morning feeds and her cries had the domino effect of triggering little Jonathan to scream along in tandem, as they both tried to get our attention. It was a sign of things to come from that pair and as they grew up together, they became thick as thieves.

Whenever Audrey needed to busy herself upstairs, either tending to chores or doing the shop's accounts, she would often come down to the shop and leave little Jonathan with me, having already put Patricia down for a nap. With my son beside me in the shop, it must have looked to the outside world that I was training my successor and in a funny way I suppose I was, but really I just enjoyed having his company throughout the day.

When Jonathan was not causing mischief out in the yard, he was on the shop floor with me and there he would rival the freshest fruit and vegetables as the star attraction for the customers. In fact, he was the recipient of so many pats on the head and ruffles to his hair, that I spent half my working day flattening stray strands back into place before his mother saw the state of him.

Old ladies with shopping bags would ask Jonathan if he would like to help them to pack away their purchases and they would coo and clap with delight as each item landed safely inside.

"He takes after his father, this one," they would say with a smile.

The blooding of youngsters is not always plain sailing of course and I recall one particular instance when little Jonathan caused one hell of a rumpus in the shop. In fact, I almost got a thick ear because of it. You see, if there was one way in which Jonathan was taking after his old man, it was in his inherent ability to annoy and displease a certain Mrs. Kirwin.

Out of laziness, rather than loyalty, Mrs. Kirwin continued to frequent our shop several times a week and she would buy much the same order each time. I am ashamed to say that I used to give her extra in her basket, in the hope that she would have enough food to warrant one less trip to my shop each week, but no, in she came regardless. The extra produce she received was clearly just being consumed with the rest of her dinner, which was unsurprising really, as she amounted to a woman of considerable size.

When a familiar shadow was cast over the shop on the morning in question, I knew that her presence was imminent, so I braced myself for a few moments of unpleasantness. Seconds later, I watched her squeeze in through the shop's door, planing its frame as she entered, and she then waddled up the aisle towards the counter, where I greeted her with proper shopkeeper etiquette.

"And how can I help you today, Mrs. Kirwin?" I asked.

"You can start by helping me sift through those withered old cabbages out front, or better still by showing me the fresh ones that you keep hidden out the back!" Mrs. Kirwin said sharply.

"All my stock is displayed, Mrs. Kirwin and it's fresh as the day it was picked, I can assure you of that," I said in truth.

"A likely story, I'm sure. I think I recognise some of those cabbages from last week!" Mrs. Kirwin said dismissively.

Undeterred, I decided to humour her, which I always felt was best as far as that woman was concerned and we set about the foolish task of dismissing perfectly good cabbages, in search of those she deemed "more suitable".

As we rummaged through the produce, I felt a gentle tug on my clothing and when I looked down I saw that little Jonathan was clinging to my trouser leg. He was obviously keen to assist as before, so I asked him if he wanted to help the "nice lady" with her shopping, to which he enthusiastically nodded his head in response.

I hoisted Jonathan up into my arms, and I playfully and proudly reintroduced him to Mrs. Kirwin as our latest member of staff.

"Yes, you Soap lot do like to start them young, don't you?" Mrs. Kirwin said, no doubt, in a sly dig at my own early taking up of the reigns.

I decided to ignore her trite jibe and instead I took from my son's example, by politely nodding my head in agreement. Acknowledging Jonathan's happy little face, I playfully tapped the tip of his nose with my index right finger and we lovingly exchanged smiles and the deepest of eye contact.

"He's the sorcerer's apprentice this one, make no mistake," I said, with great pride.

"Well, I don't know about sorcerer. Perhaps that's a stretch of the imagination. Con artist, maybe!" Mrs. Kirwin barked back.

Jonathan and I dutifully helped Mrs. Kirwin select her wants and we moved through the aisles together, choosing as we went along. When we reached the middle of the shop's floor and having revealed that she planned on baking an apple tart on her return home, Mrs. Kirwin then demanded six of my very biggest cooking apples.

"I want proper cooking apples, not the grape-sized ones you sold to me the last time. I barely had enough to make an apple bun, let alone a full-sized tart. Now do you think your boy can handle that, Soap?" Mrs. Kirwin asked.

"I'm sure that he can, Mrs. Kirwin. He's very clever, you know," I added boastfully.

"I know no such thing. But I'll leave my bag here and he can set to work. We'll go over there, Soap, and blow some of the dust off those pears and we'll see if any of them are still edible!" Mrs. Kirwin said with contempt laced in every syllable, as she pointed across the shop.

Having agreed to her demands, I knelt down until I reached eye level with Jonathan and from there I picked up a large cooking apple and showed it to him. Next, I carefully and quite deliberately placed the apple into Mrs. Kirwin's shopping bag and with the use of the fingers on my left hand, I instructed him to add five more.

"There's a good lad. I'll leave you to it, while I go and help the nice lady to pick out some pears," I said to Jonathan, before following Mrs. Kirwin across the shop, where we painstakingly selected the pears that she deemed satisfactory.

"Finished," proclaimed Jonathan moments later from across the aisle, and I turned just in time to catch sight of the back of his little head, as he toddled off upstairs in search of a new adventure.

Mrs. Kirwin, once happy with her own selection, gathered up half a dozen plump pears into her arms and then made her way back along the aisle, where she clumsily deposited the fruit into her shopping bag, which Jonathan had left in situ on the floor. Despite her having spurned my offer to help carry the pears, I accompanied Mrs. Kirwin up to the till, where she paid for her groceries without even the faintest bit of small talk, before hastily exiting the shop.

Relieved to see the back of her, I went about my business as before but barely a half an hour later the shop was again cloaked in darkness, as for the second time that day, in barged Mrs. Kirwin.

"I've a bone to pick with you, Soap!" announced Mrs. Kirwin midway up the aisle.

"What seems to be the problem, Mrs. Kirwin?" I asked out of politeness, tinged with an element of fear.

"The problem is that I've been sold a pup here. And not for the first time, I might add. I clearly asked for six apples, I paid for six apples, but I only received four," she stated coarsely, before depositing four cooking apples onto the counter.

Patiently, I tried my best to calm her down and I attempted to reason that as her bag had been quite full, there was always the possibility that the apples may have fallen out on her way home. Mrs. Kirwin did not take too kindly to this notion, and she was not afraid to tell me as much.

"A likely story, Soap. That boy of yours is a cheat!" she raged.

"Ah, now, there's no need for that, Mrs. Kirwin, he's only a child and besides, my boy is no cheat. He takes after his father on that score," I said, as I tried to defend Jonathan's honour.

"Oh, he takes after his father all right. He can't count either!" replied Mrs. Kirwin.

"Mrs. Kirwin, I told Jonathan to put five apples into your bag and as I had already placed one in, six apples is what you got," I replied.

"I'm surprised you both didn't take a bite out of the ones you gave me. Bunch of crooks, the lot of you," Mrs. Kirwin added, somewhat nonsensically.

Well, I was not prepared to have this woman speak ill of my son, so for the first time in my life, I stood up to the old goat. I defiantly informed her that not only had she received six shiny apples, but she had also received customer attention above and beyond what was required from me. And by way of dismounting my high horse, I finished by telling her that if she was not happy with the service provided, she was welcome to take her custom elsewhere in future.

Clearly taken aback, Mrs. Kirwin was now like a rabbit in the headlights and without restitution, she turned and marched at pace out into the street, leaving four cooking apples in her wake. I stood delighted with myself during a moment's reflection, before I continued my day's work, until closing. Work, which I carried out with the air of a man who had just stood up for something, and someone, he believed in more than anything.

With the shop locked up for the night, I dragged my weary bones up the stairs for a spot of dinner. At the top of the stairs my nostrils were met with the homely smell of beef stew and as I walked into the kitchen, little Jonathan ran joyously towards me and flung himself into my arms. Audrey told me that she was almost ready to dish out before asking me, if I would go and check to see if Patricia was awake. Eager to help, I placed Jonathan securely at the kitchen table, before then going off to stir our sleeping beauty.

Audrey had put the little one down for a nap but it was now time for her to wake for a feed, so I opened the bedroom door and walked over to Patricia's cot, smiling as I always did. On reaching her side, I was met by a most unexpected sight. As there, standing guard each side of her, buried deep within her cot, lay two large cooking apples.

I removed the apples in near disbelief before gently waking Patricia up and following a brief bout of justifiable crying, she soon settled back into calm. Wasting no time, I took her into the kitchen to join the others, where Jonathan as always ran to greet our arrival. As he did so, he looked like butter wouldn't melt in his mouth. He was clearly delighted with himself for having lavished his little sister with such lovely gifts and his good mood continued over dinner, as he spent more time waving across the table to Patricia than he did eating from his plate.

Over tea, I told Audrey all about our son's latest escapade and we both sensibly agreed that there was no point in punishing a little boy whose only crime (whether intentional or not) was that of loving his sister with all his heart.

And later, while discussing Mrs. Kirwin, Audrey and I both somewhat flippantly joked that perhaps little Jonathan, in depriving her of apples, had inadvertently done her a favour. As surely the last thing that poor woman needed, was another dessert!

CHAPTER 20

FATHER

MY FATHER, DANNY SOAP, WAS VERY much a man who became a victim of circumstance. Indeed, had he been permitted to lead the existence he craved, without pain and sadness woven in through it, he would have gladly spent his years just sitting on a park bench, holding his wife by the hand. But, like most dreams, my father's never saw the light of day and often it's a cruel rule of life that prevents even the simplest of wishes from becoming reality, no matter how much we desire a change of fortune.

In his later years, a dependence on alcohol seemed to rob Father of his rightful train of thought and often to me it appeared as though his mind simply was not his own as his inner demons lurked inside him, hell-bent on wreaking havoc whenever they saw fit.

Despite all this and following several brief bouts of sobriety, each unceremoniously interrupted, Father appeared to turn a corner once and for all, when almost eighteen months passed without a tempting drop touching his lips. It was a special time for the Soap family, as he returned to being the man I once knew. His reawakening was credited, by all who knew him, to the responsibility of becoming a grandad and the new sense of self-worth that came with seeing his grandchildren growing.

But just like the rarest of flowers in bloom, my father's moments in the sun passed all too quickly and when he eventually succumbed to his vice once more, I was again left to curse the fragility of human nature.

In the strangest of ways, I believe that I said goodbye to both of my parents on the day of my mother's passing, as the strong man I knew my father to be appeared to wilt almost immediately when faced with incalculable loss. Life's cruelty and lack of empathy had identified a weakness in my father, and it took from him not only the love of his life, but also the motivation to accept and come to terms with what had happened. It changed him profoundly.

I remember one such occasion, following one of his wildfire sessions, when Father arrived back at the house and proceeded to cause the sort of commotion that only a drunk person can when they are trying to be quiet. Once startled, I got out of bed and went into the sitting room where I found Father slumped in an armchair. My initial efforts to rouse him ended in failure. When I did manage to wake him, he had a lost look in his eyes and I could tell that the problems he wished to wash away with drink, resiliently remained intact.

"You never talk about your mother, son!" said Father, with both a longing and an element of truth.

He was, for the large part, right of course, but I hardly felt that now was the time to start discussing such matters. Yet, against my better judgement, I began to tell Father my reasoning for such a selective silence. The first of two main reasons was perfectly simple, in so much as anytime Father wanted to talk with me about Mother, he was heavily under the influence of alcohol and I felt that she deserved better than to be the subject of mindless patter. If we were to speak of Mother, I would rather it be with fondness and warmth, rather than in a blaze of drunken ramblings, muttered on a constantly repeated loop.

The other reason, I am at pains to say even now, is that by not confronting the issue head-on, by not talking about it out in the open, I could, on occasion, convince myself that Mother's death had not happened at all. I learned pretty early on to trick myself into thinking that heartbreak and loss had not intruded in on my life and by keeping my sorrow at arm's length, where it could do the least amount of damage, I could prevent it from ravaging my fragile emotions even further.

It was clear that my father was of a similar mind to me in this regard but when his emotions got the better of him, as they always did in tandem with his alcohol intake, he would open the floodgates and reveal his true vulnerability and despair.

After much debate, I eventually got Father into his bed, having promised him that we would talk about Mother from dawn to dusk the following day. Before he drifted off to sleep, he himself repeatedly promised that "things will be different from tomorrow, you'll see, son".

The next day saw neither sight nor sound of Father. Things were exactly the same.

I must say that it was hard to see my father lose his way in life once more. He lost a lot of weight during the many months that followed and while he still cut something of a dash, he was a shadow of the man he was in his pomp. Father's clothes, forever smart and beautifully turned out, made way for more casual attire and the garments he now donned perfectly encapsulated his, by now, threadbare attitude to life. I knew I was losing him, but I was powerless to prevent it, and much like the ending of a bad film, it became as predictable as it was inevitable.

Things came to a head one Sunday afternoon, when Father arrived home from some drinking den or another and whilst visibly unsteady on his legs, he attempted to fix himself a sandwich. A calamity of drunken errors ensued, resulting in him tripping and falling straight into the kitchen table, sending all sorts of foodstuffs and crockery crashing to the floor. The whole family was present in the kitchen at the time and the sight witnessed brought tears to all concerned. Sensibly, Audrey rounded up the little ones and brought them into the next room. While I, once again, found myself the victim of obligation.

I stayed back to help Father compose himself and I tended as best I could to a cut on his forehead, which thankfully looked a lot worse than it was. Once settled, we sat and spoke at length and I made plain the situation, by telling him that his behaviour had now descended to the point where his actions were frightening the children. And in my attempt to talk some sense into him, I repeated myself time and time again, as if I were the drunken one. I told him that his behaviour was disgraceful, and I drilled home the point that I would simply not tolerate having my wife and children exposed to such a troubling and upsetting scene again.

Father then promised me heaven and earth, before again rolling out his well-trodden commitment that he was "going to give up the drink" once and for all. I tried to believe him, I really did, but his failure to deliver on such promises in the past now robbed him of any chance of credibility.

When my doubts were proved well founded and Father's drinking continued unabated the next day, I took no satisfaction whatsoever in seeing him march down his path of self-destruction. As I helplessly watched his life unravel before my eyes, his fate became apparent and all that was left for me to do was shed a tear for each step he took away from me.

Two days later and on my return from a stock trip, I routinely manoeuvred the van to the back of the shop and once I had climbed out, I endeavoured to open up the back gates. Having prised them apart, I allowed momentum to swing the gates to the wall and while doing so, my eyes probed in search of the two concrete blocks I used to keep them securely in place. It was then I caught sight of Father.

He was lying perfectly still on the ground at the far side of the yard, his right arm draped across his chest. I screamed out his name. Several wooden pallets were strewn in my path and I was forced to leap over them as I ran. On reaching his side, I hastily knelt down beside him. His eyes were closed, his skin felt cold to touch and in a fit of blind panic, I grabbed him and pleaded with him to wake up.

He didn't hear me.

He didn't react.

My father was gone, lost to me and the world and just like a flame that was once thought of as eternal, he ultimately faded into darkness. There, on the cold concrete yard, I remained on my knees, overcome with grief and for the second time in my life, I knew of a sadness I had never thought possible.

It was only later on that evening, after a day as long as any I had ever spent, that a shaken Audrey mentioned that she had spoken with Father earlier that morning while I was away getting stock. She told me that Father had already eaten his breakfast by the time she entered the kitchen and after bidding her a good morning, he informed her that he was all set to do a bit of work around the shop. Audrey admitted that she didn't think he looked up to it and she said as much to him but he laughed off her concerns and told her not to worry.

"I'll get that yard tidied before Joseph gets back. Make myself busy. It won't take me long," Father told Audrey, as he set off down the stairs.

Thinking of that time now, I really wish that I could have been there with him. Maybe I could have done something before it was too late. Perhaps if I hadn't pushed him so far or criticised his ways so much, he might have been okay. For years, I lived with the worry that Father's body simply could not cope with the sudden shock he put it through when he abruptly stopped drinking. I worried that the emotional guilt I placed upon him had forced his hand and that maybe he had pushed himself too far too soon for fear of letting his family down.

I was housed in complete shock for most of that day, yet still I knew that I was duty-bound to inform my brothers. At that time we did not own a telephone so I walked the short distance to a neighbour's house, a kindly lady by the name of Mrs. Sullivan, who permitted me the use of hers.

Breaking such terrible news over the phone is far from ideal. The two calls I placed to Michael and Edward were extremely difficult to say the least, and the telephone receiver trembled in my hand throughout. Both of them shed a tear over the phone and I'm not ashamed to say that their cries triggered yet more of my own to flow.

Michael and Edward duly set about plans for their trips home, while in Dublin work on the funeral arrangements commenced. A combination of air, road and sea brought my brothers back to me and more importantly, brought sons back to their father. Edward travelled the short journey home from England by ferry, while Michael, brave as ever, made the trip across the pond by aeroplane and in doing so he became the first ever Soap in the sky. On his arrival, he told me that a recent promotion at work and the increase in wages that came with it had enabled him to raise part of the airfare home. Heart-warmingly, he added that some of his co-workers, on hearing of Father's passing, had chipped in some cash to cover the remainder of his fare. I know that Michael greatly appreciated the gesture, as did I, and I dare say that knowing my father, he too would have been touched by such a show of goodwill.

For Father's wake, we all gathered above the shop and laughter rivalled tears, as stories were passed around like cups of tea. Michael, Edward and I, for the most part, sat around the kitchen table and it wasn't long before Father's absence loomed large. While we were growing up, in the midst of rambunctious behaviour and clanging noise, our two parents had been ever-present in our lives, yet now three grown men sat subdued, gazing longingly at two empty chairs whose rightful occupants would be forever missed.

During the funeral, I stood side by side with my brothers and at its end, we received handshakes and condolences, which seemed to go on forever. A fine turnout of people came up to pay their respects to my father and I was heartened that all of his years on this earth, years spent being a pillar on which to base one's community, had not gone unnoticed by the part of Dublin he held most dear. Father would have loved and appreciated such a fine turnout and looking down from above, I'm sure that he did.

In the days that followed the funeral and before my dear brothers crossed back over waters both east and west, we all found a quiet corner where we discussed all that needed discussing.

With pain still very much raw, the departures of my brothers soon after hit me for six and I was left to come to terms with feelings of sadness and isolation. Selfishly, I had wanted my brothers to stay but deep down I understood that they no longer considered Stepaside, or indeed Ireland, their home.

Despite being surrounded by my own little family, I will confess to feeling quite lonely and without the support and great efforts of my wife, I honestly feel as though I may have crumbled under the sheer weight of the grief I was experiencing. Audrey, to be fair, kept me going throughout and as a consequence I put my name down on a very long list of supposedly strong men, whose strength has been reinstated by an even stronger woman.

It is often said that an Irishman views his mother as though she were a saint or an angel sent from heaven and as we have discussed previously, this is largely true. Similar notions are not usually afforded for the man of the house; however, this should not be seen as a slight towards the feelings held for ones father as, without question, a deep love and affection is also held.

For a young boy, his father is his hero. He should be someone who not only provides for the family, but also protects them and keeps them safe, no matter what issues they face or villains they may encounter. My father was one such man. And while not without his flaws, his imperfections were all the more noticeable because he was perfect in every other way.

Looking back on Father's bleakest moments, as he struggled with loss and a thirst for alcohol, I believe that his choices were not entirely of his own making. Instead, I opt to lay blame on the doorstep of his inner demons, leading me to absolve Father of culpability for his actions.

Age has given me the opportunity to reflect upon my father's situation and although my findings remain inconclusive, they may yet show that he had remained the strong, determined man I knew him to be. There is a chance, albeit a small one, that in later life, Father's bravest trait was that he accepted who he was, warts and all, and that he obstinately refused to change despite others, including me, telling him that he had to. He was, after all, a man of conviction, stubborn to the core, and do you know what? Maybe he was right all along. He didn't have to change. He was the man he was and I loved him for it.

Alcohol had gripped my father, make no mistake about that, but perhaps instead of failing to fight it off, he instead embraced it and went along for the ride. Life, after all, had taken him to a point where perhaps he felt that his job on earth had been completed as his wife had passed over to the other side and his boys had grown into men. Maybe he felt that we no longer needed him.

If that were the case, I would now respectfully wish him to know that he was very much mistaken. We did need him back then, very much so in fact and in many ways, even all these years later, we still need him today.

Father was a dignified man, a man of quiet wit and respectability, who stayed for the most part on the periphery, silently observing and enjoying the goings-on around him. He had the ability to light up a room but resisted. Instead he chose to sit back, confident and safe in the knowledge that he could if he wanted to.

That was his way, that was his wont and that is how I will always remember him.

I both love and miss him still.

CHAPTER 21

HIGH STAKES

THE TRYING TIMES FOLLOWING THE DEATH of a loved one can bring an entirely new set of challenges to bear and having previously hurdled life's little bumps in the road, you are now left facing a seemingly insurmountable climb over a mountain so high that its peaks reach into the heavens.

Your mind also becomes riddled with doubts and worries, while fears for the future wrestle to and fro with longing for the past. It can be incredibly hard to think straight and often it is only the strength of those around you that keeps any sort of purpose to your days. Death is an unwelcome heartbreak that all families must face but following the loss of a parent, the awful practicalities of dividing up the estate need to be addressed and it is as sensitive a topic as one can imagine.

When our time came for the dreaded conversation, a day or two following Father's funeral, Michael, Edward and I were left with little choice but to broach the delicate subject that was the shop.

Since Mother's death, Father had often spoken about making a will but my brothers and I all agreed that it was highly unlikely that he had ever gotten around to it, as alcohol had robbed all formality from his life. But if, by chance, he had met with a solicitor, the whole process would have been as straightforward as can be. You see, Father had neither money nor a host of possessions with which to trouble the solicitor's fountain pen, so any will made would have been a short one and one that would centre on our home and shop.

I remember the hope I held that a will would turn up and I prayed that Father had somehow managed to get himself to a solicitor's office. I knew that was the only way in which three young men, unable to think straight, would be freed from having to make some awfully tough decisions. Without a will in place, I feared that my views on the shop's future would be outnumbered by those of my brothers and that the decision to sell would be made, leaving me without work and more importantly, my family without a home.

I was also well aware of the fact that I possessed no formal skills to speak of and were I to lose the shop, I would be faced with the prospect of adding further length to the dole queue. Memories of my schooldays reappeared and as I lay awake at night lost in thought, feelings of 'what might have been' ran riot around my head.

The situation also had far-reaching implications as Audrey and I really wanted to add to our family. However, faced with the very real possibility of losing our home, there was a chance that this would have to be put on hold. Shamefully, the thought even crossed my mind that should the Lord himself somewhat less cautiously, choose life over practicality, his kind blessing would leave us in one hell of a pickle.

In a quiet moment, in the kitchen, I confided my concerns with my brothers and I was so relieved that they seemed genuinely sympathetic to my situation. Nothing but truth was spoken around that table and when the thorny issue of money reared its head, I could not have hoped for two more honest points of view. Michael put his cards on the table and admitted that with a growing family back in the States, he could really do with some extra money, adding that due to the birth of two more children, Orla and Liam, Una had been forced to give up her job, leaving them to understandably tighten their belts somewhat.

Edward, for his part, was quick to point out that if Father had wanted just one of us to have the shop, he would have ensured that a will was made out to that effect, but in the absence of any such document, it was clear that Father had no such desire. From Edward's tone, it was obvious that by "one of us" he was referring to me. Indeed, his barbed comments prompted Michael and me to exchange mutual shakes of the head at his ever-decreasing sense of morality.

In truth and despite still wanting to give him a clip around the ear, I couldn't help but agree with Edward. Even though I had laboured for many years to make a go of the shop, it was just one part of the property. The building, as a whole, was also the Soap family home; a home now belonging to my brothers, as much as myself, and I had no divine right to lay claim to something that did not entirely belong to me.

Thankfully, however, they agreed that I should remain living beneath its roof and we collectively set about finding a solution that would suit all parties. I pointed out that as the property was to be split three ways, my third was already secured so I broached the idea that I would buy the remaining two thirds from them. We discussed the matter at some length before an agreement was reached and I was pleased and relieved in equal measure when we shook hands in conclusion of settlement.

When the time came to make things official and following confirmation that no will existed, an agreement was drafted and signed in the offices of the respected Rogers, Kinsella and Bannon solicitors in Stepaside. With all necessary paperwork completed, Michael and Edward were free to return to their respective homes but before they departed Irish soil, I assured them that they would receive their payments promptly once I had the money in place.

I was thrilled to have come to an amicable arrangement with my brothers, as I knew of too many families who had fallen out over money. I value people above profit any day and when it comes to family, it is not even a debate worth having. Greed should only circle the outer perimeter of a family and it must never be allowed to encroach on its core.

Of course, the agreement reached with my brothers was not to be the end of my problems, far from it in fact, as Audrey and I simply did not have the means necessary to fund such a purchase. Thankfully, Michael and Edward were happy to take my word that I would complete the deal and to their credit they did not insist on a specific timescale, leaving us with a bit of breathing space in which to try and raise the money.

Granted, due to Audrey's endeavours, the shop was turning over a tidy little profit but financing its overall buyout was on a different scale altogether.

I was adamant that asking Mr. Healy for the money was out of the question, leaving us little option but to seek a loan of five thousand pounds from the bank, a fortune in those days. Such astronomical figures caused alarm bells to ring for Audrey and me, and sleepless nights were spent in panic as the fiscal tide began to rise, inch by inch, around our necks.

What if the bank refused to grant us a loan? We would then be forced to sell our home and business, the very idea of which was unthinkable.

On the other hand what if the bank actually gave us a loan and we were then indebted to the tune of a small country's national debt? The mind boggled.

I also worried that if our customers decided to shop elsewhere, we would soon find ourselves unable to keep up the repayments and the bank would then circle our home like vultures.

Audrey bravely took it upon herself to speak with the bank and having arranged a formal meeting for the following week, she returned home with a list of things we needed to provide with our application. We both sat down and put our thinking caps on but having perused the extensive list of requirements, I barely recognised a single thing on there. The bank sought records for this, that and the other and I found myself skimming aimlessly over words so long that I dared not even hazard a guess as to their meaning.

"We don't have any of those things, Audrey," I said with despair.

"No, Joseph, you didn't have any of those things. Until I came along," Audrey added with efficiency.

"You mean we're sorted then?" I asked.

"No, Joseph. We're far from sorted, but we have given ourselves a fighting chance. I have being handling the accounts for a while now and I think we're in good shape overall," Audrey explained.

Ahead of our meeting with the bank, Audrey compiled all of our documents and she even managed to familiarise me, as best she could, with a few relevant terms and a spot of legal jargon. This was done in order to give the illusion of knowing, should any tricky questions happen to come my way, but 'plan A' was undoubtedly for Audrey to champion our cause and lead the conversation.

When the time came for our meeting, we met with a nice man named Mr. Kent and during what proved to be a long, drawn-out conversation, most of what was discussed flew right over my head. We did however agree that the loan, were it approved, would come in the form of a mortgage, with the monthly repayments spread evenly over twenty years. It was some commitment to make but as it was the only show in town, we reluctantly bought two tickets. Throughout the meeting, I dutifully nodded along as though I was listening to a favourable tune and when finally prompted by both Audrey and Mr. Kent, I signed the application forms where instructed.

Mr. Kent told us that, by his reckoning, we had a fairly decent chance of approval as not only had our business banked at his branch for many years, we had also presented "excellently kept records" which he said were among some of the finest he had seen. Foolishly, I tried to point out that this was all down to my wife and if left up to me we would have walked into his office, wheeling a wheelbarrow full of crumpled-up dockets. But Audrey, showing the foresight of Nostradamus, quite rightly cut me short mid-sentence by informing Mr. Kent that we had always felt that bookkeeping was an important part of business life.

Mr. Kent shook both our hands and wished us well in our application following which we returned home none the wiser about our future prospects. On the way home, Audrey and I discussed the meeting and we replayed it over and over. We wondered if Mr. Kent had cleverly concealed signs of horror and disgust on viewing our accounts or had he perhaps given the game away, by disguising a snigger of contempt as an impromptu sneeze?

As is a husband's duty, I tried to reassure my wife that everything was going to be okay and I promised her, without foundation, that we would get the loan, no question about it. Audrey, much more sensibly, opted to carry out a wife's duty, by bringing an air of common sense to proceedings and she quite rightly pointed out that the bank could just as easily say no as it could yes.

It was several weeks of worry later before an official-looking envelope dropped through our letterbox and the importance of its content was suggested by the perfectly aligned stamp on the back. Having picked it up, I nervously brought the letter upstairs to Audrey who, sensing its relevance, dropped what she was doing immediately. We both sat down to open it. I tore at the paper, slowly at first, but found myself finishing at the pace of a child unwrapping a Christmas present.

"Well?" asked Audrey.

"Loan approved!"

I sank into my chair with relief, while Audrey began to cry as she thanked God for heeding her prayers. The whole process had been a great strain on both of us and it's a truly horrible thing to be faced with the prospect of having the rug pulled out from under you. Indeed, it is only in such circumstances that you realise just how much you have in life and how heart-breaking the thought of losing it really is.

I put my arm around Audrey to comfort her and I pointed out that everything was going to be fine now that we held our destiny in our own hands. I told Audrey that I shared in her relief and I confessed that my hopes had been up so high and that rejection would have seen me wailing like a banshee.

"I can just picture you, Joseph, and I'm even happier now that I don't have to see it," Audrey said, as she dabbed tears of relief with a tissue.

The vast mountain of debt was to be climbed over twenty years but on that momentous day we had at least taken our first steps in our expedition and daunting as it now was, we knew that it was the best thing for our family to undertake.

I moved my chair around further to position myself even closer to Audrey and I gave her a little cuddle as I thanked her for making all things possible.

"You know what this means? We can have another baby now, seeing as we still have a roof to put a little one under," I said, hoping to raise a smile; a smile which sadly never came.

"Oh, Joseph, I don't know how to tell you," cried Audrey.

"What's the matter?" I asked, instantly concerned.

"Joseph, I've been meaning to tell you. But with your poor father, your brothers and then the bank, I didn't want to worry you further!" said Audrey, her words beset with emotion.

"You're scaring me now Audrey, what is it?" I asked.

Audrey went on to tell me, that a visit to Dr. Kelleher's office some four weeks previously had all but ended our hopes of having another baby. Following prior examinations Dr. Kelleher had revealed to Audrey that, due to complications which arose during the birth of little Patricia, she was now unable to conceive any more children.

Audrey and I had been trying to conceive for many months without sign of success before her visit to the doctor and now it appeared that we had been fighting a losing battle all along.

"So all our efforts were in vain," I said, struggling for words.

"Oh God, Joseph, the things you say. It was hardly effort now, was it?" said Audrey, with a hint of a smile breaking through her sorrow. "Are you disappointed?" she asked, having taken me by the hand.

"Oh, of course I am. But as long as I have you, Jonathan and Patricia, I can cope with anything. We are a team, you know. I would have loved to have added to our family too and I know that we would have given a little baby a loving home to grow up in. Not to mention the best mother in the world," I offered.

Audrey then shared with me the fact that she now felt a strong loss of womanhood and that if she couldn't reproduce and add to her family, her role on this earth was greatly diluted. Cradling my wife in my arms, I reminded her that she had already created life and that our two beautiful children were testament to her having fulfilled and exceeded any expectations that she may have felt were placed upon her.

"Are we not good people, Joseph? Why would the Lord not smile on us again?" Audrey lamented.

"We are good people, Audrey but the Lord has already blessed us. He's blessed us by giving us more love than most people get in a lifetime and I bet that from heaven, he sees our little family and probably thinks to himself that we have all the happiness in the world already," I said, to no reply, as I held my wife close.

Audrey had transformed my life and her presence would be forever felt in the hearts of her children and those of our future grandchildren. She really had so much love to give and my heart broke for her that day, as I tried to stay strong to help shoulder her burden. Yet, behind my words of reassurance lay a sorrow at having just witnessed my wife confirm to me that her dreams would never again come true. And not for the first time, my eyes were opened up to the fact that realisation of the truth can be a most cruel and harrowing thing.

Long term, of course, I knew that Audrey's heart would need to be mended but, bit by bit, we managed to keep moving forward. Several weeks later we drew down the money from the bank, and we were finally able to settle up with Michael and Edward. The solicitor even arranged for the money to be transferred directly to my brothers, via some banking trickery.

I later received a charming letter from Michael, confirming that he had received his payment and in it, he even went as far as to detail out his plans for it. He told me that in light of Orla and Liam's births he was going to add a small extension to his home, which I thought was fantastic. He went on to thank me for arranging everything before signing off graciously by wishing myself, Audrey and the children many years of continued happiness in Stepaside.

I never did receive word from Edward but, in a way, his silence was deafening and no doubt some barman of the day or perhaps even a lady of the night, benefited in kind from his windfall. Still, Edward's life was his own to lead and were I to dwell on that very subject I would mourn the fact that the proceeds of my parents' lives were being spent so frivolously and with little regard shown to their memory.

As a trying time, in more ways than one, came to a close, I will admit to being hugely relieved when the buyout finally went through and it felt wonderful that Audrey, Jonathan, Patricia and I, now had a home we could call our own. It also meant a great deal to me to be able to keep the shop within the family, as I was all too aware of the hard work and dedication that had gone into it over the years.

From its very creation to its daily grind, our family's shop has been kept alive as much by passion as by commerce and as its guardian, I was more determined than ever to keep the home fires burning. Daunting as that prospect seemed, I at least knew that by having a courageous wife, two beautiful children and the spirits of my parents at my side, our little shop would remain in caring hands, where it would be loved and appreciated by all those fortunate enough to have ever called it home.

CHAPTER 22

BALANCING ACT

THE SUDDEN AND TRAGIC LOSS OF my father had not only left a gaping hole in my personal life, it had also left two well-worn size nines that needed to be filled in the shop. In his later years, Father's efforts with the business were not exactly what you would call consistent but God love him, he did what he could and those hours, no matter how few, now had to be made up somehow. With a wife and two children to support, the hiring of additional staff was out of the question, so I was left with little or no option but to up my own workload and kick on as best I could.

Balancing work with rearing a family was not without its testing times but I am proud to say that after a few teething problems, we eventually found a system that comfortably balanced both aspects of our lives. Audrey, as I knew she would, rose to the challenge and we both managed to continue running the shop as a going concern.

If there was one silver lining that appeared through the occasional dark cloud, it was my relationship with Audrey. An already rock-solid relationship seemed to coat itself in gold during this period and although we probably didn't realise it at the time, any little arguments or stresses we had, simply served to make our marriage even stronger. As a young couple, we struggled to find what they call nowadays 'quality time' as other commitments often divided our attention, but I do believe that we never lost sight of the fact that we were at our strongest while together.

Tending to the needs of the children and the shop understandably had a monopoly on our daylight hours, but at night-time, when the shop's demands were satisfied and the children were curled up on a cloud of dreams, Audrey and I found tiny moments of time to just be together and talk. Those are some of my happiest memories and each conversation reminded me why I fell in love with her in the first place. Any negative issues or cross words traded during the day were cast aside and nothing in the world could intrude on us in those moments. Tucked up in bed, our focus on each other was without distraction and we were free to be serious, to be silly or to just do what folk do.

"Things are going well aren't they, Joseph?" asked Audrey, as if wanting me to confirm what she already knew to be true.

"Things are going great. Granted, we may never hit the nail squarely on the head but we'll at least clip the side of it!" I said with a smile and cuddle to emphasise the point.

Aside from bouts of silliness, a commodity hugely underused in most marriages, Audrey and I would use this time wisely and we both afforded each other every opportunity to confide any issues that may have been preying on our minds.

"Do you really think that things will always stay this way, Joseph?" asked Audrey, while nestled in close.

"I really do. Sure why would God interfere? He has blessed this house and the people in it for a long time now and although I don't understand all of his ways, I do believe that he has a plan for each one of us," I said in truth.

"Well, I hope he continues to look upon us with favour. I really do. And we won't let him down, sure we won't Joseph?" Audrey reasoned.

"No, we won't. He's in safe hands with us, pet, and that's for sure," I said, before kissing her on the forehead.

During these moments, of which there were many, Audrey never once brought up the subject of our inability to add to our family. I knew how much it had pained her when Dr. Kelleher informed her that she would no longer bear children and I was always amazed that she never seized upon those quiet moments to discuss the news that had led her to shed so many a tear. Audrey, it seemed, had either lost or at least kept very well hidden, her desire to have more children.

Of course, I suspected that she still longed to have another baby, in truth so did I, and it greatly saddened me that I could do nothing to help the situation. I wanted so badly to be able to talk to her about it, to at least try and help her come to terms with things, but at the same time I also understood completely her decision not to speak of it. A woman's true feelings are not something into which you should ever pry so I respected her right to hold a secret close to her heart, while I remained content in the knowledge that I would always provide a wanting ear, should she ever feel the need to lighten her load.

With work stealing six days a week from us, Sunday was the day we all looked forward to, the Soap family day out, and we would spend that precious time at the seaside or at the local park. Each week we would prepare a picnic and bright and early, we would take up position in the great outdoors.

During breaks in play, Audrey and I would wisely sit, gathering our breath on an old red gingham blanket we kept for such occasions. From there, we would watch on with great pride as the children continued to scamper about at a pace which we both resignedly accepted was beyond us.

I am most fortunate to relive the pleasure I gained from those carefree days time and time again, by looking over old photographs of us all. And indeed, anytime a sea breeze rushes my face or the aroma of freshly cut grass chases up my nostrils, I feel as though I am brought back to a time when my legs could run at a respectable speed as I gave chase in hopeless pursuit of my delightfully exuberant children.

In fear of Jonathan or Patricia injuring themselves, Audrey was always much more cautious than I was and if the children's behaviour ever became overly boisterous or unruly, she would insist that they settle down and behaved in a more dignified manner. Certainly a manner more restrained than was usually expected of children with sand or grass in between their toes.

I, on the other hand, would let them run wild as jackrabbits, as I figured that the odd bump along the way would do them no harm at all, in the big scheme of things. Audrey would sometimes pass comment at my perceived lax attitude when it came to the children's high jinks but overall we found a happy medium and combined to great effect with regards to their raising. I always attributed Audrey's stern outlook to parenting to her own upbringing and I imagined that having Mr. and Mrs. Healy as parents would have forced even the softest of rose petals to harden in amongst such thorny surroundings. I always suspected that given half a chance, Mr. and Mrs. Healy would steal a dream from a child's mind, so whenever Audrey was strict with the children, I would take a temporary vow of silence and just chalk her stringent approach down to her own rearing.

The children grew at a rate that paid little or no regard to the new shoes that we were forever buying them and as they both shot towards the sky, they did so hand in hand. Right from Patricia's birth, she and Jonathan were inseparable and they shared a relationship, which entwined both family ties and friendship to perfection. It was a lovely thing to witness and in many ways it reminded me of Michael and myself, from way back when.

Simple ball games or good old-fashioned 'tag' seemed to be particular favourites with the children and Audrey and I took great pride when on occasion Jonathan would deliberately slow down, in order to let his sister's shorter legs catch up with him.

When we had inhaled every last breath of fresh air available to us, we would pack up our things and head for home. On one such journey, I recall Audrey and I having to sit through constant badgering from the children and all the way home two little voices were joined in unison, expressing a great craving for treats. Chocolate-based ones, no less. Audrey stood firm in defiance and she made plain to them that their greedy wants would not be forthcoming.

"There'll be no treats this evening. Your dinner will be treat enough. We have a home bursting its walls with fruit and vegetables and you can eat as many of those as you want. And besides, you both know full well that chocolate is bad for you," Audrey said, in no mood for debate.

Feigning similar sentiment, I exaggerated the nodding of my head in solidarity with my wife's decision. That is, until the opportunity arose for me to sneak Jonathan and Patricia a lightning-fast wink to indicate that my stance on the matter may not be quite as rigid as their mother's.

Sunday dinner usually consisted of a lovely roast and Audrey outdid herself time and time again when it came to putting on a good spread. When my bacon and cabbage was off the menu, chicken or beef were staples and they came with broccoli, carrots, potatoes and peas to keep them company on the plate. The children had an indifferent attitude towards those types of meals back then and the great love affair I had and indeed still have with fruit and vegetables had yet to influence them in any way, shape or form.

Later that day, when we sat down to eat, Jonathan and Patricia barely touched a bite of their dinner and they clearly took more pleasure from moving it around their plates, than they did from actually eating it. Castles were made out of mashed potatoes, goalposts from carrots, while peas masqueraded as tiny footballs, aimlessly distracting two children who were unaware of the efforts involved in preparing such a meal.

"Jonathan and Patricia, stop playing with that food and eat your greens!" Audrey bellowed from across the table.

In response, Jonathan, ever the scamp, and still sulking from his lack of chocolate, manoeuvred his fork and prised a lone piece of carrot from his plate and held it aloft.

"Eat my greens? But this is orange!" he said, causing his sister to giggle.

Little Patricia was not doing a very good job in hiding her laughter and such was the shaking of her shoulders that the glass of milk she held to her mouth was almost churned to butter. The chewing of a piece of chicken offered my mouth all the distraction it needed to avoid laughing and I pressed my forearms onto the kitchen table in the hope of steadying my own shoulders, which had involuntarily started to tremble.

"Jonathan, I don't care if it's BLUE... EAT IT!" Audrey roared.

Now, little boys the world over tend to react in one of two ways when they find themselves in trouble. Firstly, and some would say traditionally, they stay quiet and hope that their parent's anger passes with minimum fuss. Alternatively, they cry bucketloads, whilst pleading impassionedly for forgiveness. Both of these are well tried and tested measures and they have saved the skin of many a rascal and quite how boys from the four corners of the world know about them, is a puzzle too complicated to even contemplate.

Young Jonathan, however, decided to go down an entirely different path and he chose to face his mother's annoyance head-on, armed with only giddiness for protection.

"BLUE!" Jonathan squealed. "Carrots aren't blue, Mammy!" he added in hysterics, as he slumped forward on to the table, simply lost to wild fits of laughter.

Milk suddenly rained from across the table as Patricia roared at the funniest thing she had heard in all of her five years of life. The chorus of laughter prompted me to let out an untamed chuckle, an act that all but sealed my fate, as it drew a disapproving glare from my wife.

Audrey was by now livid and she let it be known.

"Jonathan and Patricia, leave the table immediately and go to your rooms till morning!" Audrey commanded.

After a second or two, the children quietened down and sensing their mother's discontent they sat rigidly in their chairs, still as statues. Their indifference to vegetables was one thing but the fear of their mother's wrath, combined with the prospect of going to bed with hungry bellies, quickly made their 'greens' seem all the more appetising. So, it was with bowed heads that Jonathan and Patricia remained defiantly in place.

"Leave now!" Audrey loudly reaffirmed.

Quiet as mice, Jonathan and Patricia got up from the table and headed sluggishly for their rooms. Watching from the table, I thought I heard a faint "Sorry Mammy" as they toddled off and I like to think that I did.

The tension continued in the children's absence, until Audrey rose without comment and began to tidy the table. I offered to help, but I was told that I had "done enough".

While doing the washing up, Audrey looked genuinely let down and looking back on it now I can understand why. Like all mothers, Audrey held the keys to her children's future and the concern she had for their wellbeing simply didn't warrant such behaviour.

Much like Jonathan and Patricia, I would often bask in those funny moments and on many occasions, I was guilty of showing little regard for the life lessons that were lost as a consequence. Regardless of the fact that the children's playing up had been amusing to all but Audrey, the point remained that they had blatantly disobeyed their mother by refusing to eat good and wholesome food. With their impressionable heads turned by the faint lure of chocolate, Jonathan and Patricia cared little for its side effects, nor indeed for the long-term benefits provided by the vegetables. But their mother cared.

Silence echoed around the Soap household that evening and the general feeling of gloom lingered, before seamlessly blending into the darkness of the night. Tucked up cosily in my nice warm bed, I could have been forgiven for thinking that all was well, but the biting chill emanating from my wife's cold shoulder, soon put paid to such fanciful notions.

The lack of conversation between Audrey and me caused me to look towards my thoughts for company and I soon became troubled with visions of little Jonathan and Patricia, in bed with two rumbling bellies, and with only food for thought.

Deep down, I knew that Audrey deserved an apology. She had after all been let down by those closest to her so, in a belated effort to thaw relations, I sheepishly extended an olive branch.

"I'm sorry, Audrey. I should have supported you," I said, my words simple but heartfelt.

To her credit, she accepted my apology, before going to great lengths to emphasise our role and the fact that we had the responsibility of safeguarding our children's best interests. I listened intently to everything Audrey had to say and, for the most part, I agreed with her entirely. The brief discussion that followed thankfully brought the matter to a close, and our truce was sealed in warm embrace.

Having allowed sufficient time for the children to adequately digest their food for thought, we decided to call them from their rooms, to face the music. Jonathan and Patricia came out somewhat hesitantly at first, but when they saw that Audrey and I were not exactly red with rage, their grip on each other's hands seemed to loosen ever so slightly. Sensing their unease,

I walked over to where they were standing barely a foot inside our bedroom door, and I coaxed them in closer to their mother.

"Now, Jonathan and Patricia, have you anything to say to your mammy?" I asked of the subdued pair.

"Sorry Mammy," the children said simultaneously.

Clearly appreciative, Audrey smiled an all-forgiving smile and with pursed lips and a raised hand, she sent two kisses hurtling in their direction. Before the kisses had even reached their cheeks, Jonathan and Patricia darted across the room like whippets and with a hop, skip and timely jump, they landed into their mother's embrace.

"I bet you're both hungry, aren't you?" I asked moments later.

"Yes, Daddy," the children replied in perfect harmony.

"Okay, I'll tell you what. Go down to the shop and pick yourselves a nice big apple each, and bring it to your rooms. Don't forget to make sure you look at the bottom of the box, because that is where the really shiny ones are," I offered knowingly, before following my words up with a well-timed wink to the children, when their mother was not looking.

Initially, Jonathan and Patricia looked disappointed at the measly offer of an apple but my disguised wink soon triggered a charge in them, which was usually only seen on a Christmas morning. They ran straight out of the room and as they did so, they left to the sound of Audrey telling them to slow down.

Five minutes or so later, Jonathan and Patricia returned to the landing from downstairs and the first sight of them revealed that they were both grinning from ear to ear. Without stopping they skipped merrily at pace towards their respective bedrooms and as they passed our room, they politely waved two green apples in our general direction.

"Consider yourselves lucky you two, and make sure you enjoy those apples... they don't grow on trees you know," I shouted after them, needlessly adding a joke I often used (with varying degrees of success) to amuse my customers.

Predictably, the children failed to laugh at my well-trodden-out joke. Instead they closed their bedroom doors behind them and we didn't see them again until the next morning.

Audrey and I then settled in for the night and we spent an hour or so talking about the children and how important it was to teach them the importance of good food, as well as the dangers of giving into chocolate cravings and the like.

"There's hope for them yet, Joseph. Did you see how excited they were to have those apples?" Audrey asked, with her head resting on my chest.

Stroking her hair, I replied by telling Audrey that she had done right by the children, before adding that I fully respected and supported the firm stance she had taken. Cradled tightly within my arms, Audrey began to settle in to her sleep and as she did so she reasoned contently, that Jonathan and Patricia were "a good pair really". I wholeheartedly agreed.

I remained awake for a little while longer, all the time watching Audrey as she slept and while doing so, I couldn't help but wonder what she was dreaming about; she looked beautiful. Lying perfectly still, so as not to disturb her, I did nothing but add further weight to the still of night and the only sound defeating the cold silence came in the form of a faint rustle from across the landing.

The looks on the children's faces, not to mention the bulge in the breast-pockets of their pyjamas, had been all the indication needed to know that they had found their real treats at the bottom of the apple box. Knowing that that was the last place in the world in which the children would ever seek sugary snacks, I had set aside two bars of chocolate, which I placed there in the midst of the extended hush earlier on in the evening.

Before falling asleep, and whilst reviewing the situation, I smiled with satisfaction at the thought of how happy Jonathan and Patricia must have been, as they secretly devoured their less than wholesome supper. And having once again realised the importance of an apology, I said a prayer to God, hoping that the children had learned a similar lesson. Shrewdly, I also made sure to tip my cap towards the merit of a little white lie, which when used correctly has the power to extinguish a whole host of fires.

Continuing to engage the Lord, I also somewhat opportunistically prayed that Jonathan and Patricia would have the good sense to hide the chocolate wrappers, as well as the undoubtedly uneaten apples, before their mother discovered them the next morning. Fortunately, both prayers were answered.

Young Conor, regardless of how we got there and in spite of a few bumps along the road, the Soap family, each in their own way, went to bed happy and contented that night and at the end of a long and trying day, who could ask for anything more than that?

CHAPTER 23

REARING IN THE YEARS

THE 1970s FINALLY SAW THE ARRIVAL of modern trends into Ireland and I must say that I found that whole decade to be most peculiar indeed. The country was swept by an invading wave of change both in terms of fashion and overall approach and, as far as I was concerned, too much bloody change flooded our shores.

Flowers inexplicably moved from people's gardens to their wardrobes, while a generation of people's silly notions betrayed the last bit of respectability that was left over from a bygone age. Flower-power clothing was permitted to run riot against the norm and the famed 'Sunday best' look of my youth quickly fell foul, as its first victim. Good taste in general simply evaporated amid a cloud of suspicious-smelling smoke and it could be argued that, as of today, it has yet to mount a serious comeback.

Looking back on that time now, 1970 to 1979, I honestly cannot recall seeing a single well-pressed suit or blazer jacket adorn the backs of the local youth; which is to say nothing of hairstyles, which absolutely lost the run of themselves. I saw only cavemen roaming the streets of Dublin, yet proudly I stood defiant with my 'short back and sides'. I continuously spurned the unwelcome suggestion to "Move with the times, man," and in the face of what were clearly flippant attempts at persuading me to break from tradition, I remained loyal to the only style of cut I have ever sported. In fact, such was my loyalty to it, I can honestly say that it is a hairstyle I would still employ today, had baldness done the decent thing and just let me be.

I was, after all, too busy a man for such nonsense and during that period I barely had time to leave my twenties for my thirties, but somehow I managed it. I had a young family and business to take care of, and each day spent working for the well-being of both was a day well spent in my eyes.

I would love now to be able to say that the Soap family years were packed to the rafters with exciting times and stories that would leave a receptive ear craving for more, but in truth, they were played out much the same as any other family up and down the country. Audrey and I worked hard and did all that we could to provide a safe family nest in which to raise our children and while the years rolled routinely into the next, save for one reminder each year, I grew older without pausing to notice.

I did, however, note with great interest as Jonathan and Patricia grew older and there was not a single day that I was not amazed at how they each took the world in their stride. It was just wonderful to see both of them developing personalities of their own and to watch as various interests caught their eye and engaged with their imaginations.

Patricia became an avid reader, a pastime also enjoyed by her mother, and she would read cover to cover anything that she could get her hands on. Although slight, even for a girl of eight, she was not averse to more strenuous activities but by and large, her adventures were lived out through print, where her stories took her from the ocean's floor to the surface of the moon.

Jonathan, for his part, was very much a chip off his father's block and happily he continued to share my interest in all things shop related. Much less welcome, however, was his inherited aversion to school and his focus often seemed to centre on pottering around the shop floor, where he would treat the place as though it were his own little enterprise. As Jonathan knew the owner quite well, the shop was available to him even when the sign on the front door read 'Closed' and often he would continue his imaginary trading right up until his bedtime.

Jonathan, at ten years of age, would spend many happy hours playing shopkeeper and not once did he let the noticeable lack of real people hold his fledgling business empire back. While packing bags with whatever was closest at hand, he would engage with his imaginary costumers on topics such as vegetables in season or the changing weather, and time and again he would answer knowingly to his own questions, having paused a second for thought. I often stood silently in the background, observing him as he went about his work and it always both amazed and delighted me how, even lost in play, he was courteous and engaging to all.

For a young pair, Jonathan and Patricia had great confidence and they had that lovely combination of fearlessness and innocence which all children have, when they know of only simple matters and kindness. That is something which is lost in every adult and few can say for sure when they lost it, yet each one of us lives with the sad effects of its passing. To be pure of heart is a blessing and as parents, if we can help keep a little bit of heaven alive in the hearts of our children, we will have done right by them.

Audrey and I took great pleasure from raising Jonathan and Patricia, but we were always acutely aware of the importance our guidance was to them as we helped them along the way. Children are so impressionable and we carried out our role as parents knowing that one slip of the tongue or lack of judgement could have a negative influence on their lives.

While Audrey and I knew of Jonathan's dislike of school, we also knew of its importance so each and every day, we would try and encourage the boy with his homework. Audrey would sit with him to coax him along and she would add valuable input and a view of the world, which made sense to a young lad struggling for answers. When Audrey wasn't available, I would peruse his homework and with little or no clue as to what I was actually looking at, I would quietly rue the fact that the price of vegetables rarely, if ever, came into the equation.

Patricia was a lot more focused on school than her brother was. She would start her homework as soon as she arrived home and it would take at least three prompts for her to pause in order to come to the kitchen table for her tea. She expressed quite early on a desire to become a schoolteacher and her reasoning for this showed what it is like to be controlled by the mind of an eight year old, in which all things are possible.

"Daddy, I'm going to be a teacher when I grow up. So I can stay in school forever and teach all my friends," Patricia stated, with the seriousness of a flat tyre on a rainy day.

Audrey and I frequently pressed home to the children the importance of spending time together as a family and as a result, our weekly outings still took pride of place on the Soap calendar with our tendency now favouring the beach over the park. As parents, we felt strongly that this time was important, not only to build family values and unity, but also to keep alive a tradition which had come to mean so much to us.

The years continued to pass by at what could be described as an alarming rate, and days which in truth often seemed mundane at the time now seem like a life lived to its fullest.

As we approached the end of a demanding decade its effects became more and more apparent, and a pronounced broadening around my waist crept up on me, whilst my hairline receded to a point where I was receiving a discount from my barber. While I had everything a man could wish for, I did briefly mourn the loss of my youth, but thankfully I soon accepted that the predictability of living one's life to the ticking of a clock invariably means that time waits for no man and that change comes to us all, regardless of want.

The children, however, did not skip a beat as the years progressed and they embraced each day as though it were the opportunity of a lifetime. Jonathan, at fourteen, had grown to tower over his old man (not that that was hard of course, with me standing at five feet seven inches, on a good day) and even Patricia, at twelve, was not far off giving me a run for my money.

Children grow, it's their only job really, yet regardless of increasing age, a parent will always see their child as a babe-in-arms. Like everything we hold dear, time gradually and quite sneakily changes the world around us and we as people are exposed as mere pawns in a game too complex for us to ever understand.

Although change is a natural part of life, many parents remain emotionally unprepared for when their children reach the cusp of independence.

Audrey and I were two such people.

We watched as Jonathan and Patricia grew older and built friendships of their own and we quietly lamented the fact that they increasingly spent less and less time by our side. Indeed, as they branched out into life, Audrey and I both clung on desperately to what we still saw as two fragile birds about to take flight.

Our weekly family day out had now all but vanished and in its place came a hurried walk along the coast once a month or so. Audrey and I saw no deterioration in the beauty of the Irish coastline nor did we feel that the sea air was any less exhilarating but the children's own views on the matter had by now altered greatly. Scenery which once enthralled was reduced to commonplace, while family time was now a poor relation to the excitement of meeting up with their pals.

Each Sunday, I would suggest coming for a walk with their mother and me but Jonathan and Patricia would, more often than not, politely decline. Their reasoning always involved an adventure or two with their friends and as time went on, I eventually, if somewhat reluctantly, accepted the change of tide. Audrey, however, refused to accept it and each week she would try to disguise her disappointment, as we left the house just us two. Of course, we still had some lovely walks and some wonderful times but when you take two from four, a sense of loss is inevitable.

On the stroke of 1980, the world waved goodbye to a decade which will go down in history as being most unusual, yet remarkably, and with a wave from the same hand, an even stranger decade was immediately ushered in. In no time at all, footballers' shorts shrunk to the point of indecency, music turned electric and what were already poor haircuts now went out the window altogether, as 'the Mullet' adorned the heads of people who really should have known better.

Amidst all this change, some old issues still stubbornly managed to follow us into the new decade, as shortly after his fifteenth birthday, Jonathan made clear his disinterest in school and in no uncertain terms, he told us that he wanted to leave. It was a conversation I had always feared as I knew that by leaving school, he would also be leaving behind the ability to shape his own future and fond as Jonathan was of the shop, I worried that he was choosing the safe option, rather than pushing himself out into the unknown.

Having sat the boy down for a heart-to-heart, I told him of the longstanding regret I held for my own unfinished education and of how, with the benefit of hindsight, I would have loved to see it through to its natural conclusion. Were he to apply himself a bit better, Jonathan had the ability to go on to college and I went to great pains to try and convince him to knuckle down and persevere with his studies.

"But you didn't go to college, Da, and you turned out alright," Jonathan said in retort.

"I want you to be more than just alright, son. All I have ever been, or am ever likely to be, is alright, but you can be more than that, you and your sister. You can be whatever you want to be," I said, as I tried to open up my boy's eyes.

I so dearly wanted to ensure that Jonathan refrained from turning his back on his education and armed with Audrey's support and her power of persuasion, we both set about trying to talk further sense into the boy. A verbal tug of war ensued over the next number of days and it wasn't until both sides were exhausted, and with no victory in sight, that we finally settled upon some middle ground. Thankfully, Jonathan eventually agreed to stick it out at school for a while longer having been appeased by our promise that we would look at things again at the end of the school term.

Audrey and I, as always, would spend hours discussing our family, with our best chats usually reserved for past bedtime. Yet on one blustery Sunday afternoon, while walking along Dollymount Strand, she confided in me what I had long since suspected, that she still longed to have another baby.

This sudden airing of opinion was no doubt influenced by Jonathan and Patricia's ascent into adulthood but given the harsh reality of life and the stern stance it had already taken on the issue, I knew that barring a miracle of biblical proportions, the situation would sadly not be for changing. I, too, would have loved to have added to our family, but the words of Dr. Kelleher replayed over and over in my mind, yet such was the pain the diagnosis had caused Audrey, I figured that she had somehow banished it from her mind.

Audrey admitted that, at thirty-eight years old, she was approaching a now-or-never situation and as each year rolled into the next, her chances of conceiving dwindled away to the point of no return. Her beauty cast doubt over the numbers on her birth certificate and she had freshness like no other, but the brutal truth remained that my wife had no chance of conceiving another baby.

"But there has to be a way, Joseph, there has to be. Maybe we could get a second opinion, a better opinion," Audrey said, in hope.

Our failure to add to our family in the years following the doctor's cold diagnosis, had extinguished any flame of hope that lingered in my mind. Audrey, however, was different and almost blind to reason, it appeared as though her heart refused to accept the limitations of her body.

With this in mind, I was now faced with the harrowing choice of either cruelly ending my wife's dream, by killing it with biological fact or offering a grain of hope to a desperate woman who had so much love left to give. I chose the latter.

"We can go and see someone else if you like, of course we can, pet. Doctors can do great things these days," I said, in an effort to appease my wife.

"Maybe if God sees the extra effort we are making, he'll bless us again, Joseph," Audrey said, as a tear ran past her lips. "Maybe he'll grant us our miracle," she added.

"Maybe he will, maybe he will," I said, as I shielded my wife from the biting wind that suddenly chased across the unforgiving Irish Sea.

As we stood together, with the wind making us increasingly unsteady, we both silently wondered what the future held in store for us. Regardless of whether we were to be granted a miracle or whether we would be forced to deal with the ramifications from the ending of a dream, one thing was certain – we would face it together.

As we walked from the beach that day, Audrey and I had no way of knowing the heartache that lay in store for us. Our search to create life would ultimately lead us to encounter death and were we to know the future that awaited us, we would not have taken another step. Rather, we would have remained on the sand, holding on to each other with all the might we could muster.

Young Conor, I know that fate would have continued on its path regardless and it would have done so without compassion. But Audrey and I could have at least lived our lives in the land of blissful ignorance, if only for a little while longer, instead of blindly running into a world of true sorrow and pain.

CHAPTER 24

WHAT CHANCE A LIFETIME?

As AUDREY AND I MADE OUR way back from the beach, heading towards our van, the conversation continued without relent and all along the journey home, we set about making plans to take our quest a stage further. We both readily agreed that time was of the essence, as matters of such importance can rarely wait and over supper that Sunday evening, we settled upon troubling Dr. Kelleher at the start of business the following day.

At a stroke past nine the next morning and while I tended to the shop's needs, my wife loitered with intent inside kindly Mrs. Sullivan's hallway, having once again acquired permission to use her telephone. Despite having paced the floor incessantly, Audrey commendably managed to compose herself before formally sitting down upon the old dear's smart telephone table-seat. It was of rich mahogany-build, quite decorative for its day and its red velvet cushion offered your bum all the comfort needed to tolerate a call of any length. From there she placed a telephone call and once connected, an appointment was promptly arranged for us to attend the doctor's surgery later that same day.

As was often the case when Audrey and I were both required to be somewhere at once, we deposited the children safely with Mrs. Healy and having turned the shop's sign to 'Closed', we headed off for a meeting that had the potential to stretch our emotions both north and south.

We arrived at the doctor's surgery shortly after lunchtime and with plenty of time to spare and amid the usual chorus of coughs and sneezes you find in such places, we took up a seat and waited to be called. There, Audrey and I sat patiently and, save for the odd exchange, we remained in relative silence until an unseen lady from behind a pane of frosted glass bellowed "Soap!"

In response, Audrey and I rose cautiously to our feet and we walked what must have been all of ten yards to the doctor's door, at a pace that was laboured at best. Our sluggishness was of course unintentional, but with each step we racked our brains in search of a suitable response to what we knew was an inevitable, "Now what seems to be the problem?"

Although we already knew what the problem was, Audrey and I both wondered just how he would react to our seemingly brushing aside his original diagnosis, and brazenly seeking a second opinion to what in all likelihood was a complete flight of fancy.

Dr. Kelleher for all intents and purposes was a very nice man, one who was polite, courteous and genuinely interested in the well-being of his patients. He was a pillar of our community, a man held in high regard by all of Stepaside, and as a result I imagined that it was quite seldom indeed that anyone saw fit to question his findings. So it was with brass necks and bated breath that Audrey and I entered his office and took a seat.

"Now what seems to be the problem, Mr. and Mrs. Soap?" greeted Dr. Kelleher.

"Doctor, Joseph and I have being trying to conceive a baby and so far, we have gone unblessed," Audrey said, as an opening gambit.

"Mrs. Soap, having reviewed your file prior to this appointment, I cannot say that what you are telling me comes as too much of a surprise. From my case notes, as well as my recollection, I seem to recall speaking with you with regards to this very matter. And I thought, with regret, that I made your situation perfectly clear to you," Dr. Kelleher replied.

"We were hoping that, with time, perhaps things may have changed somewhat, Doctor," Audrey offered, in way of an explanation.

"Do you know, Mr. and Mrs. Soap, when I saw you both walk in through my door, looking fit and healthy, I half suspected what it was you came here to see me about. I see it often, too often in fact, where couples such as yourselves let emotions get the better of you and hearts begin to rule heads," Dr. Kelleher said, with an air of legitimacy.

"We're just looking for a second opinion Doctor," Audrey clarified.

"You are looking for an opinion other than fact, Mrs. Soap!" Dr. Kelleher said.

"We're only looking for a referral, to maybe see someone who might be able to help us, that's all!" Audrey said, with increasing desperation.

"You are seeking news which you will not find, Mrs. Soap, that I can promise you!" Dr. Kelleher replied.

"All we are looking for is a chance, Doctor," Audrey near pleaded.

"You are looking for a miracle, Mrs. Soap and I'm afraid I cannot prescribe miracles. I deal solely in facts and scientific certainty," Dr. Kelleher affirmed.

As I sat quietly and watched while Audrey and the doctor traded verbal punches, I could not help but find myself agreeing with the man who was crushing my wife's dreams. He spoke with logic, with reason, whereas Audrey spoke with nothing other than wishful thinking and a passion for something beyond her reach.

Like a keen-eyed referee with a vested-interest in the bout, I sat and watched as both sides exchanged blows and, highly engrossed, I struggled to predict an outcome. Being a reasonable man, one who could ultimately see a battle being fought with neither side destined to win, I knew that I would have to intervene at some point and when that time finally came, I came out fighting with my wife's best interests at heart.

"Look Doctor, we didn't come here today to offend you or question your expertise, we came here for help. You can help us. All we're after is a simple letter of referral, to see someone of your recommendation and choosing, and then we will be on our way. A stroke of your pen will give us the chance to move forward, and I may as well tell you, that we're not leaving here without that chance!" I said, wedging my way into what was already a heated debate.

Dr. Kelleher looked unmoved.

Just as I was building up a full head of steam and ready to unleash another impassioned tirade, Audrey broke down in tears. Not out of duty, but out of want, I reached across to my wife and placed my arm around her shoulder, which only seemed to heighten her distress.

I suspect it was at that very moment with emotions dancing wild around the room that Dr. Kelleher saw the true pain behind my wife's eyes, and it was her sorrow, her passion and her blind faith that ultimately lead him to break away from best practice.

Dr. Kelleher averted his gaze for a moment, as if lost in a train of thought, before he too let his heart overrule his head.

"Look, Mr. and Mrs. Soap, I can refer you on to a colleague of mine who practises in the Coombe. He will see you on my request," Dr. Kelleher said.

"Oh thank you, Doctor, thank you and God bless you!" Audrey said, as she waited for her tears to retreat following the answering of her prayers.

"I'm afraid you do not understand me, Mrs. Soap. I'm happy to refer you on, but I am doing so in the belief that you will be told once and for all, that the creation of life is no longer within your means. It is with deepest regret I might add, but that is my honest view on your situation. You may very well get the miracle you seek, that is beyond my control, but please know that that is what it will take for you: a miracle," Dr. Kelleher said, before putting pen to paper.

"We understand, Doctor, and we thank you for your time and patience. You've at least given us a chance of a miracle and that's more than we had before we came to see you," I added, as I rose to my feet to take the letter from the kind doctor's hand.

"I sincerely hope you find your miracle, Mr. Soap, and I'll be sure to say a prayer for your cause," Dr. Kelleher said, as he handed me the letter.

In the car park of the doctor's surgery, Audrey and I both felt a new-found sense of achievement, as though we had somehow successfully leaped over the first of many hurdles that littered our path. Secretly, I even allowed myself to believe that the impossible may just be possible, after all.

We both agreed to transport the referral letter to the hospital straight away and showing little or no regard to the vegetable cravings of the people of Stepaside, we mounted the van and headed towards town.

It was several weeks before we received word from the hospital but when the letter finally arrived on our doorstep, the appointment was dated promptly for the following week. Audrey and I were thrilled that we would be seen so quickly and that with the help of God each passing hour would take us closer to the good news we sought. The appointment was to see a Dr. Mark Philips and instantly Audrey's and my nightly prayers included a man that neither of us had ever met.

It wasn't long before the appointment date arrived and on presenting ourselves at the hospital, we found Dr. Philips to be cordial and polite, if not blessed with a charm of any particular sort. Professional as he was, he appeared to lack the compassion you would imagine such a role requires and from our very first meeting with him, Audrey and I were left in little doubt that Dr. Philips was not a man who suffered fools lightly.

It was evident immediately to Audrey and me that he had been well briefed by Dr. Kelleher and from the instant we walked into his office, he dealt us a hand of cold, hard facts. He explained that he concurred with Dr. Kelleher's diagnosis and having read Audrey's records from cover to cover, he felt that we stood little or no chance of conceiving another baby. Dr. Philips, did, however, agree to run some further tests, which appeased our mood slightly, and I was duly asked to step outside.

As I sat alone in the corridor, I so badly wanted to be there for my wife and to hold her hand in support but such things were thought of as inappropriate in those days. When Audrey eventually came out of the room, I noticed that she looked slightly uncomfortable and sensing her unease I simply embraced her lovingly and said, "Well done". Without further ado, we left for home and we did so sandwiched between hope and nervousness as we prepared to wait for the results to come through.

During that period, our general lives and those of our children continued to play out much as before. Yet at the back of it all, Audrey's and my thoughts were drawn every which way but loose, as we constantly debated the outcome of the results, which hung over us like a ruling judge's gavel. Our minds would race each time we discussed the matter and at times Audrey's enthusiasm, if only for a second, would make me believe that I lived in a world in which miracles had already been granted.

Less than three weeks had passed when, quite out of the blue, an officially branded envelope landed through our door and given that Dr. Philips had suggested a period of a "couple of months" for the results to filter through the system, Audrey opened it up without giving it due care and attention.

The letter read:

> *Dear Mrs. Soap,*
>
> *Please make contact with this office at your earliest possible convenience.*
>
> *Regards,*
>
> *Dr. Philips, M*

Audrey read the letter out to me before I read it for myself and as I did so, I hurriedly scanned it for clues as to explanation. She then asked me what I thought it meant, but I was unable to answer knowingly and even after reading it for a second and then third time, I could do nothing but shake my head in bewilderment. The only suggestion I could muster was that we contact Dr. Philips right away. Audrey, in response, reclaimed the letter, before heading straight out of the door to Mrs. Sullivan's, in the hope of again using her telephone.

At Mrs. Sullivan's good grace, Audrey placed a telephone call to the number detailed on the letter, and it was subsequently arranged for her to go and see the doctor the very next day. Despite persistent querying from Audrey, the hospital staff refused to shed light as to the letter's meaning and they stubbornly refused to lift the veil of secrecy their professionalism demands of them.

On her return home, Audrey seemed strangely pacified and clearly believing Mrs. Sullivan's reckoning that "good news travels fast", she now refused to look upon the letter as anything other than a positive sign. But I wasn't so sure. While I agreed that good news does indeed travel fast, I was also aware that, more often than not, its old running mate 'bad news' has the ability to pip it at the post.

Although I am by no means a man consumed by negativity, I am unquestionably a realist at heart and when it comes to my wife's welfare, I view life from every possible angle, to ensure that I always have her best interests covered. After all, it is my belief that a husband's role in life is to protect his family, to stay one step ahead of the game and to consider every eventuality with the view of finding a solution to whatever life throws at them.

Thankfully, the next day came around at pace and when

Audrey and I reached Dr. Philips' office, I trawled the receptionist's face for an indication of what lay in store. But her pleasant and jovial manner failed to let the cat out of the bag either way.

"Audrey Soap!" bellowed the receptionist a short time later, triggering my wife and me to our feet.

On entering Dr. Philips' office door, my eyes bore straight through those of the learned man sitting behind the finely polished desk and immediately I saw concern strewn across his face, as he readied words that would darken our world.

"Mr. and Mrs. Soap, I'm afraid that I have news which will be of some concern to you both," Dr. Philips said, ominously.

Audrey and I looked nervously at each other and instinctively we joined our hands in support. Squeezing our fingers together with the strength that only fear can generate, we both sat silently as we listened to an honest man struggle with the hardest part of his or any other job for that matter.

"Mrs. Soap, I'm afraid your test results show the presence of ovarian cancer cells. How far along it is we cannot say at this point, but it is essential that we carry out further tests to determine its extent," Dr. Philips said bluntly.

Audrey raised her free hand to her mouth and a look of total disbelief instantly distorted her face. Frozen, we both sat rigidly in our seats for a moment until Audrey bravely broke the silence I had thought would never end.

"But this can't be, doctor, this can't be. We just wanted a

baby, a little baby. Tell him, Joseph, tell him what we wanted!"
Audrey said, as tears struggled to force their way past shock.

"Doctor, there must be some mistake, a mix-up." I said, wishing for common sense to prevail.

"I'm afraid there's no mistake, Mr. Soap, I only wish that there was. Please understand that it is vital that we conduct further tests this very instant, as time is of the essence as far as cancer is concerned," Dr. Philips said plainly.

"Stop saying that, stop saying that word!" Audrey cried.

I embraced Audrey, I embraced her like never before and in between the numerous drawn-out pauses that came to litter the conversation, we discussed the options that were available to us as we tried to find the best course of action for moving forward.

It was during this discussion that Audrey and I started our fightback, and if cancer wanted a battle then it had found for itself two people who were determined to stare it in the eye, slap its belligerent face and kick its arse back through the gates of hell.

"What do we need to do to beat this, Doctor? And beat it we will!" I said with intent.

Dr. Philips again emphasised the importance of additional testing before talking us through, in some detail, the various stages of the illness. His descriptions of the first three stages failed to allay our fears and indeed, harsh words such as "aggressive" and "intrusive" served only to heighten our despondency. So much so, that I was forced to cut him short when it became more than apparent where the latter stages were heading.

"Mrs. Soap, are you willing to have the tests carried out here today?" Dr. Philips asked with a gentleness that Audrey and I both appreciated.

"I am, Doctor, of course I am," Audrey replied.

Clearly approving of her decision, the doctor's attention then turned to me and he suggested, in no uncertain terms, that I wait outside while the tests were being carried out.

"I'm going nowhere, Doctor," I said, matter-of-factly.

"Mr. Soap, it would be most irregular for a husband to be present for such an examination," Dr. Philips stated.

Sensing rising tension, or at worst my imminent departure, Audrey suddenly spun around in her chair and grabbed my hand tightly for support.

"Stay with me, Joseph, please," Audrey asked me, as our eyes met.

"Mr. and Mrs. Soap, I must stress that it would be highly inappropriate. It is convention I'm afraid," Dr. Philips informed.

There I was, with my life coming apart at the seams, and as well as watching Audrey weep at the most devastating news she or I had ever received, I was now being told that society's unofficial rule book was to force me to leave my wife's side, at a time when she needed me most.

"Convention can go and shite, Doctor. I'm staying put!" I said, turning the air a light shade of blue.

Stubbornly, I remained in the room while the slightly perturbed doctor carried out his tests and I stood silently by

Audrey's side throughout just holding her hand and occasionally moving her hair away from her eyes. I tried to maintain
a calm facade to show Audrey that everything was going to
be okay, but behind my show of apparent strength lay a man
petrified to his core.

With the tests completed, Dr. Philips informed us that
chemotherapy may be needed, and having lowered his voice
sufficiently, he went on to reaffirm in even greater detail the
gravity of our situation.

"Mr. and Mrs. Soap, I owe it to you both to be as frank as I
possibly can and I feel it is crucial that you understand exactly
what is happening. With all cancers, early detection is vital and
at this stage we simply don't know how far it may have spread.
I only pray that we have caught it in time and that it can be
contained. We must stay positive," Dr. Philips said.

"And if it has spread?" Audrey asked softly.

"One step at a time, Mrs. Soap, one step at a time," the
doctor replied.

Moments later, Audrey and I left the doctor's office and
as we did so, we walked out into a different world. We now
inhabited a world that was not without limits, a world that no
longer stretched into infinity and a world that contained evil
strong enough to tear us apart. For the first time in our lives
we were faced with the prospect of our own mortality and the
fact that 'old before young', while probable, was certainly not
a copper-fastened rule. Audrey was scared, I was scared and
we embraced as we wept for each other's troubles.

Back in the van, Audrey and I both agreed that it was best not to concern the children or indeed her parents at such an early stage of her illness and later on, when collecting Jonathan and Patricia from the Healys, we sported painted smiles.

That night, when sleep understandably eluded us, Audrey and I lay silently in bed and neither of us dared to move an inch for fear of ruining the other's chance of finding rest. As my mind raced, I knew that if I possibly could, I would have taken Audrey's cancer for myself, and if it meant relieving her of a single moment's pain and worry, I would have done so gladly. Of course, those were fanciful thoughts, unrealistic dreams while wide-awake, and in the harsh throes of reality, I was faced with the unthinkable: the frightening possibility of losing my wife, my Audrey.

That one fear continued to grip me and it clung on relentlessly throughout a night of endless worry. The darkness at least gave me time to think without distraction and it helped reaffirm what I already knew to be true, which was that I needed to be strong for Audrey, no matter what. With each passing hour, I became more and more determined and I promised myself that come daybreak, I would face the battle head-on, in wild defence of my wife. I would rise even earlier than usual, to attend to any household chores that usually required my wife's hand, and I would do so to ensure that she could conserve the energy she would undoubtedly need in her own much more perilous fight.

As the sunlight began to peek through the tops of the curtains, I eased myself gently from the little sleep I had somehow managed to find and I endeavoured to silently prise myself from the bed, so as not to disturb the sleeping beauty who lay next to me. Having placed my feet quietly on to the floor, I turned around to check that I hadn't roused Audrey but my tired eyes were greeted only by the sight of an empty pillow. I yawned out loud amid confusion, before tentatively creeping across the hall and into the kitchen, where I found Audrey up and about, hurriedly attending to some porridge oats.

"What are you doing up at this time, pet?" I asked in astonishment.

"The show must go on, Joseph. And besides, this porridge won't make itself now, will it?" Audrey said, in a determined tone.

My wife's resolve made it clear that during the sleepless night gone by, she too had come to her own conclusion as to how best to approach this devastating illness and it became obvious to all who later bore witness that she had decided to fight it tooth and nail.

Young Conor, my wife was made of strong stuff, stronger stuff than I was, that was for sure, and as I readied myself to be at her side during her fight, I knew that I would have to quicken my step in order to keep pace with her. Audrey was charging forward into battle with the passion, determination and single bloody-mindedness of an Irish woman on a mission and although I thought it impossible to love her any more than I already did, my heart grew ever fonder for a lady who was nothing less than an inspiration.

CHAPTER 25

BATTLING

IN THE DAYS THAT FOLLOWED OUR crippling news, Audrey and I somehow managed to carry on with our lives as though neither of our hearts had skipped a beat and we steadfastly upheld our pact not to inform the children of their mother's illness. And knowing that tears can always wait to be cried, we further agreed that there was little point in raking up yet more upset, when we had more than enough of our own to cope with as it was.

Although our efforts at protecting Jonathan and Patricia had added an extra layer of complexity to our situation, Audrey and I both felt strongly the need to put on a brave face, despite the fact that we ourselves were cowering behind an invisible shield which we held aloft to protect us. We were scared, scared for the present as much as the future, but we knew that our feelings would pale into insignificance when compared to the fear and anguish that the children would experience at the very thought of losing their mother.

The summer holidays had freed Jonathan from his schooling servitude and when he wasn't up to mischief with his pals, he was of great help to me on the shop floor. Whilst Patricia, who often felt torn from school during its extended breaks, would shadow Audrey in the hope of learning the little tips that are generationally passed down from mother to daughter.

Audrey, of course, continued her role as master of all trades by attending to bookkeeping, household chores and the never-ending task of looking after our family. Following the completion of each task, I had, however, begun to notice that she would do the previously unthinkable; in so much as she would now sit down for a short break in order to draw breath. Alert to her troubles, I would brew a nice cup of tea and leaving her in little doubt that she was loved like no other, I would garnish it with a biscuit and a peck on the cheek for morale.

During quiet moments, Audrey and I would ponder just what was happening to us. After all, her illness had come as a complete shock to us both, not least because she hadn't felt unwell prior to her initial appointment with Dr. Kelleher. She had, on occasion, mentioned experiencing the odd abdominal discomfort, albeit in a dismissive way, and unconcerned she went about her business as before, chalking it down to 'women's troubles'.

God love the pair of us, but we later laughed through tears on recalling a day when Audrey complained about having a bloated stomach and I replied by telling her that she was "still lovely to me".

We both really tried to put her condition to the back of our minds but no matter how hard the attempt, we failed miserably. It consumed our minds, our hearts and the very foundations upon which our little family resided.

The day finally came around for Audrey to return to see Dr. Philips and as was routine, we included him in our prayers that morning before setting off. We were due to receive the test results following Audrey's examination and fear gripped us tightly as we drove to face our future. Dr. Philips had warned that chemotherapy may be required and the very thought of my wife having to face such a gruelling course of treatment was enough to panic the angels.

With the doctor's foreboding words still ringing in our ears, Audrey and I pulled anxiously through the hospital gates. On arrival into reception, we were ushered into Dr. Philips' office and his grim expression made his words redundant.

"Mrs. Soap, Mr. Soap, I am afraid I have some sombre news for you both and I will spare you any unnecessary small talk. The tests reveal that the cancer has spread to both ovaries and it is also present in your lymph nodes. It appears to be at a fairly advanced stage and I recommend treatment as a matter of some urgency," Dr. Philips informed, leaving us in little doubt.

Audrey and I remained silent with little if any expression adorning our faces, while inside our heart rates quickened by the second. Dr. Philips appeared almost puzzled by our seemingly calm exteriors and in turn he too fell silent as words temporarily eluded him.

In truth, the doctor's diagnosis had come as little or no shock to Audrey and me as by the very nature of human beings, we had already exhausted every possible outcome with worry. Following the initial findings, we had both managed to make peace with the fact that this disease was not going to go away without a fight and we had subconsciously prepared ourselves to battle our opponent, from whichever angle it attacked us. Remarkably, we found a strange level of acceptance in this and although the cancer left little grounds for optimism, we defiantly grew ever closer because of it.

"Right, Doctor, what do we need to do? Chemotherapy, is it?" Audrey asked, brave as a lion, fracturing the haunting silence.

"Mrs. Soap, as I said, your condition is at an advanced stage so I am recommending surgery to remove and hopefully contain the cancer. Chemotherapy may well reduce the size of the tumours, but that is of irrelevance at this point. Surgery will involve the removal of both ovaries, as well as any other contaminated tissue we find. Mrs. Soap, I must also inform you that by removing both ovaries, you must understand that, for sure, your childbearing days will be no longer," Dr. Philips said almost apologetically.

"Surgery it is then, Doctor. Can you please tell me the most suitable date, as we'll have to make arrangements for our shop?" Audrey said casually, as though making a luncheon appointment.

"I will schedule you in at the first available opportunity, Mrs. Soap. I can assure you of that. I know this must come as an awful shock to you both but I must stress the importance of trying to stay positive," Dr. Philips said.

Seizing the opportunity to speak, I moistened my lips, which were dry from idleness, and I told the doctor that, "If positivity is important, then positivity will get every chance to succeed". And having collectively discussed the matter further, we thanked the doctor before heading for home.

In bed that night, Audrey and I were left to discuss this most harrowing turn of events and we embraced each other tenderly while doing so. There, our earlier declaration of positivity proved to be short-lived and we allowed ourselves the opportunity to cry for our plight. We held onto each other tightly, determined never to let go, and into the night sky we again let loose our hopes and fears for both present and future.

"Joseph, it's all gone wrong. Everything has gone wrong," Audrey said with her head resting on my chest.

"Everything will be OK, you just see if it isn't," I tried to reassure.

"But we only wanted to add to our family, Joseph," Audrey sobbed.

"The doctor said that our trying for a baby and your illness are in no way connected and if anything, your desire to create a life may well prove to be the reason that you save your own. Something, somewhere, led you to discovering your condition and maybe it is God who showed you the way. Maybe he has blessed our family that way, instead of adding to it," I said in a near whisper.

"The Lord will help us through this won't he, Joseph?" Audrey asked.

"Of course he will, pet, he'll see us right," I replied.

Audrey and I were left to contemplate how life can totally change without warning, almost on the flip of a coin, and having gone from praying for the creation of a new life, we now found our prayers laden with pleas for the continuation of an existing one. It's funny how events beyond your control can alter your outlook on life and leave you praying inexplicably for something which you almost take for granted; your health.

The next day went by like all those before it and the shop went about its usual business. Our daily tasks were carried out as if on autopilot and we were grateful that we at least had familiarity to thank for not causing us further quandary.

When six o'clock came, I closed the shop's front door and I made my way upstairs to join the rest of the family who had gathered around the kitchen table for dinner. Conversation was pleasant, if a little strained, and Audrey and I exchanged brief looks across the table, by way of offering each other the strength to push on through the remainder of the day.

Midway through our meal, the chit-chat quietened somewhat, but soon the children revealed a hidden agenda of their own.

"Mammy, why were you crying last night?" Patricia asked, with concern across her face.

"I was crying because I banged my toe on the bed frame Patricia, now eat your dinner up, please," Audrey said, in a hurried tone.

"But Da was crying too," Jonathan interjected.

"Your father banged his toe as well, Jonathan, now less of that talk," Audrey snapped, before pausing for reflective thought.

Audrey and I again looked to one another, however, this time we were not seeking strength, rather we were looking for approval to break our children's hearts. Having previously agreed on keeping the news of Audrey's illness to ourselves, perhaps now the time had come for us to put Jonathan and Patricia in the picture.

When my eyes met with Audrey's, she slowly nodded her head.

"Jonathan, Patricia, your mother and I have something very important we need to speak to you about. Now, we don't want you to worry because everything is going to be fine. We just need to stick together on this, OK?" I said, as I struggled for the right words.

"What's wrong, Daddy, have we done something bad?" Patricia asked, with words tinged with worry.

"No, of course not," I replied.

As best I could, I explained to both Patricia and Jonathan that their mother was feeling quite poorly and that she had to go to the hospital so that the doctor could make her better.

A look of concern immediately washed over their faces and, as only a mother can, Audrey reached out to both of them and instantly tried to make their fear her own. Slowly and calmly, she tried to explain a situation, which to be fair, both she and I were at a loss to understand ourselves.

The children quickly grasped the seriousness of what was being said and without prompt they rose from their seats and embraced their mother. Surprisingly, Patricia then started to tidy up the spent dishes. Jonathan, too, got in on the act and offered to cut us a slice of Madeira cake, which he said he had seen in the back of the cupboard. Audrey feigned surprise at its presence, even though it was she who had housed it there three days previously, but we soon graciously accepted two coarsely hacked slices.

Jonathan and Patricia were brilliant throughout and their reaction to the most trying of news was simply a privilege to witness and it roused such a sense of pride within Audrey and me. If they were to cry, they bravely did so in private and they selflessly placed their mother's needs well above those of their own. They were two little stars.

The fateful day of the operation came around a lot quicker than expected, as no doubt the severity of the illness had cut its way through the usual miles of waiting lists. I must admit that the previous night I prayed harder than I had ever done before and the anguish in my words left me begging the Lord to show my wife mercy.

Audrey and I went to the hospital alone that day after I had explained to the children, while dropping them off at the Healys', that their mother would be fine and that her hospital visit was all part of her getting better. I even half-convinced myself that everything really was as simple as that but the other half of my mind rang with alarm bells. The fear I had of losing Audrey was almost overwhelming but I stayed focused on the task at hand, which was to do all I possibly could for her.

Audrey was placed on a ward that was shared with three other ladies. Two of those ladies looked very poorly indeed, while oddly enough the other lady looked to be the picture of health. Audrey and I chatted quietly away to one another and while holding my hand, she shared with me her deepest fears, which I must say, were understandable given the circumstances.

"Joseph, I'm scared. I'm really scared," Audrey said.

"You're in the best possible place, love, and you'll be right as rain when this is all over. Try not to worry yourself," I said while stroking the back her hand.

"What if the operation doesn't work, Joseph? What if it hasn't been caught in time and it has spread further? What if it's too late?" Audrey asked, as panic came to the fore.

"It will work. We're not too late, and besides it is never too late for anything. You must believe, pet, you must believe that everything will be OK. If not in me, have faith in God," I said by way of reassurance.

"I'm trying Joseph, I really am. I'm trying to stay positive like the doctor said, but it's hard," Audrey explained.

"I know it is but you're doing brilliantly. Just try and stay positive and you won't go far wrong," I said before kissing her on the forehead.

Moments later, two female members of staff arrived in and I was practically shooed outside while Audrey was prepared for her procedure. A short time later, as she passed by me on the corridor, I stopped the trolley she nervously lay upon and I kissed her gently on the cheek before whispering softly that I loved her with all my heart. There was never a truer word spoken. Before disappearing down the end of the long corridor, Audrey told me that she loved me too and, in the blink of a tear-filled eye, I was then left to fret and hopelessly pace the floor for hours on end.

Later, whilst back on the ward and curled up on a chair beside Audrey's belongings, I somehow managed to nod off for a good hour or so, only to be woken by a cup of tea being placed in front of me by a kind nurse. The nurse, a smiley lady in her early fifties, informed me that Audrey was on her way back from the operating theatre and that she should be along in no time. I excitedly drank the tea in an effort to dismiss any cobwebs that lay prominent and I sat bolt upright, eagerly awaiting my wife's arrival like a needy pup awaiting its master.

When Audrey appeared, my heart sank and sang all at the same time. She looked so fragile and small in the middle of the bed and although she was unconscious, the relief I felt just to see her was beyond measure. I hurriedly cleared a pathway so that the trolley could be repositioned against the wall and as they did so, I thanked the orderlies for the gentleness they showed.

Before too long, Dr. Philips appeared and he informed me that the operation had been a success and that the cancer had been removed. Naturally, I was thrilled beyond words at this news and I shook his hand with great gusto, while at the same time thanking him profusely. Brushing aside such sentiment, he said that he would speak with both Audrey and me tomorrow when she had regained consciousness and before going on his way, he considerately wished me a good evening ahead.

I sat on guard for what remained of the night and I held Audrey's hand throughout as I spoke to her about anything that came to mind. My words, of course, went without reply but I just hoped that they reached her and provided her with some comfort during her time of great need.

When Audrey stirred briefly early the next morning, she was greeted by the sight of me smiling back at her and again to no response, I gently kissed her and I told her that she had done brilliantly. Then, as tenderly as I could, I held her hand as she fell back into rest. Three hours or so later, Audrey had woken fully and we spoke without topic for the best part of an hour.

Shortly before lunch, Dr. Philips arrived back in on his rounds and he greeted us warmly before pulling the curtain around Audrey's bed, cocooning us away from the rest of the world. This time addressing Audrey, he again explained that the operation had been a success, with both ovaries and the other affected tissues removed without complication.

Sensing our relief, he prudently reminded us that Audrey was by no means out of the woods, as with cancer there is always the risk of it returning even more severely in some cases. Bringing us down to earth with a thud, Dr. Philips then pointed out that another exploratory operation would be needed in due course, one which would determine if the cancer had come back or indeed, if it had spread to other parts of her body. He explained that Audrey would need six to eight weeks of recovery before we could even think of a second operation, adding that her first week of recuperation was to be spent in the hospital, where he could keep a close eye on her. As the doctor bid his goodbyes and walked to the door, Audrey and I both thanked him sincerely for his efforts and once alone, we then tried to banish our worries to another day.

During her week convalescing in hospital, Audrey received as many visitors as her strength allowed, with Jonathan and Patricia as well as the Healys, in through the door each day. And when she was finally deemed fit enough to return home, her friends and family ensured that she was greeted as though she were the Queen of All Ireland. Which was fitting, as that was how I had always viewed her.

With Audrey recuperating and under strict orders to put her feet up, Jonathan, Patricia and I did our very best to keep our business and home ticking over but in times of need, I was privileged to be able to call upon the help of a dear old friend.

Fully abreast of our family's situation, Donal, now a fitter at a local plant, had kindly offered to help us out in the shop and in between his energy-sapping night shifts, he would yawn his way through a couple of hours, whenever required. He was a true friend and like the very best of friends he provided help when it was needed most. Over the years and in a large part due to my shop duties, I had not always been as good a friend to Donal as he had been to me, yet nonetheless we had managed to stay close. And therein lies the power of friendship, I suppose.

Peter, our other great partner in crime, was like my brothers, limited to offering support via post during this time but it was still always greatly appreciated when it came. Years earlier, a discovered love of all things fitness-related had led him to join the Irish Army and a subsequent posting to the border region had caused our paths to divide. As a result, his presence in Stepaside became something of a rarity but we remained in touch throughout. Regardless of circumstance, when you make a connection with someone it becomes a resilient thing, a bond not easily broken, and a true friend is someone to cherish whether near or far.

Somehow we all managed to muddle through that terrible time and, bit by bit, Audrey began to regain her strength. Through collective effort, the shop itself even managed to avoid going the way of the dinosaurs and together we cemented a unity that not only reinforced our family walls, but coated them in protective steel.

Eight weeks later and following a check-up with Dr. Philips, Audrey was considered well enough to undergo the exploratory surgery and arrangements were soon put in place. We were reassuringly told that this procedure would be less taxing than before but like all serious operations, we were reminded that it came with its own set of risks. Despite our obvious fears, Audrey and I both knew that this operation was vital, as it was imperative that we establish the full extent of her situation.

As before, Audrey and I went to the hospital alone and the procedure was carried out with the goodwill of Stepaside still ringing in her ears. Our daily prayers, as you would imagine, included all of our life's blessings and woes, but a special place was found for all those who showed love and support by sending flowers, cards and best wishes.

The procedure thankfully took less time than before and the waiting game for answers commenced the second that Audrey was wheeled safely back onto the ward. A dutiful nurse then informed me that the operation had been completed and that Dr. Philips planned on speaking with us early the next day, by which time Audrey would have had sufficient time to come to. Taking my eyes ever so briefly off Audrey, I thanked the nurse for her time and efforts and I then settled in for the night, curled up on a chair, which, like myself, had seen a better day.

The unnatural setting of a hospital ward is no place for a married couple to spend a night and while functional, it lacks the warmth, privacy and familiarity of one's own bedroom. Knowing my wife's thoughts on the matter, I longed to be able to take her home to where she felt most comfortable but through utter misfortune that hospital bed was now the best place in the world for her to be.

A night of twists and turns was spent beside Audrey's bed but I was only too pleased to be by her side as I drew all the comfort I needed from watching her sleep. My eyes rested only while speaking to the Lord and through spiritual conversation,

I'm pleased to say that the clock seemed to tick a little faster than it should have.

Mine was the first face Audrey saw when she eventually stirred and if my expression in any way matched the joy I felt at seeing her awake, she would have seen a man with the look of an excitable child at the foot of a rollercoaster. Audrey slowly gestured her hand to wave me in closer, to which I rose to my feet and kissed her. After a moment or two's whispered chat, I tentatively mentioned that Dr. Philips would be along in a little while, but only if she was up to seeing him. Unsurprisingly, Audrey said that she would make it her business.

Audrey and I then prayed out loud together for the first time in our lives and we paused only through disbelief, when a passing nurse and patient stopped to bless themselves to our impromptu service. I had always considered a person's prayers to be the most private thing in the world, but seeing as we were now both praying for the same thing, I really didn't think it mattered all that much.

Dr. Philips came to see us shortly after lunchtime and with one fluid swish of the taupe curtain that hung to the side of the bed, he was able to fashion a cloth wall between us and the rest of the ward. As we had come to expect from him, he cut right to the chase and in doing so, he broke our hearts beyond repair.

"Mrs. Soap, it is with the greatest possible regret that I must tell you that your condition is more serious than previously thought. I'm sorry to say that the cancer is at a most highly advanced stage, a stage four in fact, and not only has it returned to some previously affected areas, it has now also spread elsewhere in your body," Dr. Philips said crushingly.

"Oh, Joseph," Audrey said, grabbing my hand.

Dr. Philips paused to allow Audrey and me to gather our thoughts, before going into further detail on the rapid spread of the cancer. We both listened intently, or at least as best we could and while doing so I found my eyes drawn onto his mouth, in the hope of getting an early glimpse of an optimistic or encouraging word. None of which passed his lips.

"Mrs. Soap, the cancer has spread to your lungs and to the inside of your liver, while the surrounding tissue from the initial operation also shows a presence of cancerous cells. The awful truth of the matter is that a further operation to remove these growths is out of the question, as too much damage would be inflicted, and the organs simply couldn't cope with such trauma. Were the cancer to be on the outside of the liver, there may have been some hope of removal, but as it is on the inside we must look at an alternative course of action and hope it has an effect," Dr. Philips said in clear detail.

"Hope it has an effect? What is the alternative course of action, Doctor?" Audrey managed to ask.

"Chemotherapy, Mrs. Soap. There is a possibility that it may shrink the tumours and at the very least it could offer you some more time," Dr. Philips said.

"More time? How long, Doctor?" Audrey cried, as she sank deeper and deeper into the mattress.

"Pending treatment, it's impossible to say, Mrs. Soap," Dr. Philips replied.

"So there is just a 'possibility' the treatment may work?" Audrey asked.

"I'm afraid so, Mrs. Soap. And a small possibility at that," Dr. Philips said earnestly.

Standing, observing what was the most frightening and distressing horror show imaginable, I simply couldn't believe what I was hearing – 'a possibility?'

My mind was spinning out of control as I searched for a solution to an unsolvable problem, and not for the first time, I was struck silent by the bravery and dignity shown by my wife. Suddenly, a question popped into my head but almost immediately, I was too frightened to ask it. I was frightened of the reply it may get but knowing its importance, I forced my own hand.

"Doctor, what if the chemotherapy doesn't work? If it's ineffective, do we keep trying?" I asked, before bracing myself for the response.

"I'm afraid that were the cancer to remain unresponsive to the initial rounds of chemotherapy, further treatment would be little more than a throw of a die. We could of course proceed, but should the cancer once again remain unresponsive, I would be forced to tell you that there was nothing more we can do. Our next step, Mrs. Soap, would be to make you as comfortable as possible. I'm sorry for being so blunt, I truly am, but that is where we stand I'm afraid," Dr. Philips informed us both.

Audrey and I remained silent.

"There is one very important thing you must remember, Mr. and Mrs. Soap. Chemotherapy is a harsh treatment. Often patients are left feeling that the negative side effects outweigh the positives and for some, most in fact, the treatment can be most unpleasant," Dr. Philips explained, again holding no punches.

Audrey and I looked at one another and I could sense that we both felt as though we had somehow let the other down. Nothing, of course, could have been further from the truth but at that moment we both realised that we had arrived at a place where neither of us had ever intended to go. And through no fault of our own, we were now at a loss to understand how a marriage of such promise could end up caked in such misery.

Dr. Philips endeavoured to continue on his rounds, or perhaps he just wanted to give us some space and the opportunity to come to terms with what he had just told us, but Audrey wasn't finished with him yet.

"Doctor, I want you to arrange for the chemotherapy to start as soon as possible. I have obviously no time to be sitting around idle, so we shall act immediately," Audrey said plainly.

"Of course, Mrs. Soap, anything you say," Dr. Philips replied without hesitation, before nodding his head in solidarity and turning on his heels.

For a second or two, Audrey and I remained stunned behind the bed curtain and in lieu of words, I cradled her up in my arms and kissed her gently on the temple. I could feel her shake slightly as I prised my lips from her skin, while my concerned eyes soon saw tears rush down her face. The toughness of moments before had quickly faded and Audrey now found herself alone with the one person on earth with whom she did not need to put on a brave face.

I loved my wife for exactly who she was and whether radiant in happiness or lost in sorrow, she was perfect to me. On our wedding day, I had promised to love her "in sickness and in health" and with God now seemingly testing my vow, I became more determined than ever to stay true to my word.

Still holding Audrey in my arms I looked up to the heavens, and right there and then, I dared God to even try and take her from me.

CHAPTER 26

BORROWING TIME

WITH AUDREY'S CANCER AT SUCH AN advanced stage, an aggressive course of action was prescribed from the outset and less then seventy-two hours after leaving the hospital, we returned for the commencement of chemotherapy. Sessions were scheduled to take place on a two-week cycle, as opposed to the preferred three-week cycle often used in milder cases.

Audrey was to receive three hours of therapy each day, for three days straight, followed by what was sure to be a welcome rest period of two weeks and once recuperated, the gruelling cycle would start all over again. It was a vicious circle in the truest sense and in a world devoid of other angles left to explore, Audrey and I found comfort within each other's arms. From day one, I accompanied her to each session and we would sit and chat our way through the whole horrible experience, something which had become a hallmark for us making the best of a bad situation.

The treatment room itself was something of a blank canvas, with little or no imagination shown when choosing the colour of its off-white walls and if its aim was to avoid distraction from the matter at hand, it achieved its goal tenfold. I would sit on a chair beside Audrey and watch in awe as she remained dignified and unfazed, despite the fact that she was surrounded by all manner of bleeping gizmos and space-age contraptions.

Audrey seemed more comfortable than I was at the presence of a tube running from a bag of gunk into her slender arm, although I grew to appreciate it, when I realised that it was very much on our side in my wife's fight.

For each of the three days we were marooned in the hospital, we would try to keep our spirits as high as we possibly could and given the situation, we felt that it was imperative to seek light amid such darkness. Conversation amongst the other patients and their companions was often lively and I always made sure to seize upon the energy from those early moments before the medication tightened its grip.

I recall an impromptu sing-along to the Frank Sinatra number 'Come Fly With Me', which we had early one morning before the ill effects became apparent. It was a lovely moment to share with complete strangers but regrettably a rather stern-looking nurse had other ideas and she brought the joyous sing-song crashing to an end, caring not a jot for the morale of the patients under her charge. Perhaps she saw singing as an unwelcome waste of energy, or maybe it was hospital policy to keep noise levels to a minimum but whatever her reasoning, I thought it short-sighted. If a tiny fleck of happiness can be found during the direst of circumstances, then the very least of her chores should have been to join in mid-verse and lend support to a much-needed distraction.

This nurse, however, showed what I must say was an unusual lack of compassion in her field, when without explanation, she swooped in on her broomstick and switched off the wireless that sat innocently upon a sideboard, condemning our little sing-along to memory. Clearly wishing to fly solo, as opposed to with Frank and the rest of our gang, the surly nurse then left the room, amid an air of officialdom. Silence then briefly ensued among the chastened few but I was not for defeat.

"I do a lovely Elvis. Shall I sing us a song, Audrey? Sure I don't need a radio," I offered, in an attempt to humour her.

"No, Joseph. Things are bad enough already, without you singing and making it worse," Audrey said truthfully, but with a faint twinkle of mischief in her eye.

In life, sometimes you just need to smile and if ever a smile was needed, it was during those distressing periods. We collectively settled back down into quiet chat and as liquid hope flowed through the veins of those so desperately in need of a change of fortune, I watched as the zest in the room wilted before my eyes.

When the sessions became somewhat more subdued, limited conversation was used as a further tool of distraction and encouraging head nods were exchanged across the room, as each patient fought their own individual battle. Surprisingly, for a room filled with so much heartache, there was a warming sense of camaraderie and witnessing it was more than enough to restore one's faith in humanity, were such a thing ever needed.

The course of treatment rolled perilously on and following completion of the second cycle (and before the third got underway) Dr. Philips asked Audrey to return in two weeks' time for a scan which would hopefully show that the cancer was reacting to the therapy. Refusing to demand miracles from him, Audrey and I both noted with caution that the doctor was as quick to remind us "not to get your hopes up", as he was to tell us to "stay positive".

At home the side effects of the chemotherapy, although not immediate, came, as we knew they inevitably would, and Audrey was struck with a lack of appetite and a near intolerance to food, which was most out of character for her. Although slight and with a good figure, Audrey had always loved her food and it was perhaps this simple change of events that really brought our chickens home to roost. Hearty meals were replaced by tiny morsels and before long, even those proved to be a struggle for her.

With a lack of proper sustenance, Audrey's energy levels dipped at an alarming rate and the fatigue that came as a consequence, forced us to revaluate any initial positivity we may have held. I gradually began to notice that Audrey took just that little bit longer to scale the stairs each time, while naps become all the more frequent and even the dazzling shimmer in her eyes worryingly dimmed, to the point where they almost lost perfection. But we stayed strong.

It was around this time that Jonathan again approached us and laid bare his desire to leave school once more. By way of appeasement, Audrey and I had previously agreed to reconsider earlier refusals and young Jonathan, clearly waiting in the long grass, had now decided to ambush us with yet another push for academic freedom. As parents, Audrey and I had already discussed this very issue at length and now and in spite of our best beliefs, we eventually decided to trust our boy's judgement. Jonathan, in all truth, had become vital to the running of the shop and with no end in sight for his mother's struggle, his would be a welcome pair of hands, on a full-time basis.

Audrey quite rightly pointed out that Jonathan's stubbornness showed traits of his father and at sixteen years of age, he joined the ranks of the employed. And in fairness to the lad, he has worked hard ever since.

During this period, getting either of the children to leave the house at all had become an almost daily chore, as the family's needs took priority in their lives and both Jonathan and Patricia were at pains to never leave their mother's side.

Patricia used the opportunity of the school holidays to take on her mother's role in the family and she did all she possibly could to carry the burden while her mother struggled with illness. All of Patricia's stoic efforts were greatly appreciated by Audrey and me and really helped to keep the house spick and span and on occasion, she even prepared some delicious family meals for us, albeit with the aid of her mother's tried-and-tested recipes.

Jonathan and Patricia's friends would still come calling to our door but requests for their time now fell upon deaf ears, as they both opted to remain inside in order to help their mammy in any way they could. Their pals seemed to understand and while I'm sure that it wasn't easy for all concerned, each would have done exactly the same if placed in a similar situation.

Before the next three days of treatment were due to commence, Audrey reported back to the hospital for an assessment with Dr. Philips, with the view of establishing how the cancer was reacting to the treatment. We had, of course, both hoped for good news but once again devastation came our way, as the examination showed that not only had the cancer failed to reduce in size, it had actually spread further around her body.

"Mrs. Soap, I'm afraid I must tell you that the chemotherapy is not having the desired effect and in hope of improvement, I recommend that we alter the administered drugs and begin a fresh cycle. I know it's not the news you both wanted to hear but that is where we stand at the minute," Dr. Philips said clinically.

Audrey and I, both lost for words, nodded silently in agreement and as our world came apart at the seams, we shed a tear for the innocent young couple we once were.

Two days later, when the time came for Audrey to receive the next phase of treatment, she and I faced the challenge as always before, united as one, and while our hopes for a positive outcome remained unchanged, it seemed as though grounds for optimism were fading elsewhere.

On entering the treatment room that morning, I was immediately taken aback by the sight of the other patients, two of whom I recognised from previous sessions. Good people, the best of people, now appeared to be almost worn down and weakened beyond repair and they had visibly declined to an extent that alarmed me. I tried to brush aside my anguish for their suffering by offering a pleasant 'hello', but I couldn't help but think that my eyes gave away my deep sympathy.

I began to wonder if they viewed Audrey in the same light and I prayed that the effects of her illness had not crept up on me and that the familiarity of seeing her every day had not clouded my judgement when assessing her frailty.

The treatment that day played out exactly as the previous ones gone by and with gritted teeth, we saw it through before returning to Stepaside. At home, I helped Audrey up the stairs and I tried not to cry as my arm wrapped around her frame, which felt as fragile as glass. When we reached the bedroom, I gently sat her down on the bed and once suitably comfortable, I popped to the kitchen to fetch her some tea.

When I returned to the room my heart wept.

Audrey was sitting up on the edge of the bed with her hairbrush in one hand and fine strands of brown hair in the other. When I left her side moments earlier, she had wanted to straighten herself up following her return from the hospital and, as was often the case, her trusty hairbrush was put to task.

This time, unlike every time before, the bristles cruelly lifted the all-too-delicate hairs from Audrey's scalp and each one, once removed, made her look all the more vulnerable and exposed. Our eyes met and I began to cry.

"None of that blubbing now, Joseph, we knew this day would come," Audrey said, as she continued to comb at her beautiful brown hair, while occasionally gathering up all that clung to the bristles. Brave as she was being I could still see tears trying to escape from her eyes, but stoically and quite wonderfully, she managed to hold firm.

That night I asked God, begged him, yet again to end my wife's suffering and rid her of that terrible disease. Yet once more, my words fell upon deaf ears, or perhaps they just disappeared into nothing at all.

Back in the treatment room, the next two days seemed to drag like never before as desperate people laboured through a desperate situation. I, along with the companions of the other patients, watched as those brave souls fought for their lives and I am ashamed to say that I too felt as though a toll was being taken on me. I really felt worn down by it all, drained even, and the sight of constant hardship shamefully led me to believe that I was as much a victim as my wife.

When Audrey's eyes closed to rest, as they now frequently did, I would ease from my chair and excuse myself to all those present. Having made the short walk down the hospital's corridor, I would shed a tear or two in the privacy of a bathroom cubicle. When all cried out, I would straighten myself up as best I could and return timidly to my wife's side, more mouse than man. I know that I really let myself down in those moments and I hated myself for showing such weakness in the shadow of my wife's strength.

With the three days of treatment over, we again faced into another torturous waiting period, as Dr. Philips had informed us that Audrey should return in two weeks' time for another assessment. It proved to be as testing a time as any I have known and our little family strained but somehow didn't buckle, as my wife's illness held onto her and attempted to wring the very life out of her.

Whilst Audrey was recuperating at home and tucked up safely in bed, I would sit guard over her like a dutiful night-watchman, all the time, painfully observing how the little sleep she managed to get was frequently disturbed by bouts of vomiting and terrible sweats. Indeed, such was her struggle that every moment's rest was viewed by me as though it were a win on the pools.

Despite all that was going on around them, Jonathan and Patricia were real troopers, however, on occasion and when needed, we found time for heart-to-heart discussions, during which many a tear was cried as we attempted to make sense of what was happening to our family. I often wondered how the children continued to function in the way that they did but I put it down to the fact that they were just following the courageous example being set by their mother.

As a father, I knew all too well that I was duty-bound to teach my children all that I knew to be true in life, yet during those trying times, I began to realise that they, too, could teach me in return. If two frightened teenagers and their ailing mother could stand toe-to-toe with cancer, then it was imperative that I follow their example and continue on my search for personal strength in amongst the mire.

With the passing of days, Audrey became so weak that she no longer had the strength to go outside on a whim and her body began to totally betray her long-held enthusiasm for fresh air. Each day proved challenging, yet still we continued to move forward and on reaching the day of reckoning (Audrey's latest assessment), we were both much the poorer for her struggle.

Donal was again conscripted to watch over the shop, while not without dread, Audrey and I, along with an insistent Jonathan and Patricia, headed in the direction of the hospital, where we took up residence in the waiting room.

Once called, the examination was understandably thorough and on completion Audrey returned to our side while the results were confirmed. There, as a family, we collectively prayed for continued strength as well as for God's mercy in our hour of need.

Audrey's name was called a short time later and leaving the children to peruse magazines of various interests, I accompanied her in to see Dr. Philips. Somewhat unusually, a nurse on duty escorted us to the office door and while letting us in, she explained that the doctor would be along momentarily. Audrey and I took a seat in the empty office and with our hands clasped together tightly, we nervously awaited our fate.

Almost immediately, the door opened behind us, and we turned at pace to face the doctor, who just continued to his chair and took up his seat.

"Mrs. Soap, with true regret, I have most unfortunate news," Dr. Philips said with compassion, a mere second after adjusting his position in his chair.

Audrey and I immediately closed our eyes in readiness for heartache, a heartache that duly found its way into a room where its presence was feared like no other.

"Mrs. Soap, I am afraid that the cancer has continued to spread across the affected organs and tissue. The damage is now widespread, with your liver and right lung past the point of recovery. At this rate of metastasis, I must sadly tell you, that there is no more we can do. I am so terribly sorry," Dr. Philips said, as our world came crumbling down.

"Oh God," I cried, clinging to Audrey.

"How long, Doctor?" Audrey asked, her hand trembling in mine.

"Six months, maybe less," Dr. Philips said bluntly.

Moving closer, I hugged Audrey like never before and we both wept as though we were a million miles away from the gaze of a man who had just set a ticking clock to the time we had left together.

"Surely there is more you can do, Doctor. There has to be

something. An experimental treatment, something, anything! Oh, please God," I pleaded, in desperation.

"I'm afraid not, Mr. Soap. We could put your wife through another round of chemotherapy but that may only buy her weeks, if even any time at all. You must now consider quality of life in the time your wife has left and another course of treatment will only distress her body further," said Dr. Philips.

"We'll do whatever it takes!" I said fervently.

"No, Joseph. I can't take it. I just can't take it anymore. I feel so terrible all the time and it's not fair on any of us: you, me, or the children. I've had all I can take, Joseph," Audrey said, as she moved her hand to my face to calm me.

After a moment or two, Dr. Philips spoke favourably of palliative care but I was barely even listening. He was speaking about the end while I still clung to dreams of a future. After all, our future had been written in the stars and it was one in which we would be together forever, loving and laughing with each other, for all the world to see.

How could we have only six months to live out a lifetime?

With nothing left to say, Audrey and I dejectedly left the doctor's office and linking on to one another for support, we slowly made our way towards the waiting room to gather Jonathan and Patricia. En route, we hastily decided to delay telling the children details of the prognosis, at least until we got home, as there was no way of knowing how they would cope with such news.

On the way home, Audrey and I somehow managed to hold ourselves together and having skilfully deflected the children's probing questions, we pulled up outside the shop with our secret still intact.

A tired-looking Donal greeted our arrival as we walked through the door and the measured look he gave us seemed to suggest that he understood our decision not to stop for a conversation. Having made a beeline for the adjoining door, we disappeared upstairs where we sat Jonathan and Patricia around the kitchen table and broke the terrible news.

Their poor little faces.

As a family, we attempted to deal with the consequences of the most devastating news imaginable and we did so in the only way we knew how: together. The Soap family had now come face-to-face with the devil himself and it appeared as though the Lord had forsaken us when we needed him most.

Damn him.

Over the weeks that followed, Audrey's condition continued to deteriorate further and although the palliative care she received did at least bring her some degree of comfort, it proved to be the most harrowing of times.

Audrey had bravely chosen to spend her remaining time at home and from that moment on, only close family members were granted audience. Other than myself and the children, only the Healys were permitted into the inner sanctum for our bedroom, where Audrey now resided, and each visit paid was tinged with disbelief and sadness for what was to come.

Audrey really did become so terribly frail. Her suffering made me question the very point of life at all and I wondered how a young woman, in the prime of life, could suffer such an awful and undeserving fate. Even now, all these years later, just typing the word 'fate' leads me to think about other aspects of life, namely the belief in a God above. And while spiritual faith is indeed blind, so too it seems is the 'all-seeing Lord' who so insecurely craves our worship, without ever providing proof of his existence.

The Soap and Healy families learned to struggle on as one and even though our defiance at Audrey's plight had long since been replaced with reluctant acceptance, we tried to remain strong for her. Yet still it was with heavy hearts that we conceded to losing our fight, a fight in which the odds were always stacked against us.

Audrey's light began to fade and less than three months after her final bout of chemotherapy, I knew she was not long for this world. As had always been the case, we continued to speak at night just us two and although it was I who was now doing the majority of the talking, Audrey smiled when she could and seemed content just to listen.

It was on one such night that she mustered the strength to tell me that she longed to visit the seaside one last time.

"You'll take me, Joseph, wont you?" Audrey asked, in the softest of whispers as she drifted off to sleep.

"I'd take you to the moon and back, pet, you know that," I said, with truth laced in each word.

Alone with my thoughts that night, I set about planning to make Audrey's final dream come true and the following morning, I hastily arranged a trip out to the coast. As Audrey was barely able to leave her bed, I was conscious not to place too much strain on her in terms of travelling so I chose Killiney beach as our destination as it was within easy reach of Stepaside.

Having made arrangements for the shop, I duly announced details of our trip, to Audrey's obvious delight, and soon afterwards, a small group of family and friends pooled at the doorway to wave us off.

So determined was I to get Audrey to the seaside, I was prepared to carry her there if need be. But thankfully such an indignity was spared as the hospital had provided a wheelchair as part of her palliative care, which I carefully stowed in the back of the van before setting off.

With Audrey by my side, we made the journey to Killiney and I drove at a snail's pace every inch of the way, as I was conscious of the delicate flower I was transporting. When we arrived, I helped Audrey from the passenger seat before gently placing her into the wheelchair, which I had retrieved moments earlier.

Having placed our old red gingham blanket on her lap for comfort, I slowly brought Audrey as close to the sand as I possibly could and although I couldn't see her face to tell, I could sense the tiniest tingle of exhilaration as it rushed her body.

"What do you think of that, Audrey, beautiful, eh?" I asked, while surveying the crashing waves.

"Help me get closer, Joseph, just for a minute," said Audrey, as she signalled for me to raise her from the chair.

"For you, anything," I said.

Reaching down, I gently placed my arm around Audrey, raising her ever so carefully from the chair, before then tentatively walking her over towards the water's edge, where the waves kissed the tips of her toes through her sandals. There we stood in perfect silence, save for the crashing waves, and Audrey's minute's pleasure passed all too quickly as did the couple of minutes more, which her strength somehow allowed us to savour.

"Do you know, Joseph, I think that in some way, I'll always be by the sea," said Audrey.

"You will, pet, and I'll be there with you," I replied, before kissing her temple while the waves continued to crash around us.

"That's it. That's it now, Joseph... I'm ready to go home," Audrey said quietly, before filling her lungs with the sea air one last time.

In the days that followed, Audrey's condition worsened dramatically and we eventually reached a point where we hurriedly sent for Dr. Kelleher. On his arrival, he quickly decided that Audrey's immediate family should be called to her bedside, while the decision to send for Father Fitzgibbon, was also made.

Four days on from our embrace at the beach, surrounded by people whom she loved and who loved her so very dearly in return, Audrey Soap, my wife, my love and my best friend, passed away.

We, her family, watched helplessly as the life slowly left her and it was through utter sorrow that we collectively prayed for her soul to enter the gates of heaven. While part of me was relieved that Audrey's suffering was no more, the overwhelming pain I felt ate away at my core. And if the world had opened up and beckoned me into its crevasse, I would gladly have leapt into the bowels of hell in order to escape the sorrow I felt on seeing my wife's eyes close without opening.

Later that evening, as grief gripped ever tighter, Audrey's father approached me on the landing as I returned upstairs, having just shown Father Fitzgibbon to the door. Standing nervously in front of me, Mr. Healy was not the tyrant I had known him to be, rather I was faced by a broken man whose heart had been torn in two.

"Joseph, I need to talk to you. I need to talk to someone," he said, his eyes red from crying.

"Now's not the time, Mr. Healy. I'm sorry, but I can't take any more upset," I said, as I attempted to walk by him.

"It has to be now, lad. I need to ask you something," Mr. Healy said, while forcibly taking hold of my arm.

With a weighty shrug, I freed myself from his grasp but instead of marching off and leaving the chore of a man behind, I reluctantly gave him a hearing.

"Joseph, let me take Audrey back home. It's not proper to wake someone above a shop, I'm sorry, but it just isn't right," Mr. Healy said, to my disbelieving ears.

"You bastard," I replied, staring straight into his eyes.

To my surprise, Mr. Healy began to weep uncontrollably and as he broke down into a fit of desperation, he again took hold of my arm. This time, however, felt different and I opted to remain perfectly still as he clung on to me for support, lest he fall to the ground.

"Joseph, I didn't mean anything by it, honestly I didn't. I just want what's best for Audrey. That's all I've ever wanted. You must understand that," Mr. Healy said, as his emotions overran him.

"Joseph, please, please let me take my daughter home. I just want my baby home one last time, Joseph, please," Mr. Healy said, weeping hysterically.

Mr. Healy then released his grip on my arm and I suddenly felt his trembling hands claw wildly at my lapels. He then slumped forward, as though grief had robbed his legs of their function, and I found myself cradling his full weight against my chest. I remained motionless at first, before embracing him in solidarity and for the very first time in our lives, we found common ground in the depths of sorrow and despair.

I had just lost my wife, the children their mother and as for Mr. Healy, well he had lost his little girl.

I would grant him his wish.

CHAPTER 27

GOODBYE

An Irish wake truly is a most peculiar affair, in so much as it is an occurrence as old as the hills themselves, and one which is practically unique to our little nation. Its familiar lure entices family and friends alike to gather as one, often around an open casket, and there they sit for hours on end while respects are paid to the faithful departed. On viewing the remains, grieving folk innocently comment that the deceased has never looked better in their life, that they really look like themselves or that they look as though they are only sleeping.

People sit together and reminisce about times gone by or laughs once shared and before long new stories, new laughs rise out from the darkness. There must surely be no stranger method of dealing with grief in the world and, in my own humble opinion, there is no finer way of handling it.

Staying true to my word, I bowed to Mr. Healy's wishes

and on the night before we committed Audrey to the soil, her wake was held back in her childhood home.

In truth, I saw nothing wrong with holding the wake above our shop, not least because it had been good enough to wake both of my parents (and it'll be good enough for me when my time comes), and I also surmised that Audrey herself would have quite liked to have held it there. She was, after all, a very house-proud lady and I think she would have loved to use the occasion as a means to showcase her beautiful home. But ultimately, I knew that she, more than anyone, would have honoured her father's wishes.

The Healys owned a spacious home, spacious even by today's elaborate standards, and for Audrey's wake, it was positively thronged with her extended family, old school friends and neighbours who came to pay their respects.

Mr. and Mrs. Healy welcomed Jonathan, Patricia and me, but their time plainly wasn't their own that afternoon and their attention was divided by high demand amongst fellow mourners. An orderly line of dejected-looking people passing on condolences occupied their every second and I watched as countless unfamiliar faces wept openly for the loss of my one true love.

Mr. and Mrs. Healy, together with their two daughters, stood guard over Audrey, who lay in repose in the corner of the living room and from their position of authority, they received sympathy and reassurance in equal measure, from those who had queued patiently to shake their hands.

Jonathan, Patricia and I sat at the opposite end of the room, and we watched as a never-ending precession of strangers walked in and dutifully lowered their heads. A path was almost worn into the carpet as people moved from the Healys' side to Audrey's coffin and once the appropriate blessings were bestowed, a discreet and dignified exit was made in search of tea and sandwiches.

The children and I remained disconsolate right the way through and for five hours or more we played the role of scene extras to the Healys' star turn. Several mourners did however approach us throughout but largely we went unnoticed, seemingly dismissed as just three of the many faces. Unable to circulate for fear of leaving the children alone for too long, I was left to sit and contemplate the curious situation we found ourselves in.

During that reflective time, I realised that we were living out exactly what I feared might happen and, rightly or wrongly, I felt that Jonathan, Patricia and I were being cast into the shadows, while the spotlight of sympathy and compassion illuminated only the Healys.

Audrey was, after all, only a matter of yards away from us yet it felt as though we were a million miles from her side. And even though the children and I had little to say, in truth we had no words left, we would have loved to have had the opportunity to feed off some of the goodwill that was circulating around the room.

Music, as much as chat, plays an important part on such an occasion and many a song that nobody knows is sung by a person who nobody really knows either: a song whose sole purpose is to unify spirits and rouse hope in those in dire need of it.

Audrey's wake was no different and coarsely sung music frequently filled the air as the children and I sat alone in the corner, listening without choice. There, words of little or no personal meaning invaded our minds, driving us off into our own private thoughts and with each questionable note, we grew ever more distant from the world around us.

It was only when the Healys announced that they were going into the kitchen to retrieve some sandwiches for the older people gathered that I suddenly snapped back into dreaded reality and from a distance, I watched quietly as they walked in unison from Audrey's side.

Not wishing to disturb Jonathan and Patricia, who were lost in quiet thought beside me, I decided to watch over Audrey from across the room and although on high alert, I remained anchored to my chair. From there, my view was disturbed only momentarily by passing souls and my focus lost only to faint glimpses of a time when laughter came naturally to me.

It was during one such moment that I inexplicably found myself rising to my feet as though commanded to do so from the heavens and even now, all these years later, I am convinced that it was my wife's gentle hand at play.

An older man, not a kick in the backside off sixty-five, who had been sitting opposite me for most of the evening and who I believed to be a brother-in-law of Mr. Healy, had sung over the course of the evening two songs, which had received little or no attention. Yet, with his third choice of verse he struck a chord with me in a way I cannot explain when, in a room where deep-rooted emotion was only ever one second away, he broke into an unaccompanied version of 'The Town I Loved So Well' by Phil Coulter.

Each word hit me with force and reminded me of when my life was awash with music rather than an existence in which I was hopelessly drowning in tears and sorrow. Audrey had always loved that particular song and the desire to share it with her one last time was simply too strong to ignore. Having risen to my feet, I made my way across the room to Audrey. My Audrey.

When I reached the opposite end of the room, I positioned myself next to the casket and placed my hand tenderly onto Audrey's and in a house filled with people, I somehow felt completely alone with her. I savoured each second of magic and, once again, I was privileged to experience the kind of love, in which all things are possible.

I continued to hold Audrey's hand in mine and using my free hand, I wiped away a tear as my emotions began to get the better of me. With my gaze trained on my wife's face, I listened intently to the words of the song and in my most wanting heart I could almost hear Audrey's voice, singing along in the distance.

Without prompt, Jonathan took his place by my right-hand side and he gently reached out and touched his mother's fingers through mine. Patricia then followed suit, positioning herself to my left and her gentle hand joined those of Jonathan and mine, in embracing her mother's.

The Soap family, once again, stood together as one, united in love and loss while the music that echoed all around us, spoke words we could only hope to muster.

Audrey's funeral took place the very next day and Our Lady of the Wayside was thronged with people who turned out to help ease her path to the other side. Michael and Edward, however, were unable to attend as despite her long illness, Audrey's passing had come relatively quickly in the end, leaving both of my brothers unable to make the required arrangements to come home. I will admit to missing their presence that day and during unaided times, I couldn't quite ignore the feeling that my family was getting smaller and smaller with each passing year.

In truth, I remember little else of the day and such was my heartache, I happen to think that I am quite fortunate in that regard.

Young Conor, death is a cruel and inevitable part of life and one can only hope to pass over to the next world quickly and without pain.

I continue to pray that those very clever medical people (out there trying every day) manage to find a cure for cancer, as I simply dread to think of all the misery it has caused before, during and after I encountered it so very closely with Audrey. I truly believe that they will beat it one day because I believe in people, I believe in humanity, and I simply refuse to give up on my belief that all things remain possible for those with good intentions.

I wish, more than anything, that I could go back to a time when Audrey would return my embrace and that her body was as alive as her now liberated soul. In place of her touch, I live with the burden of patience. Still, I spend my time safe in the knowledge that one day I will be reunited with her and when that moment comes, it is one which will last for all eternity.

Although, it has taken me time to make peace with the situation, it is now for that very reason that I go to bed a contented man and it is why I sleep soundly and without fear each night.

I love you Audrey.

CHAPTER 28

DOWN BUT NOT OUT

In the months that followed Audrey's death, I was left to live an almost impossible life and I felt as though I was living out an existence devoid of hope, fairness and, most cruelly of all, the love of the one person who treasured each of my imperfections. I found myself living each day with fears for the present as well as the future and any focus I had in my life had now disappeared into the heavens. I had previously lived my life as though I were a sidecar attached to one of those old motorcycles with Audrey the industrious driver that drove us forward, whereas now, I had become decoupled and I was rapidly careering downhill, destined for disaster.

I also had a burning fear of being alone for the rest of my life and having left certainty for unpredictability in one fell swoop, I now saw nothing but hardship and confusion ahead. Together, Audrey and I had our path almost set in stone and the very first golden brick in our road had been laid the instant I cast my eyes on her all those years ago. We had met, fallen in love, gotten engaged, gotten married and had children, all the things you are suppose to do. We were all set for a lifetime together, a life of love and affection played out into old age, but, like everyone else, our happiness teetered on a knife's edge.

Audrey and I had so many great plans for our future and we often spoke at length about how we would fill our days when the children were reared and the shop was out of our hands. As parents and business owners, our time was not for our choosing but we always pictured a time when each second belonged to only us. We planned to go travelling around Ireland and once we even lost the run of ourselves by briefly speaking about going abroad, on a cruise no less, but we quickly thought better of it, as we wagered that the coastline was probably the best bit of the sea anyway. So, with common sense back in play, a trip around Ireland was to be the pinnacle of our adventures, yet the very idea of it thrilled us both to no end.

The thoughts of dreams unfulfilled now haunted me on a daily basis and they weakened me further every time I even attempted to look into the future. All I could see was missed opportunity and each milestone ahead only served to remind me of what I had lost – my Audrey. I rued the missing out of conversations on topics unknown and laughing at jokes that would sadly never get told. I also realised that Audrey and I still had so much more to find out about each other and in my prayers, I sometimes ask her a little question or two, but to no reply. I guess she is waiting until we are reunited before she answers.

I wonder what she will say.

I must admit that my initial concerns for the future were purely selfish ones and such was my level of grief that I withdrew inside myself where I was able to keep my troubles firmly under lock and key. Denial became something I grew to know well and I am deeply ashamed to say that my heartache led me to selfishly place my own feelings above even those of my children.

As the sole parent of two grieving teenagers, I knew that Jonathan and Patricia would have little option but to turn to me for guidance but I had doubts as to whether or not I was up to it. Like a coward, I chose not to meet the issue head-on and instead I opted to stand back with my head in the sand, as everything began to unravel. Temporarily blinded by indifference, my attitude towards my family's needs was deplorable and if given the opportunity to rectify my mistakes, I would do so with fervour.

With regards to Jonathan, my view was that things would be relatively straightforward with him as he was already well on his way to becoming a man. I was confident of my ability to teach him the basics, tips on shaving, minor repairs and vehicle maintenance, but I doubted that I would be able to supply the emotional support he was sure to need following his mother's passing. Shamefully, I sidestepped this issue, and the personal needs that grief had placed upon me selfishly took priority over those of my boy.

In spite of this, Jonathan, to his credit, worked really hard in the shop and he tried his very best to learn the ropes as he went along. He now rose each morning at the same time as I did, an achievement in itself for a boy prone to a sticky mattress, and we would head off together in the van to get the fresh stock in before opening. Often, our journeys were sombre affairs and to the outside world the two lost souls driving silently along must surely have seemed like distant co-workers rather than a father and son who should have been relishing each other's company.

The rearing of Patricia on the other hand was on another level entirely and regardless of any approach taken, I would never be able to adequately replace her mother. Even taking the emotional aspect aside, I was simply not qualified to dish out advice on things like make-up and dresses, let alone 'women's troubles' and the like.

You see in life, generally the father is seen as the breadwinner, whereas the mother makes the home and provides the emotional backbone needed to rear the children. There is a perfect symmetry to that and it encapsulates the very best of what can be achieved when two people work together towards a common goal.

With that and so much more whirling around my head, I began to feel the lure of the Irishman's distraction – the pub. Inside those dens of ineptitude, I found a kinship with men in similar situations to my own, decent, usually God-fearing folk who chose to practise a nocturnal habit during the day, only to then allow their troubles to fester when alone at night.

While we struggled to find our feet as a family once more, Donal continued assisting us in the shop and his efforts, combined with mine and those of the children, endeavoured to keep it ticking over as a going concern. Shamefully, however, this noble gesture led me to show further weakness and I am loathe to say that when the opportunity arose to exploit the kindness of others, I, on more than one occasion, left Donal to take up the slack while I sought refuge on a bar stool.

Jonathan had a few teething problems as he took on greater responsibility in the shop but I decided to let him get on with it as I had what I felt were more pressing matters to attend to. My disappearing act was honed to a fine art and once the stock had been gathered in the morning and the shop up and running, I would make my excuses and head out the door.

Once free of clinging responsibility, I would frequent whatever public house took my fancy, although predictably, Murnaghan's saw more than its fair share of my custom. There, I lived among the discarded betting slips that others had thrown around like confetti, while pints of plain were relentlessly washed down as though someone had just rung last orders before Prohibition.

I found peace in among all those strange characters and the weirdest thing of all was just how normal it felt to be in their company. I was by no means a heavy drinker. In fact, if anything, I was a lightweight and the few tipples I did consume were more than enough to put me four sheets to the wind. Like all those who surrounded me, I was hopelessly looking to fill a void in my life but rather than confine my problems to the barman's ear, they began to trail me home.

An evening which holds particular infamy in my mind regrettably saw me return home heavily under the influence and yet still, I sauntered into the kitchen casual as you like. I had fully expected to find Patricia sitting at the kitchen table with her head buried in her schoolbooks but instead the sight that greeted me was that of my little girl – slaving over the cooker.

"What are you doing, love?" I asked, with slurred words.

"I'm fixing Jonathan his tea," Patricia said bluntly, without turning to face me.

"But it's gone after nine o'clock, where is he?" I asked.

"He's still down in the shop. He said he won't be much longer," explained Patricia.

Puzzled, I checked my watch again to confirm the time before I returned back down the stairs and through the door that adjoins the shop. When I walked in, I saw young Jonathan struggling to secure an old shelf, which had come loose. Without announcing my presence, I approached him from the side and I took the wooden shelf from his grasp and placed it on the floor. The boy's relief was palpable. The poor lad then went on to explain that the shelf had given way shortly before closing and despite his best efforts, he had been unable to mend it.

"I'm sorry, Da. I'm trying to fix it, I really am," Jonathan said, his upset clearly visible.

"You leave it there, son, and I'll see to it in the morning. Get up those stairs and get some food into you, there's a good lad," I said, with only my boy's best interests at heart.

The next morning, bright and early, I brushed aside the ill effects of the night before and secured the shelf back onto the wall and while doing so, I gave point-by-point instruction to a watchful Jonathan, who passed me tools diligently on request.

A short time later, less than ten minutes after opening, Donal came in to the shop on his way home from a night shift and thoughtfully asked if we would be needing him that day. Sensing an opportunity to abscond to Murnaghan's, I shamefully told him that I had some business to attend to in town and I laid plain that he would be doing me a yet another favour if he could stick around for the day.

"No bother at all, Joseph," Donal said, as he tried to conceal an escaping yawn.

Donal's effort at disguising his tiredness failed to mask the fact that he was clearly feeling the effects of his night shift. Yet disgracefully, such levels of vulnerability had little or no effect on me, and my train of thought focused on finding an easy way out. By way of self-appeasement, I offered Donal a cup of coffee to blow away his cobwebs and I beckoned young Jonathan over from the repaired shelf which he was restocking.

"Pop upstairs and make Donal a cup of coffee, before he falls over and worries the customers that we're working him too hard," I said to Jonathan, who promptly made his way up the stairs, and out of sight.

By way of small talk, I told Donal what had happened with the shelf and I jokingly mentioned that as Jonathan had been unable to mend it, his old man had to step in and save the day.

"How do you think he's fairing out with the shop, Joseph?" Donal asked.

"He's doing very well all things considered and I suppose it's helping to keep his mind off things," I replied, alluding to his mother's passing.

Donal nodded along at my assessment but a few tell-tale signs gave me the impression that he was holding something back.

"You don't look convinced, Donal?" I said.

Donal's face revealed an expression of uncertainty and I could see that he was being very selective with his response. But following a short pause, during which I patiently held my tongue, he bluntly shared with me his true feelings on the matter.

"The boy is struggling, Joseph, and he has been for a while. He's unsure on pricing, quantity, stock rotation, basically everything he needs to know, and it's getting him down," Donal said, unburdening himself.

"I showed him all those things, Donal, and he told me he was fine with everything. I think you're reading too much into it. He's doing grand," I replied.

"You showed him how to do those things once and that was during the weeks that followed his mothers' passing. He's been practically fending for himself ever since and he refuses to tell you so because he thinks you have enough on your plate. He's told me as much, Joseph, and it's not just him. Patricia is constantly upset too but she won't admit it. She's begun to miss school and her class work is beginning to suffer as a result. I'm not telling you how to rear you family, pal, but you need to open your eyes. I'm sorry, but it's true," Donal said, with brutal honesty.

"Ah, Donal, they'll be fine. Things are different now, but they'll soon get the hang of it," I said, convincing no one but myself.

"Joseph, look at the shelf. Look around you. Jonathan and Patricia need their father. They need you," Donal said, before letting the truth linger.

His words quickly swirled around my mind and almost immediately, I knew them to be true. In truth, the mending of the shelf was a straightforward job, but of course it's only simple when you know how. I soon began to realise that Jonathan had stood very little chance of ever completing the task, as just like the simple act of tying one's shoelaces, it is only possible following some primary guidance.

I also became haunted by visions of Patricia being left preparing food, rather than partaking in her love of the written word, and I began to wonder how I could have been so blind to my children's struggles. I was frightened to think of what else I might have missed while languishing on torn leather seats in dank public houses and it took the placing of Donal's reassuring hand on my shoulder to stop me becoming lost in such unbearable thoughts. Footsteps on the base of the stairs suddenly resharpened my focus and Donal and I stood without comment, our words hopelessly redundant.

On his return, Jonathan carefully handed Donal the cup of coffee before continuing with the restocking.

"Are you staying for the day, Donal?" Jonathan asked, with his back turned.

"I am indee—" Donal started, before interruption.

"No son, it's just you and me today, I'm afraid. Donal only came round for the free coffee," I teased, as I discreetly placed a hand of thanks onto the forearm of my friend.

I somehow resisted the urge to shed a tear. Still, I remained saddened that I had taken my eye off the ball and allowed my personal failings to deprive my children of the basic guidance they understandably needed. It had taken the intervention of a friend, a truly wonderful friend, to point out problems which were previously beyond my gaze and whose sincere concern for my family's situation served only to highlight my shamefully inept behaviour.

Jonathan, Patricia and I had a heart-to-heart later on that evening and although it took them a little time to open up and respond to my questions, the floodgates positively burst open when they did. They candidly revealed the issues with which they had struggled to keep pace, and they even went as far as to say that they were afraid the shop may have to close down, as they were incapable of running it properly.

I tried my best to reassure them that they had done a brilliant job and that the shop was most certainly not going to close. Rising from my chair, I manoeuvred around the kitchen table and having wedged apart their chairs, I eased on to my hunkers. I then promised them truthfully that I would retake the reins and, in doing so, unburden them of the debt which they had been forced to repay in my absence. But for all of my words and promises, I knew that actions would speak loudest.

Although I was almost certainly shamed into it, I never again touched a drop or wished time away in public houses. With a clear head to now think straight with, my vision of life and its many wonders was regained and I found myself with a new sense of purpose flowing through my veins.

I had been selfish, no two ways about it, and disgracefully, I had been all too quick to downplay the needs of others in order to elevate my own. As the son of a man who had struggled with alcohol, I knew all too well of the crippling effects it can have on one's family, yet inexcusably, I allowed it to turn my head away from what mattered most to me in the world, my children, and moving forward, I knew I no longer had margin for error with regards to their rearing.

CHAPTER 29

YOU LEARN SOMETHING NEW...

IT'S MORE THAN FAIR TO SAY that I watched on with great interest as Jonathan and Patricia bounded their way into adulthood and, helping each other along the way, we faced into all of life's challenges, of which there were many. Acutely aware of my duties, I now tried to maintain a more hands-on approach to parenting than before while, at the same time, I even learned how to identify the occasions when it was actually beneficial to step discreetly to one side.

When Jonathan had a few more years under his belt, I decided that the time was right for him to face the sternest test the fruit and vegetable game has to offer – negotiating with suppliers. In days gone by, the local wholesalers plied their trade within earshot of the very vessels that yielded the produce but as the years rolled on, businesses steadily uprooted and moved closer into town. Smithfield became the hub of the fruit and vegetable world, in Dublin at least, and anyone in the trade worth their salt would converge there to stock up.

Each time I meandered its lines, I noted with sadness that a lot of the decent well-worn traders of my youth had now moved on, to either pastures new or the heavenly cloud above and in their place came a new generation, whose numbers were littered with some real cut-throats. Don't get me wrong, business was always business even back when I was starting out but in the 1980s, it seemed as though trampling over one's granny was deemed best practice. People would delve into all sorts of skulduggery in search of a pound and a fast buck could not be made fast enough, in order to satisfy the greed that dominated the decade.

With caution to the fore of my thinking, I opted to keep a watchful distance while Jonathan made his fledgling attempts at negotiating with Smithfield's finest. And I was disappointed, but shall we say not surprised, to witness some of the pretty deplorable acts that were carried out at my boy's expense, by men who no doubt viewed Jonathan (at twenty years of age) as easy prey. Several opportunistic oafs toyed with him as he tried to negotiate a fair price and any reasonable offer he made was playfully dismissed as the ramblings of a lad sodden behind the ears.

I, on the other hand, happened to be extremely well schooled on such matters and in terms of ears, well, you could strike a match behind mine such was their dryness. Of course, experience of that nature stems purely from confronting bullies and exposing them for what they are and whether Jonathan realised it or not at the time, he was learning, albeit the hard way, the ability of walking into a lion's den without a rifle.

Mr. Maurice Hughes was one such charlatan. He was a mountain of a man who hailed from the Five Lamps and he had a reputation that preceded even that of his colossal frame. Although he made his living in fruit and vegetables, he looked to me like a man who couldn't tell an apple from an orange and given the size of the leather belt that orbited his waistband, it would appear that he had a preference to eat beef steaks by the herd.

"Da, Mr. Hughes wants three pounds for a box of tomatoes. Will I pay him?" Jonathan asked me, as he returned to my side, having just spoken briefly with Mr. Hughes about acquiring some stock.

"You can tell Mr. Hughes, he can have a pound a box and think himself lucky. Those tomatoes will be worth less than a liar's promise once they're on the turn. A pound will do him rightly," I said, before sending Jonathan back into the firing line.

I again kept my distance as I watched Jonathan return to barter the price, but this time I made sure to stand in plain sight so as to make my presence known. Staring over Jonathan's unknowing shoulder, I trained my sight onto Mr. Hughes, particularly at times when he appeared most animated, and each time our eyes locked, my pronounced glare managed to subdue his uppity aggression. In the strangest of ways, I knew as well as he did, that Mr. Hughes did not fear me physically.

But as is the case with all bullies, deep down, he feared a world in which people were beyond intimidation.

After an additional moment or two's heated debate with Jonathan and a further, rather prolonged, optical stand-off with me, Mr. Hughes eventually rolled his eyes up to the heavens in agreement. And with a swish of hot air, he reluctantly turned his back to Jonathan and slowly began stacking four boxes of juicy tomatoes, one on top of the other.

Barely pausing for a second and with Mr. Hughes seemingly in retreat, Jonathan spun around, flashed me the thumbs-up sign and a smile as wide as O'Connell Bridge. Bemused beyond words at his naivety, I frantically gestured at him to turn back around to complete the deal, as it is all very well standing up to a grizzly bear, but it's another matter entirely to blow raspberries in its face and pat it condescendingly on the head.

With a 'one pound per box' deal secured and no blood spilled, Jonathan took note of his old man's approach to negotiation (the bit he was privy to anyway) and he never again asked to be shown. As the years rolled on, his questions in general became fewer and further between. His instilled robustness, together with his growing sense of personal belief, ensured that he had all the tools necessary to fend off anyone probing for weakness.

During this period, Patricia continued to harbour her desire to become a schoolteacher and I must say that the very thought of my little girl all grown up and educating the youth of the day, made me feel proud as punch. To her credit, she had given herself a sporting chance of achieving her dream, as her dedication to studying had not waned over the years and she remained well on course to become the first ever Soap to go to college.

To our great relief, excellent final year exam results followed and a college place of her choice was Patricia's reward for a lifetime spent being a good girl. After much deliberation, she settled upon a decision and in the September of 1985, at the wonderful age of eighteen, Patricia enrolled in the Carysfort teacher training college in Blackrock, County Dublin. Of course, the cost of financing such an endeavour was not inconsiderable but with a bit of belt-tightening along the way, we managed to make all of our sums add up.

As for me, well I continued to live my life without falling foul of the temptations of alcohol and my days were now spent wisely and for the most part productively. I kept up my coastal walks as before but, as you can imagine, they were not quite the same without Audrey. Free from judgemental crowds and the prying eyes of those who could not hope to understand, I would sometimes talk to her as I walked along the beach and in those wonderfully quiet moments, I had the great privilege of reliving some of our happiest times.

The routine of working in the shop continued to provide a welcome element of structure to my life and on a day-to-day basis the clock ticked an ever familiar tock, but, of course, that is not to say that I lived a life without surprises.

A notable distraction, albeit an unwelcome one, came right out of the blue one day when remarkably, I found myself the unwilling recipient of an admiring look from a lady. And, perhaps most surprisingly of all, the look was cast in my direction by a familiar face.

Deborah Kirwin, daughter of the dread Mrs. Kirwin, had been living on our street for as long as I could remember, yet for forty years or more she had barely given me the time of day. Roughly the same age as yours truly, she would accompany her mother on errands and a visit to our shop could have easily been described as something of a regular occurrence.

Through many changing years, I watched as Deborah grew from the young girl who required her mother's helping hand, into a lady who lent a supporting arm on which her ailing mother could always rely and right up until Mrs. Kirwin's passing, the fearsome duo paraded our shop's aisles in perfect tandem.

Deborah, possessing traits of her mother's fiery temperament, would in later years frequent our shop on her own and increasingly she would pass judgement as to the ripeness of the fruit or the size of the vegetables. Indeed, should a cabbage or tomato happen to be anything smaller than a family hatchback, a disgruntled Deborah would chastise me as if I had somehow shrunk the damn things to boost profits.

What remains my abiding memory of Deborah Kirwin occurred on what was up until then a quite unremarkable day and it began almost immediately on her arrival into the shop. Jonathan and I were working away as per usual, tending to a whole host of chores, when a ring of the shop's bell caused us to pause momentarily and avert our eyes to the door.

On seeing Deborah's presence loom large in the doorway, Jonathan quickly drew from all the wit and shrewdness he had learned from me over the years and he wisely, if not very discreetly, made a burst for the backdoor at the speed of a banjo player's fingers.

"I'll be off now, Da. I've a bit of work to do out in the yard!" Jonathan fibbed.

"You get back here now, boy. Us Soaps are no cowards!" I said, while jokingly grabbing at his arm.

"I'm a coward where she's concerned!" Jonathan said, as he ran at pace through the back door.

Languishing in situ behind the till, I watched a marauding Deborah make her way up the aisle and as I did so, I couldn't help but envy Jonathan and his quickness of thought.

"Hello, Deborah, what can I do for you, this fine day?" I asked warmly, but to no response. "I have potatoes here the size of watermelons if that takes your fancy, or I have watermelons the size of potatoes, but you probably won't want them," I offered, whilst probing further.

"It's not the potatoes that take my fancy today, Joseph Soap, and well you know it!" Deborah said, confusing and terrifying me in equal measure.

"Turnips?" I asked.

"I've not come here today for food, Joseph. I am a woman with needs greater than hunger," Deborah said, sending a shiver down my spine.

Alarmed beyond belief, my eyes looked left and right in the hope of a passing saviour, yet it was my ears that detected the only other presence within earshot. As coming from behind the door that leads into the back yard, I could hear a sniggering Jonathan failing miserably in his attempt at eavesdropping. Dumbstruck, I stood and bit gently down on my lip and I waited with bated breath for Deborah to come out of whatever spell she happened to be under and I silently hoped and prayed that the next words out of her mouth would be for a simple order for broccoli or the like.

"You're a respectable man, Joseph Soap, and I'm a respectable woman," Deborah said, quite matter-of-factly.

"I am that, and I plan on staying that way thank you very much," I stated with purpose.

"Joseph, it's been four years since Mrs. Soap's passing and I reckon that's time enough to mend many a broken heart," Deborah said.

"Not this heart, not my one. I'm afraid the many pieces of my heart are still beyond count and that is how it will always remain," I said in all truth.

Deborah looked despondent when clearly she saw that Audrey's presence was still very much alive inside me and embarrassment then struck us both dumb. We eventually stumbled upon the words needed to bring us back to our roles as shopkeeper and customer and, by way of changing the subject Deborah placed a small order for whatever vegetable was closest at hand. I, in turn, was generous with my scales, if not with my heart.

Awkwardly, I thanked Deborah for her custom, she thanked me for the goods and in the blink of an eye the deeply dissatisfied customer left the shop in somewhat of a fluster – even leaving her change behind.

"You're a braver man than me, Da!" Jonathan said, coming out from behind the door.

"Ah, son, Deborah is all right. Besides she's a pussycat compared to her mother. If old Mrs. Kirwin had propositioned me like that, I would have had little choice other than to drop to one knee and propose marriage," I joked, with a strange fondness for the old dear, long since passed.

Later when the dust had settled and I had time to think about Deborah's offer of relations, my initial jest at the situation was replaced by sympathy. Sympathy for what was clearly a lonely woman just trying her best to get on in life.

I wondered if Deborah had perhaps thrown an eye on me years previously, only to then see me strike gold and find love with Audrey, while she continued to nervously wait her turn at finding happiness. Were that to be the case, I imagined just how sad a time that must have been for her, to have to watch as two more young people found love, while she was once again left to smile insincerely in an attempt to conceal a longing that she feared may never leave her.

I cannot be certain whether Deborah's feelings for me were even real or imagined and there is always the upsetting possibility that she saw me as nothing more than a last resort, which would have meant that she had all but abandoned hope of ever finding true love for herself. Sadly, this too was plausible because Deborah was at that time middle-aged and having never married she was often knowingly referred to as a spinster, a term which thankfully seems to be dying out with those cruel enough to have uttered it in the first place.

Deborah, to her credit, continued to satisfy her fruit and vegetable needs within the shop's four walls and each time she entered I was genuinely pleased to see her and the warm welcome she received was most sincere. We never again spoke of romantic overtures or the like and our exchanges, while cordial, were kept pertinent and to the point.

Deborah went on to meet a gentleman friend, whose name sadly escapes me, and when she did I was as chuffed for her as she clearly was for herself. Their subsequent marriage led to a move away from Stepaside, to the west of Ireland I think, and I have not heard a dicky bird from her since the day I stood outside the shop to wave her off. I hope she is well.

Approaching the end of the decade, 1988 to be precise, the Irish national soccer team took on Europe's finest for the very first time at the European Championships and they more than made their presence felt. A great wave of pride and passion swept the nation and it was a time that all who experienced it will never forget.

It was during those wonderful crazy days, amid a sea of green, white and gold, that Jonathan met a charming young girl by the name of Laura Cunningham. They met in a packed pub in town while watching Ireland take on England and I am told that when Ray Houghton stuck the ball in the net, two perfect strangers hugged each other in celebration and never let go.

Laura had a shock of red hair and a smile straight out of *The Quiet Man* and her cheerful way and enthusiasm for life enabled her to charm those she met. I was second only to Jonathan in falling for her personality and it's no exaggeration to say that she proved to be a most welcome ray of sunshine in both our lives.

Jonathan, showing scant regard for his father's genes, had grown into a fine strapping lad and although he towered over the petite Laura, they were well matched from the very start. Theirs was a courtship that blossomed into a marriage of great love and it is one which, I'm delighted to say, seems to grow ever stronger with each passing year.

Young Conor, I hope you enjoyed hearing how your parents met one another. I know my account of their meeting and subsequent relationship is not exactly laced with great detail, but then again their story is theirs alone and my reason for writing this book, if you remember, is to tell my own story and touch on the lives of those now sadly departed.

Perhaps one day, your parents will tell you all about the life they have shared together and if or when they do so, I hope that they include all the wonderful little details that only they know. They, after all, are the only two people on earth who know for sure how they felt the first time they held each other's hands or how their hearts raced during the delicate intricacies of the romance that followed.

Theirs is a tale which ultimately led to your very creation and such an important event as that should not be allowed to fade from memory. It is too precious a thing.

Whether Jonathan and Laura actually commit their lives to paper is another matter altogether, as that decision rests solely with them. But do you know what?

I would like it very much if they did.

CHAPTER 30

BUTTERFLIES

WITH SO MUCH GOING ON IN the lives of Jonathan and Patricia, I was left with little option but to embrace the many changes that came my way and thankfully, for the most part, the changes at least seemed to be positive ones. However, an unwelcome, if somewhat expected, change came along when Patricia, at eighteen years of age, flew from the family nest at the start of her college adventure.

As our means did not quite stretch to furnishing her with a vehicle in which to travel to and from Blackrock, Patricia took up lodgings with a nice local family who lived only a stone's throw from her lecture hall. This particular arrangement, although not ideal, at least provided me with reassurance that she would have a safe and stable environment in which to learn her craft, so it suited all parties concerned.

Patricia's departure let an unwanted silence back into our

home and although she returned on what was practically a weekly basis, I missed her constantly while she was away.

Jonathan and I continued to put our all into the shop but I will admit that I struggled to compete with his stamina and if young men are guilty of one thing, it is their inability to slow down and smell the roses. Our working day was typically long but joyously rewarding and over the course of each week, we both made our fair share of trips to Smithfield, where we would replenish stock that thankfully remained in high demand with our steady stream of customers.

You see, Jonathan for his part really was and still is for that matter, the best of lads but during the years that followed his mother's passing, he showed a loyalty towards me that bordered on unhealthy. I suspect that he somehow believed that he owed me or that perhaps I would wilt when not shadowed by his company but in all honesty, I sometimes just wished him out from under my feet.

Meeting Laura was good for Jonathan, children aside, it was the best thing that ever happened to him and it proved to be the catalyst to him finally prising himself away from the apron strings. His pressing interests now resided mainly outside of the family home but rather than mourning his increasing absence, I welcomed his foray into independence.

During this time, I made a conscious effort to encourage Jonathan to branch out and each Saturday I would permit the lad to finish up early so he could go and see his girl. On his release, he would always bolt out of the shop and as he did so he would demonstrate the same flight of foot I showed in my early years of courting his mother. Laura became a frequent visitor to our home and she was always welcome as she was a joy to behold.

Of course, each second Jonathan spent with Laura was another that I spent alone but during those frequent moments of solitude, my mind would invariably dance to the tune of Audrey's laughter, so it was always time very well spent indeed.

Outside of my working hours, I stubbornly resisted people's advice to "take up a hobby" as that kind of thing is all well and good if you happen to have a particular interest or passion for something but for me, I just didn't see the point. I made plain my views whenever the subject arose, yet still the whole world and its dog continued to advise me on ways to best "fill my days". In truth, I often just wanted to be left alone and despite people's obvious best intentions, I felt as though there were too many unwanted oars trying to steer my canoe into uncharted waters.

My fondness for long brisk walks and front-to-back newspaper reading meant that, on occasion, I probably cut the figure of a loner but the views of those not privy to my true feelings were, frankly, of little concern to me.

I know that people only meant well and I do appreciate the fact that they at least cared enough about me to suggest things for me to do but the reality was that I viewed each activity they suggested as a potential distraction from time better spent having Audrey front and centre in my mind's eye.

As I crept into the 1990s, I felt for sure that nothing the world had to offer me could possibly come close to replacing the irreplaceable or make my heart sing as Audrey once did. Yet, remarkably, I had the good sense at least to try to approach the new decade with the optimism and wishful thinking that its significance seemed to demand of people.

Little changed on the work front and the sound of shutters going up and coming down started and finished each day as it had always done. The early years of the decade rolled on with that same sense of inevitability and three pleasant, if uneventful, years passed before we again had just cause to mark a Red Letter Day onto one of our calendar's many squares.

The momentous day in question, a day that saw the Soap family bloom into life once more, took place in the March of 1993 when Jonathan wed his sweetheart Laura. Their wedding was a marvellous day and it even led to a welcome visit home by Michael and Edward, reuniting the Brothers Soap once more.

Michael travelled home from the States with his wife Una and their children and they were the epitome of the all-American family, with the best of clothes and teeth so white that you could end a war with them.

As for poor Edward, well he and his partner cut completely different figures altogether. Granted, he looked reasonably well but his 'plus one' came in the unshapely form of his latest lady friend, who, in all honesty, looked like she couldn't be trusted. I never did catch her name but she stood brazenly at the reception, with a skirt up around the light fixtures and her every moment was spent worshipping glass after glass of neat vodka, as though the Lord himself had poured each one from above.

In the interests of parity and to give both of my brothers some degree of credit, I must say that Michael and Edward are as consistent as the day is long and regardless of victory or failure, I was equally delighted to have both of them by my side.

As everyone knows, a home is simply not a home without a woman's touch and in the weeks that followed their wedding I'm happy to say that Laura settled in nicely above the shop. I was only too pleased to respond favourably to Jonathan's request on the matter, and as much as I enjoyed their company, I also loved the idea of giving a young couple the chance of a good start in life.

I am pleased to say that the three of us spent many happy times time together. We ate good meals, had wonderful chats and I was touched that both Jonathan and Laura saw fit to include me in everything they did socially. Granted, I didn't actually go many places with them but that was at least through personal choice and not the lack of an invitation. You see the pub no longer held interest for me, while the picture house, much like myself, had not seen a good film since *Casablanca*. We did, however, enjoy some lovely lunches out and often I would have two nimble companions while out on my coastal walks.

On occasion, I will admit, that all was not well. After all, three adults living in such close proximity are bound to ruffle each other's feathers once in a while, and Jonathan, Laura and

I were no exception. My newspaper time was regularly inter-rupted by chattering phone calls and so on, just as Jonathan and Laura's more romantic nights in were frequently blighted by the presence of yours truly complaining about the wholesale price of celery. Despite our ups and downs, we pretty much knew that our little home was a happy one and, more often than not, we adapted well to suit all needs.

On Jonathan and Laura's first anniversary, I wisely decided to uproot myself and allow them some space to themselves. Jonathan had mentioned that he had planned on cooking Laura a romantic meal and to his credit he even asked me to join them in their celebrations. Although his heart was undoubtedly in the right place, his head was nowhere to be seen so for his sake as well as Laura's, I conjured up some imaginary plans with Donal and left them to it.

While Jonathan and Laura tucked into a home-cooked meal, which knowing my son probably consisted of beans on toast with a sprinkling of cheese, I sat alone on a familiar bollard in front of Howth harbour lighthouse.

Sitting there, tucking into some fresh fish and chips, I real-ised just how my own father must have felt all those years ago, when Audrey and I first set up home together above the shop. From experience, I could now see the difficulties and challenges he must have faced being the third wheel but through presence of mind, I was able to maintain focus on all the positives in my life rather than dwell solemnly on the minor inconveniences. My new-found situation led me to develop a further layer of respect for Father and it was with a bottle of fizzy cola in hand, that I toasted him wherever he may be.

Somehow, I had managed to survive the entire 1980s without any young bucks knocking on my door with the view of courting Patricia but I barely made it halfway through the 1990s, before a prospective suitor darkened my door. Having completed her studies and passed with distinction, Patricia had found employment at the Dominican Covent Primary School in Dun Laoghaire, where she met and fell for a fellow young teacher by the name of Andrew Kerrigan.

Some three years Patricia's senior, Andrew had a quiet demeanour and a relaxed nature that gave the impression that the world's problems were none of his concern. I will admit to being suspicious of him at first, certainly I was wary of his intentions, but his dry wit and polite manner soon won me over. Ever the young gentleman, he was courteous to my suspicions and he answered with patience and honesty, the many probing questions I threw his way.

What struck me most about Andrew was his attitude to Patricia, in so much as he seemed to hang on her every word. He would listen intently to all she had to say and it was as clear as the day is long that he held my daughter's views on life in nothing but the highest regard. Andrew became a regular visitor above the shop and whenever he and Patricia came to stay at weekends, he would retire to the sofa without complaint or even the roll of an eye.

I really was thrilled to have so much contact with both of

my children, but I was always conscious that other parents were not so fortunate. Many families simply go their separate ways once the children are of age and for lots of parents, loneliness fills the void left behind. I, on the other hand, have been extremely fortunate in that regard as I am so truly blessed to have an attentive son and daughter standing guard over me, ensuring that the isolation each one of us secretly fears never gets to within a hair's breadth of me.

The news that Jonathan and Laura were expecting their first child came right out of the blue and when the announcement was made to me in the shop one morning, I was justly elated by it. I felt a rush of euphoria not seen in this country since Jack Charlton and the lads gave it 'a lash' in the Italia '90 World Cup and such was my excitement at the thoughts of being a grandfather, I felt as though it were I, not Packie Bonner, who had made that famous save.

Six months or so later, Laura gave birth to beautiful twin girls, Claire and Roisin, and a madhouse quickly ensued. Our home was again alive with childish innocence and to the watchful eye of many a nosey neighbour, we displayed all the hallmarks of the happy family that we were.

The following year, bold as brass, young Andrew too decided to up the stakes on a personal front – by asking me if he could have Patricia's hand in marriage. Arriving unannounced into the shop early one afternoon, he discreetly asked to speak with me in private and having excused myself from Jonathan's company, I ushered the lad upstairs.

Well, poor Andrew was by now sweating buckets and without him even having to say a word, I knew exactly what he was about to ask me. Although I could see his obvious anxiety I resisted the temptation to cut him some slack and instead, I mischievously seized the opportunity to have some devilment at the young fella's expense. Andrew was, after all, playing for a big prize, the biggest prize of all in my eyes and I'd be damned if I wasn't going to make him work for it.

"What's all this about, lad?" I asked abruptly.

"Eh… Mr. Soap, there is something I've been meaning to ask you for some time now," Andrew began nervously.

"Go ahead, spit it out," I snapped needlessly, but for dramatic effect.

"It's about love, Mr. Soap. Marriage to be specific," Andrew stuttered.

"I don't know what impression I've given you, son, but I'm not that way inclined," I said sternly.

"Dear God no, I'm not asking YOU to marry me Mr. Soap, honestly I'm not, I wouldn't!" Andrew said in a fluster.

"Really! And what's wrong with me? You could do a darn sight worse than me, I can tell ya!" I said, while struggling to keep pace with my own charade.

"No, not at all, Mr. Soap, I don't mean that. Sure, I think you're lovely!" Andrew replied.

"'Lovely'? I think you may need professional help or at the very least, you should say ten Hail Marys," I impishly suggested.

At this point, Andrew had himself in something of a tizzy but unfortunately for him I was quite enjoying myself. I knew I was being cruel but I figured that if he could survive my grilling, he would at least be well primed for married life.

"Son, are you on drugs?" I probed.

"God no!" blurted Andrew.

"Don't you take the Lord's name in vain in this house, boy," I snapped back, before biting my top lip to stop smiling.

Andrew, by now, looked like a deer caught in the sights of a hunter's rifle and it was only on sensing his alarm that I decided to relinquish my puppeteer's strings and let the poor lad rest. Advising him to calm down and choose his words wisely, I then softened my stance considerably and on furnishing him a revealing smile, I sat back and gave the lad the platform on which to win my daughter's hand.

Andrew seemed to immediately sense the change in my demeanour and he began to speak in words that were both heartfelt and honest. I remained silent so as to let him say his piece and when thoughtful words eventually stumbled upon an end, I rose swiftly to my feet and shook his hand warmly in approval, much to his obvious relief.

With formalities out of the way, Andrew and I sat and discussed the responsibilities of being a husband and having ardently relished that role myself, I felt more than qualified to offer him some advice. I told him that the secret to a happy marriage lay simply in the choosing of the right partner and in sharing his life with a girl as wonderful as Patricia, he had already hit the jackpot.

Andrew, to be fair, really was a good lad, the kind anyone would want for their daughter and over the years he has done nothing but prove both Patricia and I to be excellent judges of character.

They wed late the following year, in what truly was a wonderful ceremony in Our Lady of the Wayside and, equally as delightful, some sunshine even bucked the winter's trend.

The newlyweds then set up home in Dun Laoghaire and I half suspect that Patricia's inherited love of the coast played as much a part in her decision as did the convenience of the short commute to work.

By now, Jonathan and Patricia were fully grown up and well on the way to developing little families of their own and, staying true to their mother's nature, they both became people of real worth and substance.

As for me, well I suddenly began to feel my age. Sure, I had crow's feet around my eyes as a daily reminder but without my ever really noticing, the years had crept up on me and caught me unawares.

Firmly in my mid-fifties, mine was very much a life in transition and by way of self-motivation, I made a pact with myself to at least try and keep pace with the many changes. Were I to stagnate further, I ran the risk of becoming a relic of a bygone age. And in a modern world obsessed with youth and all things shiny and new, relics today are often shamefully dismissed as neither use nor ornament, the very thought of which I cannot bear.

"Move with the times, Joseph Soap, move with the times…"

CHAPTER 31

STEPPING ASIDE

THE 2000s OR AS SOME PEOPLE infuriatingly chose to call them, 'the noughties', saw me creak my way into my sixties and each morning the Lord treated me to a new ache or ailment, which for whatever reason he seemed to think I might need. Fortunately, however, I managed to remain young at heart but the human body has an awful habit of disloyalty, as mine was to prove when it began to betray me in a most unwelcome fashion. Much like a car driven non-stop every day for more than sixty years and with a million possibilities for error, it began to let me down with increasing regularity.

As I approached pensionable age, I began to feel the effects of a touch of arthritis in my hands and wrists, while the troublesome back I had previously dismissed as just a bit of gyp, became something of a penance. These ailments were no doubt an occupational hazard, owing to the wear and tear of a lifetime spent shifting heavy loads of produce, but I learned to accept them for what they were, having reasoned that it is impossible to spend a lifetime smiling, without getting a few wrinkles along the way.

As the years took hold, I began to struggle with the heavy lifting involved in my trade and I longed for the back and knees of a younger man, without ever really holding out hope of getting them. The mass of fruit and vegetables we bought and sold seemed to grow in tandem with people's ever-increasing appetites and while I am all for healthy eating, dare I suggest, not by the shovel load as today's folk seem intent on doing.

Wholesome foods nowadays, are, of course, just a mere accompaniment to the 'half a cow' steaks that people devour for dinner and the obligatory dessert serves only to tempt diabetes one step closer. To this day I wonder how a human being can house the appetite of a blue whale, while at the same time display none of its grace and splendour.

Increasingly aware of my shortcomings, I decided to heed Mother Nature's warning by lessening my role in the shop to the point where I could consider myself part-time. With the world now seemingly travelling at a hundred miles per hour, I opted instead for a change of pace and having eased my foot gently from the pedal, I slowed things down to a much more manageable speed.

Jonathan, to his credit, was by now very much his own man and he was always quick to embrace the changing trends and, rather than following my lead in dismissing the more fanciful of modern ways, he took to them like a duck to water.

"Organic food is the future, Da!" Jonathan informed fervently.
"My eye!" I scoffed.

"People don't want modified foods these days, they want fresh produce," Jonathan added.

"People don't know what they want in that regard, Jonathan and that's the problem. It was 'people' who modified the food in the first place! We Soaps have always sold fresh produce to our customers and we pride ourselves on that, you know that as well as I do," I replied, with fervour to match even that of my son's.

Jonathan went on to say that the majority of food sold nowadays had been altered in some way and that a lot of people were now choosing to pay a premium for guaranteed organic fare. He believed that there was a gap in the market locally for that kind of thing and he told me that he had decided to make a percentage of our stock organic, so as to at least give people the choice of paying a little extra if they wished.

I must say that his argument, which was said with remarkable zeal, sounded half convincing, even to me, but ultimately I failed to see the whole thing as anything other than bewildering. I felt as though people were being asked to pay more for what they should be getting in the first place – good healthy food at a fair price.

Organic food, in my view, is most certainly not the future; it is very much a thing of the past. When my father and his father before him freed vegetables from the ground with their bare hands, they were exactly as Mother Nature had intended, yet generations later, people now feel the need to spray crops with all sorts of radioactive gloop. The intention, no doubt, is to rush growth along in order to feed insatiable demand, a goal I'm sure they achieve but shamefully, they have also succeeded in corrupting perfection. Food, like all the finest things in life, should not be rushed and, just like love, it should be allowed to grow naturally, with just a little nurturing needed along the way.

Big business has of course gotten involved, as it always does when there is the smell of a pound, and it has contrived for us the ludicrous situation where natural food is more expensive than the stuff they spend millions to manufacture.

To my surprise, Jonathan's brave new endeavour proved to be a raging success and with it came the realisation that I should completely pass on the reins of the shop. I must say that the decision proved to be an easy one to make in the end and with Jonathan I knew that the shop would continue as it always had – securely in the hands of someone who cares for it deeply.

Jonathan was now of an age where he could (and indeed probably should) put his own stamp on things and I feared that I was at risk of holding back that natural progression. I would, of course, make myself available to him whenever needed but in all truth both he and Laura were more than capable of making the business thrive by themselves. The timing felt right for all concerned and looking back now, I am pleased to say that it is a decision I have not lived to regret.

Initially, and I suppose naturally, I feared retirement as I have seen far too many good men drift away into oblivion, almost immediately after their token carriage clock had begun to count down their demise.

My own first steps into retirement met with their fair share of bumps in the road and early on, in the first few weeks and months, I struggled to fill my time away from the shop. During that brief period I felt wholly lost, as there is only so much walking a man can do, while the reading of newspapers no longer fills one's day, given some of the nonsense that now soils their pages.

Thankfully, however, I was not idle for long as Jonathan and Laura were quick to enlist me into the role of part-time babysitter and during school terms, I would promptly escort my two beautiful granddaughters to and from the school gates. I was always happy to help out in any way I could, especially where the twins were concerned, and any time spent in the company of those two sweethearts was time very well spent indeed.

Often on the way home an enjoyable visit was made to the park and, if the weather and time permitted, the beach too would feel the weight of our footsteps. On each occasion, I felt as though Audrey was right there with us. A gentle wisp of pollen or slight sea breeze was enough to confirm her presence and together once more, we would share in the great joy of watching our grandchildren at play.

I often wondered whether Jonathan and Laura entrusted me with that role as much for my benefit, as for the benefit of the family as a whole but either way, it brought me such a sense of fulfilment.

Jonathan and Laura tried their best, and from what I could see succeeded, in the age-old battle of balancing work with family life and staying true to form they continued to include me in all aspects. It is something which I truly appreciate and I remain grateful beyond words to what is and always will be a wonderful couple.

Over time the twins and I were frequently joined by more little faces, as Patricia and Andrew's marriage was blessed with three children: James, Sean and Maria, who all arrived in quick succession. Whenever crisis arose in the teaching profession, the three little ones were watched by their eager grandad and during quiet times, I would count my blessings, of which there were too many to even tally.

Retirement, for so many people, feels like a death in a way and I can see how without a sense of purpose it has the potential to make a once proud and able worker feel as though they are cast upon life's scrapheap. I want people to know that that is absolutely not the case and I would wholeheartedly encourage them to embrace all the marvellous opportunities it provides, rather than succumb to the isolation which many surrender to.

Another old codger, Donal, also fell foul of Father Time and following retirement from the plant where he had worked since leaving school, he began to perform a similar role to my own by tending to his four beautiful grandchildren.

To this day we continue to meet up, and although neither of us is as nimble as we once were, we can still give the best of them a run for their money, when it comes to having a good laugh and a joke.

Being with my grandchildren made me feel reborn and feeding off their energy, I was given a whole new lease of life. As they all grew in size, so too did our love and affection for one another and it is with great pride and good fortune that I am able to say that our bond remains intact. Family occasions and other days of note always result in an avalanche of presents and I dare say that never before has one man owned so many paisley handkerchiefs or pairs of socks.

The almost constant visits I continue to receive go way beyond that of mere routine and obligation and the relationships we have built with one another are testament to the individuals both past and present, whom I am honoured and indeed humbled to call my family.

CHAPTER 32

(S) O. A. P.

THE YEAR 2005 SAW THE INCOMPREHENSIBLE modern trend of abbreviating words beyond all point of recognition rear its ugly head yet again, when the world conspired against me and shamelessly reclassified me as an "O.A.P." or Old Age Pensioner. This new and most unwelcome guise came courtesy of a society hell-bent on pigeonholing people against their will and as I turned sixty-five I must say that I took umbrage at its very notion.

Up until that point and throughout the various seasons of my life I had happily managed to avoid such labelling. During my younger years I was never described as a 'Young Boy Worker' or even a 'Middle-Aged Breadwinner', yet post-sixty-five, people could not seem to resist the urge to ram a condescending title down my throat.

You see when you reach your winter years and the last speck of colour has drained from your hair, certain quarters of society immediately dismiss you as senile or at best doddery. Whether intentional or not, the branding of you as 'old' feels as though you are being swept to one side by a youth-obsessed culture, to clear a path for those who can move a little faster or jump a little higher.

Many times over the years I have toyed with the idea of starting a petition with the view of getting the government to drop the 'Old Age' bit from our moniker and simply refer to people of my vintage as pensioners. In the end I always abandoned the idea due to the fact that politicians rarely (if ever) listen to common sense.

So in order to seize back a little power and to march to the beat of my own drum I decided to create my own label for myself, one which was self-imposed to the point of satisfaction, and from that day forth I wished to be known universally as a 'S.O.A.P.' or 'Senior Old Age Pensioner'. Retirement gives people a lot of time to think and, no matter how old the individual, a little mischief will appear sooner or later and this mischief should be embraced, encouraged and never ever suppressed.

I make it my business to air this very fact to the awfully nice Post Office tellers each week as I draw my pension and, divided only by glass, we always share a pleasant chuckle at the absurdity of life. Perception is another important element which is often overlooked as we grow older and it's often the case that if you think you are old, you are old.

Silver periods of time rolled on as they always do and many wonderful moments were spent in the company of people, the very thought of whom I adore. School plays, communions, sports days and all things in between gave the Soap family every opportunity to get cameras out and I was always thrilled to be placed front and centre in each family portrait. What a thing it is that I am able to say, that I feel as happy as I do loved.

The decade will no doubt be remembered for the coming and going of an eventful, or should I say notorious, period in Irish history, 'The Celtic Tiger'. We as a family, unlike so many others, were fortunate not to be chewed up and spat out by the mythical moggy. We prudently paid little attention to advice from banks and building societies to "grow and expand our business" and instead we opted wisely to remain focused on what we had rather than what we could acquire. The country in the main, however, seemed to focus all of its attention on the value of people's houses. Even within the pages of trusted broadsheet newspapers, local interest stories and tales of rural Ireland made way for property supplements for holiday homes in weird places such as Turkey and Bulgaria, at prices which even to me seemed quite reasonable.

For some, those crazy and often self-indulgent years, went by in a blur of garden decking and half-price fitted kitchens and much like the champagne consumed by the bucket, with very little heed for sore heads the next day, it soon fizzled out and lost its sparkle.

In the immediate aftermath of that boisterous decade, I strolled with good step into the 2010s, and it is only by the grace of God that no one has as of yet christened these years the 'tenners' or something of equal or greater nonsense.

The nation continued to wade through the recession which had stubbornly followed us from the previous decade, but together we managed to withstand the worst of the financial storm until it eventually began to blow itself out.

Just as green shoots of positivity started to grow from the auld sod once more, the Lord it seemed had one further surprise in store for our family when right out of the blue he kindly saw fit to add to our many blessings, by placing the most delightful little cherry on top of all that we already had.

2013 saw Jonathan and Laura surprising everyone, including themselves, by announcing that they were expecting their third child, some nineteen years after the birth of the twins. When the news broke, joy struck me speechless, but it wasn't long before words of congratulation flew excitedly from my mouth. Seven months later, in the first month of 2014, the most beautiful baby boy was gently placed into my arms and my heart just melted.

Little Conor Soap, even though you turned up late to the party you were a wonderful surprise and you have brought nothing but joy and happiness to the lives of all those around you. You are a funny little lad, always smiling, and as soon as your legs are able to take your weight you will be up and away in search of all sorts of adventures.

It was your arrival that prompted me to write this very book, as the relationship I am privileged to enjoy with my other grandchildren is not one which I will ever be able to share with you. Time will simply not allow it. It saddens me that you will never be able to see me in the same light that your sisters and cousins do as my light is flickering with each passing second. Although I certainly do not wish for you to grow up any quicker and rush the wonder of childhood, I do wish to connect with you through a means on which time has no influence: this book.

When I decided to begin my story I asked your father to fetch me our old typewriter, the one used by my wife for so many years, which had been long since condemned to the attic. Without giving the game away or divulging my intent, I told Jonathan that I wanted to use it as an ornament for my bedroom.

The old typewriter, in its own way a thing of mechanical beauty, had been previously dismissed as a relic by Jonathan and Laura as they set about modernising practices. They, like everyone else nowadays, use a computer to tend to all things business.

I, on the other hand, had no desire to trouble myself with such gizmos and I went to great lengths to peddle the virtues of the much simpler machine to your father, but to no avail.

"The best things in life come without plugs, Son," I pointed out.

"Not these days they don't," Jonathan cheeked back.

I stubbornly spurned all of his advances to 'upskill' and become 'computer-literate'. Instead, I choose to remain 'computer-illiterate' as my mind has simply run out of the capacity needed to store such trivial and nonsensical phrases. After all, mine is a generation who ate 'Spam' in between two pieces of bread.

"You should use email to write to Michael and Edward. Snail-mail takes too long," Jonathan advised me.

"Snail what?" I quizzed.

"The post, Da. Nobody uses it anymore. It's too slow," Jonathan said to my surprise.

"So now even the post has fallen foul of technology, bloody hell!" I said, while shaking my head.

The great postal service had once transformed the world by keeping millions of people in touch with one another at a time when distance delivered nothing but loneliness to so many. Now it seemed that hundreds of years of loyal service was being dismissed and outgrown by people clearly spoilt with too many new and gloating alternatives. How typical of the way things are going.

It is important for the youth of today to embrace the past, and always remember that shiny and new is not necessarily better. I would like to reassure them that, despite what the media brainwashes them into believing, people really do not need to be hoisted onto a glitzy show business pedestal in order to prove that they are 'someone'.

If I were to be elevated at all I would sooner wish to be held aloft by the people who mean the most to me in the world, namely my family and friends. They are the people who I wish to impress, wish to influence and wish to take care of. In times of crisis I would seek only their guidance, because I know it is they who will always retain my best interests at heart and stubbornly refuse to see me as an unwanted burden or lingering guest who has outstayed their welcome.

My story, I am sure, is an uneventful one when compared to the intrepid tales of others. I have never wrestled crocodiles or run with the bulls, but I have in my own way achieved much more than I ever set out to in the first place. Looking back, I am both proud and in awe of the fulfilling life I have been able to tell you about and the very idea that I have been blessed with such good fortune is enough to make me feel very privileged.

I do of course still miss the company of those long since gone and I would do anything to hold the hand of your grandmother once more. Audrey has now been gone from me longer than the time we even had together and I lament the fact that I missed out on so much love from the one lady who took my heart and kept it for all eternity.

Young Conor, I hope you have enjoyed learning all about your old grandad and some of the people who you will sadly never meet. I want you to know that you have inspired me, even at this late stage of my life, to test myself, to face into the unknown and to do something which I would have previously dismissed as impossible. For that I thank you from the very bottom of my heart. I hope in turn that I can inspire you to live your life well, to be good to those around you and to never forget that they are the people who matter the most in the world.

I genuinely believe that people really do try their best but it is just that some folks are better at living their lives than others. So please remember that if you are fortunate enough to be strong in body and mind, always cradle life's weak or support those left floundering. Each one of us faces a unique set of challenges and we all, whether we choose to admit it or not, need a little help along the way.

I am sure that you will go on to accomplish great things in your life but do so on your own terms and be led solely by your own passions and beliefs. Try also to remember that only one man can be the first on the moon, the first to swim the Irish Sea or the first to scale Everest. And know that the accomplishments of those who follow years later are just as commendable, perhaps even more so, as they were achieved by those with the humility to walk in the footsteps of others.

I myself had much simpler goals, achievable goals for a quite unremarkable man, and I always believed them possible as I simply strived to be a good person and to do my best for those I cared about. I have lived a good life and have met, loved and been loved by such wonderful people, people whose decency and honour would stand up across any walk of life and in any era throughout history. I have been extremely fortunate to share my life with such people and without question the privilege has been all mine.

Perhaps on reflection I have sold myself short by referring to myself as unremarkable, as surely anyone who is lucky enough to get to live on this planet is remarkable in his or her own way. In our wonderful world, one man's Olympic gold can be equivalent to a young boy finally mastering how to ride his bicycle. Likewise, the satisfaction felt by someone achieving their first million must surely fade into insignificance when compared to the joy of falling in love with a sweetheart.

Writing this book has given me the opportunity of a lifetime in so much as it has enabled me to relive some of my most treasured moments, while at the same time, securing them eternally in print. Should time creep up on me further, allowing old age to wage its next assault on me, I at least now have a written account of my time on this planet and I no longer need to rely on a fragile mind that could cruelly erase itself on a moment's whim.

I must say that I have found this whole endeavour to be the most worthwhile of experiences and I would recommend it to anyone who would like the opportunity to revisit some old friends, or perhaps even care to lay some old ghosts to rest.

I have now reached the end of my book and I will sign off with good grace. With my legacy now committed to paper and our relationship forever set in stone, I feel relaxed enough to sit back and really enjoy what remains of my so-called golden years. While I do not know what the future holds in store, none of us do, I am certain that I will greet each day with my head held high – basking in the belief that my heyday has stretched across an entire lifetime.

And so concludes *The Life and Times of Mr. Joseph Soap*.

God bless.

EPILOGUE

My father, Mr. Joseph Soap, died on the 19th of February 2015. He was seventy-five years old.

At close of business that evening I secured the shop following the day's trade and made my way up the stairs to rest my bones as I had done a million times before. The smell of beef stew along with my wife's smile greeted my arrival and Laura swiftly beckoned me to call Dad from his room as she was ready to serve up.

I nodded in agreement and promptly changed course towards my father's bedroom door. On reaching it, I knocked loudly enough to rouse his attention. I knocked on it a second time and then a third. Several moments of deafening silence passed before I turned to see my wife's face, which by now mirrored the same concerns that were plastered across my own. Left with little option, I rapped on the door again. This time, however, I did not await a response. Instead, I just took a deep breath and entered.

Sitting in his favourite chair, newspaper within arm's reach, my father remained perfectly still. I knew. I walked slowly towards him, with a strange acceptance whirling around my mind and I now wonder if perhaps that was my own way of shielding myself from the pain that I was about to reach out and touch. When I arrived at his side, I gently squeezed his right hand, but Dad did not squeeze back.

He had passed.

Perched on his lap, as was so often the case, was one of his many photo albums. Through teary eyes I noticed that the open page contained images of me as a lad playing at the seaside with both of my parents and Patricia. I must say that we looked like a happy bunch.

Three days later, in a church packed to the rafters, we said goodbye to my father. I noticed that people smiled when they spoke of him and the man that I knew and loved would have wished for nothing more than that.

Dad taught me that love, decency and hard work can not only take a man as far as he wants to go but it can also provide more than enough happiness to quell desires for greener grass or a lifetime spent outside of the community he held dear. It is something that shall stay with me always and it is a message that should not go without heed.

Several weeks of pain and high confusion passed before I finally felt able to tend to my father's belongings. As I did so, his absence somehow made my obligation feel wrong. In his bedroom, I noticed neatly placed carpet slippers and shelves spared of clutter, while my mother's familiar old typewriter adorned a desk in the far corner. Just inside the door, on the left-hand side, stood my parents' wardrobe, which was once a favourite hiding place of mine during youthful games of hide-and-seek. Clothes that triggered a thousand memories hung inside on its rails and old winter coats which once shielded me from discovery now exposed the pain I felt and all that I had lost in the stopping of a heartbeat.

As emotion stooped my head, my eyes fell upon a plastic bag that was nestled in the bottom right-hand corner of the wardrobe. It was beige in appearance, perhaps through age, and its branding told of a shop long since closed. Bending down, I picked it up and carried it over to the bed where I placed it down gingerly to examine its contents.

Along with insurance documents, a receipt for a transistor radio, six keys without labels, fifteen pounds in old Irish Punts and a newspaper supplement from the Pope's visit in 1979, lay a stack of A4 pages with a rubber band stretching around them to near breaking point.

I carefully removed the band and, as I did so, I got to know my father all over again.

I read each page in near disbelief and over the course of that weekend I delighted in it from start to finish. In fact such was my amazement at the content that the turn of the last page led me to start the whole thing over again. As I turned each page, I learned of my father's hopes, struggles and greatest moments, and as I did so his voice seemed to whisper each word to me.

It is clear from reading my father's autobiography that he was often at a loss when it came to understanding what he perceived to be the strange ways of the modern world. He was never afraid to voice his concerns, but he did so only in the hope of finding a simpler way of doing things. A way that included everyone, without alienating those too scared of, or confused by, such change.

My father believed in people and he also believed that love and kindness were possible in all. He spoke of those for whom it came naturally and of others who struggled to make theirs known to the world. He seemed to pride himself on the fact that he gave everyone equal opportunity to air their kindness while at the same time showing patience to those who hadn't quite mastered it yet. And while he may have complained a little along the way, it is only because he cared about the world and the people in it.

Dad spoke early on in his book about not having changed the world and he stated that he never even came close to doing so. Well, I would love to let him know that he really did change the world. He changed it for me and for all those who knew and loved him and he brought kind-heartedness, warmth and compassion to generations of a family who will never forget him. I know that he is watching over us with pride as we continue to live by the lessons he taught us, lessons of hard work and family-motivated decisions, and it is these lessons that define us as a family.

Dad's book gave me an insight not just into his own life but also into that of my mother's, whose shortness of time on this earth has always led me to mourn her loss in tandem with my resentment towards the person who took her from me. Regrettably, I am not blessed with the same level of forgiveness as my father and I have always felt angry and cheated by my mother's passing. Then again, my father was always of purer spirit than I am. He believed in a God who had a plan laid out for all of us and although he seemed to struggle with his faith during testing times, he believed that one day he would be reunited with my mother.

Whenever memory lane beckons, as it often does around anniversary dates or just random moments of reflection, I thumb through Dad's photo albums and stare lovingly at the faces that smile back at me. The images of my parents cheer my heart without fail and during each night's sleep, following their viewing, my mother and father come alive once more and they are joyously reunited in warm embrace. In my heart that is how they will forever remain and the grinning face of my father is all the proof I need to know that he is at peace and in the company of his one true love.

Dad was not a man who asked for much during his life, but it's clear from his book that he held a great interest in leaving behind a legacy for future generations of his family and for them in turn to follow suit.

As for the telling of my own story, I believe that my father has thrown down a most worthwhile gauntlet for me and, having respectfully accepted the challenge, I will at least try to put pen to paper and do the best I can; as much to honour his memory, as to preserve my own.

I just hope to do him proud.

And so begins the life and times of Mr. Jonathan Soap…

Leabharlanna Poiblí Chathair Baile Átha Cliath
Dublin City Public Libraries

ACKNOWLEDGEMENTS

I WOULD LIKE TO TAKE THIS opportunity to thank my wonderful wife Siún, whose love, support and encouragement provided me with all the inspiration needed to write this book. The whole process proved to be a huge undertaking, bigger than I could ever have imagined and I simply couldn't have done it without her.

I must express my eternal gratitude to my late parents Jimmy and Patricia, two people whose kindness and decency taught me many of life's lessons, all of which helped to make each word of this book sincere. They are both loved and missed in equal measure.

To my friends and family, who may have noticed that I haven't been around as much this past while — thank you for your patience and understanding.

Many thanks to Andrew Brown and Rebecca Brown at Design for Writers for their unmatched skill and professionalism, and to Vanessa Fox O'Loughlin at Writing.ie for her much needed pointers and guidance.

Age Action Ireland: Twenty percent of the proceeds from the sale of this book will be donated to Age Action Ireland, a charity organisation whose aim is 'to achieve fundamental change in the lives of all older people by empowering them to live full lives as actively engaged citizens and to secure their rights to comprehensive high quality services according to their changing needs'. To learn more about Age Action Ireland or to make a donation please go to www.ageaction.ie.

Finally, a special mention must also go to all the Senior Old Age Pensioners out there, my fondness for whom no doubt stems from my own beloved grandparents who are sadly no longer with us. It should always be remembered that older people possess wit and wisdom like no other members of society, having lived long enough to realise that the trivial things in life really don't matter all that much. What matters to them is family, friends and trying to do one's best. Younger people, if you don't realise that by now don't worry. You will one day.

AUTHOR BIOGRAPHY

THOMAS MARTIN (b. 1980) is a native of Dundalk, Co. Louth, in the Republic of Ireland.

While on a United Nations peacekeeping tour of duty in the Middle East as a member of the Irish Defence Forces, he opted to use his free time in what proved to be the most enjoyable and gratifying of ways. Hidden from prying eyes beneath a patched-up mosquito net and armed only with his trusted laptop, he set about freeing *The Life and Times of Mr. Joseph Soap* from his imagination.

As an avid reader of autobiographies by distinguished public figures, Thomas had the idea of the 'everyday person in the street' joining the ranks of the great and the good on the nation's bookshelves, by penning his or her own life's story. Rather than relying upon epic encounters or scandalous tales often found in 'celebrity autobiographies', he wanted to write a book that proved that each one of us has a worthwhile story to tell, and free from the blinding showbiz spotlight, we all still live lives which are worth documenting for future generations to come.

In addition to reading, Thomas's interests include current affairs and travel. He married Siún in 2011 and describes himself as being very happily married.

The Life and Times of Mr. Joseph Soap is his first novel.

Find out more at www.thomasmartin.ie

Or, follow him on social media at:

www.Facebook.com/thomasmartinauthor
and
www.Twitter.com/thomasmartinaut

92810625R00242

Made in the USA
Lexington, KY
10 July 2018